The Mistresses of Charles II

The Mistresses
of
CHARLES II

Brian Masters

Blond & Briggs

for
JUAN MELIAN

First published in 1979 by Blond & Briggs Ltd
44–45 Museum Street, London WC1
© 1979 Brian Masters

Printed in Great Britain by The Anchor Press Ltd
and bound by Wm Brendon & Son Ltd
both of Tiptree, Essex

SBN 85634 099 5

Contents

1   Lucy Walter   7

2   Barbara Villiers   45

3   Nell Gwynn   95

4   Louise de Kéroualle   123

5   Destinies   179

    Index   190

Acknowledgements

The author would like to express his gratitude for permission to include pictures in this volume, both to the owners of the originals and to those who control the copyright of the prints. These include the Trustees of the Goodwood Collection (for the portraits of Charles II and Frances Stuart), the Duke of Buccleuch and Queensberry K.T. (for the portraits of Lucy Walter and the Duke of Monmouth), Pilgrim Press Ltd (for the picture of the Duke of Monmouth's cradle), the Trustees of the British Museum (for the print of Monmouth's execution), Earl Spencer (for the portrait of Duchesse Mazarin), and the National Portrait Gallery (for the portrait of the Duchess of Cleveland in old age, by Kneller, and that of Moll Davis by Lely). In addition, the National Portrait Gallery has kindly allowed the use of their prints of the Lely portrait of the Duchess of Cleveland, the Verelst portrait of Nell Gwynn, the double portrait of Nell Gwynn's children, and the portraits of the Duchess of Portsmouth by Gascar and Mignard. The print of the Kneller portrait of Duchesse Mazarin is reproduced by courtesy of the Courtauld Institute. Thanks are also happily and eagerly given for valuable help and advice to Miss Elspeth Evans of the National Portrait Gallery, to the staff of the West Sussex Record Office in Chichester, to His Grace the Duke of Richmond & Gordon, and to Lord Nicholas Gordon-Lennox. Diana Steer typed the manuscript with painstaking care and cheerfulness, and Juan Melian took the photograph of Chiswick Parish Church.

CHAPTER ONE

Lucy Walter

I n several respects, Lucy Walter deserves to be considered the most important of Charles II's mistresses. And yet, of all the women who played significant rôles in his life, she is the one about whom the least is known. Consequently, it is virtually impossible to give an account of her which is commensurate with the position she occupied in the King's affairs, without being obliged to rely upon conjecture, possibilities, likelihood. Even today, those who have explored the character of Lucy Walter differ so sharply in their assessment of her that it is difficult to realise they are talking about the same person. She was either a whore or a deeply wronged woman, a faithful companion to the young Prince in his hour of deepest affliction, or a calculating, deceitful opportunist. Most enticing possibility of all, she may actually have married him.

To begin with, Lucy represents the first romance in Charles's highly concupiscent life, and this alone entitles her to a special place. The Prince was only eighteen, and she probably seventeen, when their love affair was at its peak, and it bore all the marks of ardent adolescent passion. Though Charles retained an affectionate nature all his life, was fond of other women, and experienced lust almost as a daily event, Lucy was the only woman he really loved with abandon. Indeed, he was so enslaved by her, loving her 'to a degree of the most romantic excess', that fears were expressed for his health and sanity. 'All who were abroad with his majesty at that time', wrote a contemporary, 'knew the passion the King had for that person; so some of us can remember how, through immoderate love for her [he was] reduced to a condition that his life was despaired of.' No other woman had quite the same effect.

Lucy was the companion of Charles's early years of exile, when Cromwell held power in England, and the Prince was obliged to live from day to day, reduced sometimes to the condition of a pauper. She knew him when he was depressed and dispirited, a frequent victim of despondency. Of all his mistresses, Lucy was the only one never to see him occupy the throne, never to share the rich gaiety and sybaritic fulsomeness of the Court of Charles II. She died before the Restoration.

Finally, her son by the King was to have an infinitely greater influence on the course of history than any of the other bastards. He was the luckless Duke of Monmouth who, in spite of all his faults, errors of judgement and frailty of will, was a man of substance, an original character who made a mark. So much cannot be said of the rest of the royal progeny, who were for the most part laden with titles, married off to rich heiresses, and forgotten. Lucy Walter's liaison with the King carried formidable consequences – some say disastrous; it is a pity that she herself remains a character perceptible only in half-tones.

As a boy approaching manhood, Charles had been subject to pressures which no ordinary child is ever called upon to endure. He had been brought up surrounded by the luxury and subservience which befitted the heir to the throne, in the clear expectation that he would one day inherit the supreme authority in an orderly, predetermined manner. Suddenly, at the age of twelve, his future had been jumbled into a chaos of uncertainties, and he had quickly to assume maturity and responsibility. The next eight years of his life, when he might have expected to enjoy the gradual awakening of experience, were years of sadness and confusion, war and the degradation of exile. Forever packing his bags and moving on, Charles had seen his father the King for the last time on 4 March 1645, and had then repaired to Bristol, to the West Country, to Wales, and to the Scilly Isles in March 1646. From there he moved to Jersey, finally joining his mother, Queen Henrietta Maria, in Paris that summer, and staying close to the French court of his cousin, the infant Louis XIV, for two years. Penniless and deprived of dignity, Charles was entirely dependent upon his mother for subsistence; although heir to the throne, he had not been allowed a penny of his own, having surrendered his own small purse to her control. She was no fit company for a youth itching for redress; she spent her time living in the past, bemoaning her lost prosperity, and recalling the greatness of England and the lovely parties she gave there. Though ardent for activity, the Prince of necessity had been thrown into idleness, 'that bewitching kind of pleasure called sauntering and talking without any constraint'. Self-indulgence had been the only outlet for his abundant energies.

Charles was at this time a boy given to enthusiasms, thoughtful but not reflective enough to be discreet. He relied upon intuition more than analysis. He was generous and affectionate, an open, enchanting young man, with a gift for captivating everyone he met by the fusion of charm, loyalty, vigour and good nature. He had taste and an appreciation of finer things. He spoke with horror of Scotland, for instance, where there was not a woman to talk to and the barbarism of the men was such that they thought it a sin to play upon the violin.

The Prince was also inclined to be restless and eager, a prey, in other words, to the seductions of adventure. Totally without pomposity, Charles alarmed his advisers by making no proper distinctions among his acquaintances. In fact, he showed a preference for the vulgar, a trait which never deserted him and which was later to endear him to his subjects. A contemporary, writing in 1649, expressed alarm at Charles's propensities: 'His Majestie is of a very sweet and courteous disposition: it were all the pities in the world but he were in good company', and some years later, Sir Edward Nicholas was to remark, 'I wish the King would set a better value on himself and not use familiarity with persons of so much inferior quality.'

Lucy Walter has had the reputation, ever since, of being the first 'person of inferior quality' with whom Charles consorted, and has even been held responsible for his descent into blatant sexual hedonism. This is unfair in two respects; first, because Lucy was a squire's daughter from a good country family (albeit impoverished); second, because Charles was introduced to the vices of his times at a very early age, almost certainly before he met her. His companion in Paris was the licentious Duke of Buckingham (son of James I's favourite), and it was he who propelled Charles along the path of dissipation. Not that Charles was by any means a reluctant pupil; he was a lusty impressive looking youth, and there was not much else to do.

Though not conventionally handsome, Charles was a most attractive companion. At six feet and two inches, he was taller than many who were older than he. Naturally graceful, elegant and conspicuous, he was the kind of man who would compel attention even if he were not heir to the throne. Thick, luxuriant wavy black hair dominated his appearance, and together with his dark skin gave him a distinctly Mediterranean look. He was sometimes known as 'the Black Boy', and at his birth his mother had despaired of his swarthiness. 'He is so dark', she had written, 'that I am ashamed of him.' Now, however, there was no cause for shame: breeding and a glowing, irrepressible personality had turned ordinary looks into a spectacular appearance. Madame de Motteville described him at this time as 'well-made, with a swarthy complexion agreeing well with his fine black eyes, a large ugly mouth, a graceful and dignified carriage, and a fine figure'. Such was the youth who fell in love with Lucy Walter some time before 1648.

There is no doubt that Charles had had sexual encounters before he met Lucy. The Stuarts were known to mature early, and there was no moral opprobrium attached to the expression and fulfilment of sexual desires as soon as they became potent. At fifteen, Charles had already left behind the bloom of early adolescence. There were even stories that he had fathered his first illegitimate children soon after his arrival in Jersey, when he was only just sixteen. One of these children emerged briefly, twenty years later, to reveal his identity.

It appeared that Charles had bedded a mature young lady of twenty years, Marguerite de Carteret, the daughter of the Governor of Jersey. The child of that liaison went first by the name of Don Giacomo Stuart, and later was known as James de la Cloche. This is odd since Marguerite did in fact marry one Jean de la Cloche ten years later. Could it be that the boy assumed his mother's married name at that point? Not even tentative answers are possible, for James de la Cloche was completely unheard of, his existence unsuspected, until he joined the House of Novices of the Society of Jesuits in Rome at Sant Andrea, when he was twenty-one. He then produced letters from the King which purported to admit the royal paternity; they are letters from Charles to Oliva, the General of the Society of Jesuits, which speak of a youthful misdemeanour, the child having been born 'plustôt par fragilité de notre première jeunesse que par malice'. De la Cloche was kept well supplied with income after the Restoration, and was given a certificate by his father in which his identity was acknowledged; this document was said to be signed and sealed with the King's own seal. Furthermore, it was true that Charles gave generous honours to the Carteret family, which would allow a suspicious mind to deduce he had reparations to make.

It was even suggested that James de la Cloche was the Man in the Iron Mask, but that is a digression we can safely avoid. None of this was known until the letters were published in 1866, and were investigated by the historian Lord Acton, who risked his reputation to claim their authenticity. Andrew Lang, however, showed as best he could that the whole story was an 'audacious fraud', that de la Cloche was an 'impudent, lying adventurer' who was unheard of until he emerged 'from the subterranean depths of rascaldom' in 1668. He died in 1669.

We shall never know for certain. Suffice it to say that such stories, true or otherwise, could not have circulated unless the Prince had been known to engage in amorous liaisons when still a boy; at least the stories could not be dismissed as impossible. The only certainty is that Charles never permitted any of his offspring to bear the name of Stuart.

The next question is, when did Charles first meet Lucy Walter? We know that they were together in The Hague in 1648, but tradition, and likelihood, persist in reporting that they knew each other before then. They might have met in Exeter in 1644, or in Wales in 1645. In order to unravel the probabilities, one must investigate Lucy's background.

The diarist John Evelyn described Lucy Walter as 'the daughter of some very mean creatures' and such were the origins which history assigned to her for the next 250 years. It is difficult to square this assessment with the facts (besides, Evelyn was adding to his diary many years after the date, when he might have had political motives for defaming her). Lucy was the only daughter of William Walter, an eminent squire who had lived at Roche Castle in Pembrokeshire. The name is not Celtic in origin, but the Walters had been prominent in Wales for two centuries. Morris Walter had been sheriff of Haverford-west in 1565, and three times mayor of the town. There was a Sir Richard Walter who was High Sheriff for the County of Pembroke. William Walter himself had been Comptroller of the Household to Charles I when he was Prince of Wales. Lucy was born probably at Roche Castle about 1630, but hardly ever lived there; the castle was burned down by Cromwell's men in 1644.

On her mother's side, Lucy could boast an even more illustrious pedigree. She was Elizabeth Protheroe, daughter of Eleanor Vaughan and niece of the 1st Earl of Carbery. Going back another three generations, we find that she was descended from Lady Katherine Howard, daughter of the 2nd Duke of Norfolk, and could therefore name Edward I as one of her ancestors. Eleanor Vaughan had married John Protheroe, a distinguished astronomer and close friend of the famous Thomas Harriot. Lucy's grandfather, together with Harriot and the Welsh astronomer Sir William Lower, was one of the first Englishmen to examine the skies through a telescope. By the time Lucy was born, then, the Walter family could with justice claim an ancestry that was intellectual, aristocratic, and respectably dedicated to public service. Lucy had two brothers, Richard and Justus Walter.

When Lucy was seven or eight, the family moved to London, and took lodgings in King Street, Covent Garden. Here again, they found themselves in a district distinguished by its eminent tenants. At one time or other, they had as neighbours Sir Henry Vane the younger, a member of the Long Parliament, who lived at 43 King Street, the 1st Earl of Orford, Denzil Holles and Sir Kenelm Digby the author, diplomat and naval commander. Round the corner in the Great Piazza were William Brouncker, later first President of the Royal Society, Thomas Killigrew the dramatist, who built the first Theatre Royal in Drury Lane, Sir Peter Lely the portrait painter, Sir John Winter, secretary to Queen Henrietta Maria. The houses in Covent Garden were packed tight with aristocrats, actors, violinists, pianists, dramatists, painters, parliamentarians. In 1643 Samuel Cooper, who was later to paint the most famous miniature of Lucy's son, also lived in King Street, and Sir John Baber, physician to Charles II, would take up residence there in 1671. Hardly the neighbourhood where one would expect to find some 'mean creatures'.

Evelyn's poor opinion of them may well have derived from the unseemly litigation heard before the House of Lords in 1641 and 1646, when Mr and Mrs Walter blamed each other for the breakdown of their marriage; Lucy would then have been between eleven and sixteen years old.

Elizabeth Walter claimed that she had been deserted by her husband and left without maintenance. William Walter was ordered to answer the accusation, and he responded with a counter-petition that he had not received the £600 which his father-in-law, John Protheroe, had promised as part of his marriage settlement. He admitted that he no longer lived with his wife because he 'had more than a suspicion of her incontinency', and described her as 'disloyal and malignant'. In view of Lucy's subsequent reputation as a prostitute, this glimpse into the character and habits of Mrs Walter is illuminating. Lucy grew up in a household where marital fidelity was not the norm, and where quarrels were prolonged and vindictive.

The House of Lords ordered Mrs Walter to offer to return to her husband. He refused to take her, and his estates were thereupon sequestrated; further, he was required to pay £60 a year for the support of his wife and family.

The matter was by no means at an end. Walter returned to Wales (to live at his house in Rhôsmarket), and Elizabeth Walter moved in with her mother and sister (Mrs Gosfright) at the village of St Giles-in-the-Fields, while the children were supported by William Walter's stepfather Nicholas Chappell.

In 1646, Walter refused to pay the arrears due to his wife, accusing her of persistent adultery. Mrs Walter's submission to the House of Lords denied any such imputation, claiming instead that

> she hath so much experience of her husband's disloyaltie to her bedd and that it is alreadie publickly knowne that for the space of five years . . . her said husband kept a maid servant in his house . . . by whom he had two illegitimate children . . . and enforced your peticioner to provide for the said Children as for his own Children lawfully begotten, and if at any time she refused to doe it (as haveinge just cause) her said husband would revile her beate and abuse her for it.

Elizabeth Walter went on to say that her husband had completely abandoned and 'cast off' her children, while continuing to beget many other children on other women. She therefore besought their Lordships to grant a divorce.

The Lords evidently did not think much of Mrs Walter's veracity, for on 18 February 1647, they gave judgement that the children should be returned to William Walter for their keeping and education, and that the sequestration of his lands should be lifted. It was consequent upon this decision that Lucy, rather than be with her father, fled to Holland where she took up residence at her uncle Gosfright's house, he being a Dutch merchant. Within little more than a year she was mistress to the heir to the throne.

Examining the details of this intricate story, we see that there are two occasions on which Lucy may have come into contact with the Prince of Wales before they cohabited in Holland. In September 1644 Prince Charles was in Exeter. *Symonds' Diary* tells us that his troops were four miles away, at Broad Clyst, and that the Prince lodged there for six days. The Chappell family at that time owned a house called Brockhill in Broad Clyst, and we know from the House of Lords depositions during the Walters' divorce proceedings that Nicholas Chappell acted as guardian to the Walter children, his step-grand-children. If Lucy was at Brockhill as a fourteen-year-old girl in 1644, which is at least possible, then it is likely that she met the Prince.

Another opportunity might have occurred a year later when Charles I was a fugitive in Wales, and stayed at Golden Grove, the home of the Earl of Carbery in Carmarthenshire. Carbery was Lucy's mother's uncle, and it is again a possibility that she may have crossed the path of the royal entourage on this occasion. The fact that the Prince of Wales was not with his father by this time does not prevent local tradition from clinging to the assertion, passed down over the years, that Charles and Lucy first met in Wales. If there be any truth in the story, then Lucy may have arranged to meet Charles in Holland, although she was there before him. The strands of probability are, however, as weighty as gossamer. Even if he had known her before, it would be more than two years before they met again in Holland, and two years is a long time in the sentimental life of a young man.

Whatever the case, it was between 9 and 17 July 1648 that Charles and Lucy became lovers, and that their son was conceived. This was Charles's first visit to Holland. Lucy was now using the name Mrs Barlow (taken from a maternal uncle, John Barlow of Slebech), by which she was generally known thenceforth; no satisfactory explanation has been given to account for her need for an *alias*.

Contemporary accounts all agree that Lucy was marvellously alluring, 'perhaps the most beautiful of all the women who at one time or another enslaved the fancy of Charles'. Baronne d'Aulnoy, who had seen her, wrote, 'Her beauty was so perfect that when the King saw her in Wales where she was, he was so charmed and ravished and enamoured that in the misfortunes which ran through the first years of his reign he knew no other sweetness or joy than to love her, and be loved by her.' She relates that Charles took great care to please Lucy, and showed evident delight in parading her as his mistress; he preened himself with the pride of a young man who cannot believe his luck in making such a prize conquest, 'as he was so very young, and this was his first passion'.

Lucy's beauty would not be appreciated today. It was not so much a perfect example of feminine essence, discreet and demure, as a palpable, arrant display of voluptuousness. She was sexy, earthy, arousing, the kind of woman who knows her assets and how best to exploit them. There is no evidence that Lucy Walter was conspicuously intelligent. She was apt to express herself in violent tempers rather than with cool reasoning, although in fairness she was not nearly such a termagant as one of her successors in Charles's affections, Barbara Villiers, nor is there more than a sentence or two of Lucy's conversation which have come down to us; we have but little on which to base a judgement. However, Lucy's career shows that she could get her way with men, that she was predatory, given to sulking, and when provoked, liable to react in a demonstrative, ostentatious manner. The most famous phrase describing her is from Evelyn's diary, where she is depicted as 'brown, beautiful, bold, and insipid'. By 'insipid' the diarist means that she did not have much to say which could be of any interest, that she lacked taste and refinement. But then Evelyn was an intellectual, and rather fastidious as well; he would not approve of mistresses in any guise. The adjective 'bold' conveys a very clear picture of a shameless beauty, confident of her power to allure, more articulate in gestures than in words.

It is not, however, the beauty of Mrs Barlow that is in question, but her reputation. Evelyn uncompromisingly called her a 'strumpet', Clarendon said she was 'a private Welchwoman of no good Fame, but handsome'. After her death and the Restoration, many uncomplimentary things were said about her, and have been quoted again and again. James II in particular, in his *Memoirs*, piled accusations against her morals, giving posterity a vivid portrait of a hussy, but he of course had every interest in discrediting the mother of the Duke of Monmouth, whose claims to legitimacy threatened James's right to the throne. Nevertheless, the mud has stuck, in spite of valiant attempts by G. D. Gilbert, who wrote a long appendix in defence of Mrs Barlow which he published with his edition of Mme D'Aulnoy's *Memoirs of the Court of England in 1675.* One of Lucy's descendants, Lord George Scott, wrote a painstakingly thorough analysis of her life in which he tried to redress the balance. Gilbert and Scott both maintain that her detractors were engaged upon a defamation of character undertaken for political motives long after her death, but they ignore the fact that general opinion unfavourable to Lucy had been circulating long before.

Samuel Pepys heard from Mr Alsopp, the King's brewer, that 'it is well known she was a common whore when the King lay with her'. Pepys is an honest and punctilious chronicler. If it is 'well known' as early as 1664 that Lucy had led the life of a prostitute, then subsequent accounts which confirm this view cannot be so easily dismissed.

When Lucy went to The Hague, as 'Mrs Barlow', she was already the mistress of Robert Sidney, of the Earl of Leicester's family, and her services had previously been puchased by Sidney's brother Algernon Sidney, a colonel in Cromwell's army. Algernon had come across Lucy in London in 1644, when he was recovering from injuries sustained at the battle of Marston Moor, and Lucy herself was the rootless child of a broken home, her quarrelling parents accusing each other of promiscuity. Lucy cannot have been much more than fourteen, but Algernon Sidney is said to have 'trafficked for her first and was to have had her for fifty broad pieces'. However, his regiment was commanded out of London, and Sidney had to leave and therefore 'missed his bargain'. When Lucy went to The Hague, Algernon remembered the deal he had struck, and recommended her to his brother Robert, who was then in Holland, and whose mistress she was when the Prince of Wales arrived there in 1648. Charles, hearing of her charms, arranged to meet her and quickly took Robert Sidney's place. He, apparently, surrendered her willingly, having told his friends, 'Let who will have her, she is already sped.'

It has been pointed out that this miserable tale is hardly likely when one considers that Lucy and the Sidneys were derived from the same stock, being related to one another as fourth and fifth cousins several times over. That is a naive view. There is no overwhelming circumstance which would prevent distant cousins from having a carnal relationship. Lucy was certainly in a vulnerable position, without a stable home or any promise of permanence in her affairs; she had little alternative but to allow herself to be used in this way.

Charles succeeded Robert Sidney in Lucy's bed so hurriedly that when her son was born, 274 days after Charles's arrival in The Hague, 'the world had cause to doubt' whose son it was; the world also noted, according to James II, that the boy grew up to resemble Sidney very closely indeed, even so far as to share the feature of a wart on the face.

All this is wrong. In the first place, Robert Sidney, did not have a wart on his face, and it would require a huge imaginative leap to discern any likeness between him and the future Duke of Monmouth. Common sense alone admits a powerful resemblance between Charles II and Cooper's famous miniature of the boy when he was about seven. Secondly, Charles himself was never in any doubt about his paternity of the child; he did not always acknowledge his bastards with such resolute certainty.

Charles was evidently besotted with the ravishing Mrs Barlow, and soon his devotion to her welfare became such a talking point that rumours concerning their relationship sprang up like weeds. It was assumed by many, from the very beginning, that they had secretly married while Charles's passion was overwhelming his judgement, and so firmly established did the belief become that official denials in later years served only to reinforce it.

In 1648, when Charles and Lucy were together in The Hague, he was heir to the throne. By the time their son was born on 9 April 1649, he was King Charles II, but with another eleven years of exile, increasingly penurious and humiliating, to endure. In a gesture which may be called desperate, magnanimous, filial, or sagacious depending upon one's point of view, but certainly unique in the history of England, he had sent a *carte blanche* to his father's tormentors, with his signature at the bottom, inviting them to insert whatever demands they wished if only they would spare the life of Charles I. This odd document may still be seen at the Public Record Office in London. It was of no avail. The King was beheaded in January; the new King's son by Lucy Walter *alias* Barlow was born in April. There was a wry neatness in the sequence of events.

'The King loved Monmouth as he did his eyes.' Although it would be years before he was ennobled, before Charles felt confident enough of opinion publicly to acknowledge him as a natural son, the little James, as he was called, immediately secured a place in his father's heart which his behaviour in subsequent years could not dislodge.

The birth took place in Rotterdam, probably at the house of Gosfright, Lucy's maternal uncle, and shortly afterwards the child was removed to be nursed at Schiedam. There was a very large colony of Scottish expatriates in the area, which would permit secrecy and security if they were needed. Charles had returned from England in September 1648; the ensuing months, up to and beyond the birth of his son, were the happiest of his relationship with Lucy. The sour chapters of treachery, blackmail and kidnapping were in the future. What Charles thought about his peculiar position, or about the development of his relationship with his mistress, is not recorded: an exiled King, not yet nineteen years old, with the hopes and morale of an exiled Court to sustain, now the father of a beautiful boy, begotten on a harlot, a child who in other circumstances might be the legitimate Stuart heir. His reflections, whatever they were, ought to have been pregnant with foreboding..

Now that Charles was *de jure* King of England, the thoughts of some turned once more to the question of his future Consort. Mistresses and love affairs were all very well, but a proper dynastic match which satisfied political and fiscal requirements would have one day to be made. Charles had already had to endure a formal courtship undertaken for reasons of State when he was a boy. His overbearing mother, Queen Henrietta Maria, had thought that his cousin, Mademoiselle de Montpensier, would make an admirable wife, and Charles was made to woo her during his first sojourn in Paris. Her chief advantage consisted in her being the richest heiress in Europe, as she was the daughter of Louis XIII's brother, the Duc d'Orléans; she also counted herself

Europe's most desirable catch. She was known as 'La Grand Mademoiselle', with good reason, for she was a heavy creature built for more rugged exercise than love-making, with a large nose and a solid presence, lacking in grace or feminity. She was not at all what Charles would call *coucheable*. La Grand Mademoiselle has herself left an entertaining account of this half-hearted flirtation in her Journal, where it is obvious that both she and the Prince were heartily bored by the ritual. He behaved dutifully, she respectfully; if only they could have laughed together. She described him as 'only sixteen or seventeen years old and quite tall for his age. He had a beautiful head, black hair, a dark complexion, and was fairly agreeable in person.' She also recorded that he did not speak or understand French, which she admitted was 'a most inconvenient thing'.

Queen Henrietta Maria behaved without much subtlety in trying to advance her schemes, and the wily Mademoiselle was very much alive to her intentions. The Queen told Mademoiselle that her son was madly in love with her, that he talked about her all the time, that he had to be held back otherwise he would be forever outside her window, that he sighed and he worried and he pined; she was exactly the kind of person he most admired. Mademoiselle listened politely, without responding with the expected enthusiasm. 'I did not greatly value the opinion of another relative to a man who could say nothing whatever for himself', she wrote somewhat acidly. She was no more impressed when Charles, on his mother's instructions, always contrived to sit near her, always held his hat in his hand even if it were pouring with rain, always was the last to bid goodnight.

Mademoiselle rejected Charles's proposals, to the annoyance of Henrietta Maria, and the relief of Charles himself, who turned with relish to her beautiful Maid of Honour, the Duchesse de Châtillon. It is generally accepted that this affair remained platonic, but there is no doubt that the King's emotions were genuinely aroused, and that he cherished an affection for the Duchess, whom he called 'Bablon', all his life. Twenty years later there are cosy and charming references to her in his letters. He told his sister, for example, that he had nurtured 'more than an ordinary inclination for her'. For her part, she is said to have provoked the anger of La Grande Mademoiselle by saying that she could still, if she so wished, be Queen of England.

Then, in The Hague, Charles came into contact with his cousin Sophia, sister to Prince Rupert, later Electress of Hanover, and mother to King George I. She was living in exile with her mother the Queen of

Bohemia, and it seems to have crossed everyone's mind (except perhaps Lucy's) that she and Charles might consider an alliance. There was only six months' difference in their ages, and in every other respect they might have made a very happy couple. Sophia said that 'he and I had always been on the best of terms, as cousins and friends, and he had shown a great liking for me with which I was much gratified'. What she did not say in so many words was that Charles flirted with her, telling her she was 'handsomer than Mrs Berlo', for insincere motives; he was being King for a moment, not a cousin and friend, and Sophia was disappointed and offended. So nothing came of that idea.

Nor did the proposed match with the daughter of Lord Argyll in 1650 progress beyond speculation, in spite of its being a wise move which would have secured the satisfaction and loyalty of Scotland. The trouble with all these ideas was that they aroused no more than perfunctory interest in Charles. He was still young and lusty, and wanted to lie in a lady's arms without testing the diplomatic wisdom of his choice. He was still intent on present pleasures; let policy wait its turn. So when the name of Queen Christine of Sweden was put forward, it barely received a nod, and when later it was suggested that the King might like to select a bride from among the German princesses, he declared that he would rather remain single all his days than marry any one of them, because 'Odds fish! They are all dull and foggy.'

Meanwhile, Charles's appetite for love-making went unabated. His passion for Lucy must have subsided somewhat by 1650, for not much more than a year after the birth of his son, he had taken Lady Shannon to his bed, and had a daughter by her in 1651. She was a very pretty woman who had been born Elizabeth Killigrew and was the wife of Francis Boyle, later Viscount Shannon. Charles probably met her when she was a Maid of Honour to Queen Henrietta Maria. Eight years the King's senior, she had the distinction of being one of the few women in his life to have been older than himself. Their daughter was baptised Charlotte Jemima Henrietta Maria, and given the surname Fitzroy, the first of Charles's bastards to be so called. This Charlotte was to marry James Howard, a grandson of the 2nd Earl of Suffolk, and *their* daughter would be given the fanciful Christian name of Stuarta.

Advancing the narrative by a few years, there are two more significant mistresses who belong to the years of exile. In Bruges the King met Catherine Pegge, daughter of a Derbyshire squire, Thomas Pegge of Yeldesley, who was created a baronet after the Restoration. Catherine bore the King a son, nicknamed 'Don Carlos' owing to his affability and great popularity at Court, and a daughter called Catherine. The girl is reported to have become a nun, whereas Don Carlos was later created Earl of Plymouth and married Lady Bridget Osborne, daughter of the 1st Duke of Leeds.

The successor to Catherine Pegge was Eleanor Needham, daughter of Lord Kilmorey. She had been married at the age of eleven to Peter Warburton, soon widowed, and married *en secondes noces* Lord Byron of Newstead Abbey, Nottinghamshire. It was as Lady Byron, though again a widow, that she became the King's mistress, and thereupon used her position to extract as much money from him as was possible. Greedy concubines were one of the penalties Charles had to pay for his lascivious nature, and Lady Byron's spoils were modest compared to the vast riches enjoyed by some of the later post-Restoration ladies. Charles was ever a prey to feminine guile; he could not bear to see a lady cry, and would readily concede an unreasonable demand if it would secure a quiet life and a happy smile. In Lady Byron's case, this weakness involved giving her £15,000 during the difficult years of exile when every penny was scarce, and according to Pepys she would not leave him alone until he had promised to have made for her £4000 worth of plate, 'but by delays, thanks be to God, she died before she had it'. Lady Byron died in 1664, having experienced supreme difficulty in squeezing from the royal purse a pension of £500 a year since 1660.

Incidentally, Pepys also says that Lady Byron had been 'the King's seventeenth whore abroad' (he was quoting Court gossip), an estimate which has caused historians to start with amazement and declare that Pepys's information must have been exaggerating. Of course, it is not possible to trace them all, if indeed there were seventeen, but I do not find it so astonishing that a man with Charles II's appetite should have had seventeen encounters in fourteen years. Many men who consider themselves relatively abstemious have as many.

Like many a Don Juan, Charles preferred the conquest to the prize, and once victory was assured, he tired rather quickly of his ladies. They, however, found this cynicism allied to masculine charm irresistibly attractive, and tended to pine for him long after he had lost interest. This was probably the case with Lucy Walter. With others, he would usually give in rather than face a squabble, then move on to fresh endeavours ('it is not in his nature to gainsay anything that relates to his pleasures', says Pepys), but with Lucy, because she was the mother of the son on whom he doted, disagreements led eventually to acrimony and ultimate tragedy.

*   *   *

Lucy Walter's history would surely not have intrigued so many amateur detectives and painstaking researchers, were it not for the potentially explosive implications of her supposed marriage to the King, which alone elevates her to a position of eminence. Otherwise, she would retain a subsidiary place in the chronicles, as the object of an early passion and the mother of the Duke of Monmouth.

Quite soon after Charles II married Catherine of Braganza, and it became clear that the Queen was having difficulty in producing an heir to the throne, rumours were buzzing around London concerning Monmouth's legitimacy. As ever, Pepys caught the tone and immediacy of the whispers in a vivid entry in his diary on the last day of 1662 :

> The Duke of Monmouth is in so great splendour at Court and so dandled by the King, that some doubt, if the King should have no child by the Queene (which there is yet no appearance of), whether he would not be acknowledged for a lawful son.

Monmouth was then an exceedingly pretty youth of thirteen and the recipient of Charles's demonstrative affection (the King's new mistress, Barbara Villiers, also took a fancy to the boy, but that is a story which belongs in another chapter). However, in circles close to the King, these were not by any means fresh sprouts growing on virgin soil. Even before the birth of the Duke of Monmouth in 1649, there had been talk of a marriage between Charles and Lucy.

On 7 March 1647, the minutes for Sir Edward Hyde's day declared one of his preoccupations : 'Is not sure that the intelligence of the Prince's marriage is false.' Hyde expanded this cryptic remark in a letter to Secretary Nicholas :

> I am far from being secure, for many reasons, that the intelligence from London of the Prince's marriage may not be true; we were apprehensive of it before he went, and spoke freely to him our opinions of the fatal consequence of it.

This letter is of considerable importance for, though it says little, it does say enough to indicate (a) that the Prince had considered marrying, and was sufficiently in earnest to alarm his advisers and provoke from them severe remonstrations, (b) that he was the kind of headstrong youth who might well ignore the advice and go ahead with his romantic project, hence they did not immediately dismiss the persistent rumour as nonsense, but entertained it as a serious possibility, (c) that Hyde and others knew in advance what a disastrous move this would be. It seems that ministers were always *aux aguets* for an impulsive act of this nature. Anyway, the date is interesting, for it must refer to a marriage which took place in Jersey or in Wales, long before Charles and Lucy were known to be together in The Hague.

Hyde was eventually convinced that Charles *had* married, as is demonstrated by a remark reported thirty-three years later, admittedly at second-hand and from a partisan source :

> And yet that very Lord Chancellor [Hyde], being in danger of an impeachment in Parliament for advising and perswading the King to a Marriage with Queen Katherine, excused himself from all sinistrous ends in that affair by affirming, that His Majesty had a lawful son of his own by a former marriage (specifying by name the D. of M.) to succeed to his Crown and Dignity.

The people of Haverfordwest, where the Walter family had home and influence, have passed down a tradition that the marriage took place there in 1646 or 1647, and a local history published in 1882, while seeking to offer further information, in fact compounds the mystery :

> Some time antecedent to the middle of the last century,* under High Warrant from the Home Office, the marriage register of the Parish of St Thomas, Haverfordwest, where the family of the Walters resided for a time, was sent for to headquarters. No reason was assigned for the requirement by those who applied for these documents, but it was afterwards asserted, and with considerable confidence, by some who were likely to be well informed on the matter, that the register contained a record of a marriage which was solemnised a century before, which, if it had been proved, would have been of some consequence as regards the succession of the House of Brunswick. It is now, of course, only a romance of history, *but the register was never returned.*

It seems that whenever there is a disputed marriage, the relevant page of the church register is either obliterated, torn out, or stolen; there

* *i.e.* before 1750.

are a dozen other such cases in history, and they are all infuriating, for they preclude any approach to the truth. All we can say in support is that the Walters of Haverfordwest never doubted such a marriage had taken place; on their family genealogical tree, next to Lucy's name was printed MARRIED KING CHARLES YE SECOND OF ENGLAND.

The next time the rumour surfaced it was initiated by Mr Gosfright, brother of Lucy's uncle by marriage, who maintained that Lucy and Charles were joined at an inn in Liège, some time in 1649, and that Sir Henry Pomeroy was a witness. Pomeroy denied all knowledge of such an event, so that was pursued no further.

Other supposed witnesses who were put forward at various times included the Bishop of Winchester and the Bishop of Lincoln, who was credited with having performed the ceremony. Then, in 1696, the former Archbishop of Glasgow made a maddeningly laconic entry in his Journal :

Sir J. Corke told me that the Earl of Newburgh told him that he was witness to King Charles's marriage with the Duke of Monmouth's mother, and that Progers and another were so too.*

Newburgh was abroad with Charles in his exile, and would have every cause to be privy to the King's secrets; while Edward Prodgers was even more likely to have confidential information, since he was a Groom of the Bedchamber, and enjoyed by long habit and tradition the personal relationship with the Monarch which that position affords. Still, there is nothing to corroborate, except perhaps the story that Queen Henrietta Maria consented to Charles's marrying Lucy 'rather than he should consume and perish in his otherwise unquenchable flames', a hyperbolic remark which smacks of mockery.

It is nevertheless true that Henrietta Maria showed an interest in Lucy's son, taking him to stay with her outside Paris and treating him with the honour and esteem normally reserved for a prince of the blood. In Paris he had even publicly been greeted as Prince of Wales. The Queen Dowager never paid the slightest attention to Charles's other bastard offspring. She allowed Lucy to be present at her sick-bed, which was a very great honour indeed. Still more pointed was the inter-course between Charles's sister Mary and Lucy Walter in Holland; no one was more conscious of her rank and royalty than Mary, in fact she was rather a prude, and it is suggested that her acceptance of Lucy

* Entry in shorthand, here expanded.

is witness to her belief that Lucy was legally tied to Charles; for Mary to consort with a mere strumpet would have been unthinkable.

A journal called the *Mercurius Politicus* reported that Lucy 'passeth under the character of Charles Stuart's wife or mistress', which at least indicates that Lucy was not slow to claim her status, and it was said that Queen Catherine herself was convinced that a marriage had taken place, all of which shows that the rumours had spread, by 1656, from the highest to the lowest in the kingdom. Lucy's servants were seen to serve her on the knee, in a manner which befitted royalty.

During the course of 1654 and 1655, Princess Mary wrote letters to Charles which, when they were published, served to darken the mystery to the point of total obfuscation, by reason of their ambiguous references to a person whom she calls 'your wife'. These letters continue to confuse historians.

On 9 November 1654, Mary wrote :

Your Mothere says that the greatest thankfulness she can show for the honour of your kind remembrance is to have a special care of your wife for feare her husband here may make her forget them that are absent. Your wife thanks you in her own hand and still though she begs me very hard to help her.

The first problem with this is that 'Your Mothere' cannot refer to Henrietta Maria, who was not with her daughter in Holland at the time. So who does it refer to? That must ever remain Princess Mary's secret. It is perhaps a private nickname for someone who cannot be identified. And if 'Mothere' is not mother, then 'wife' presumably does not mean wife.

The next letter, in May of the following year, contains another curious paragraph :

Your wife is resolving whither she will writ or no : therefore I am to say nothing to you from her; but will keepe open my letter as long as the post will permitte, to expect what goodnature will worke, which I find now dos not at all : for 'tis now eleven of the clock, and noe letter comes.

And in June she says :

Your wife desires me to present her humble duty to you which is all she can say. I tell her 'tis because she thinks of another husband, and does not follow your example of being as constant a wife as you are a husband : 'tis a frailty they say is given to the sex, therefore you will pardon her I hope.

'Wife' might mean sweetheart (one of the seventeen mistresses who have never been discovered?), or it might refer, in sisterly banter, to Mary herself. The letters are clearly written in a teasing spirit, for Mary would be unbalanced if she really thought constancy was among her brother's qualities, and they must therefore reluctantly be dismissed as serious evidence of any kind. Besides which, as the King had terminated his liaison with Lucy in 1651, any attempt to identify her as the 'wife' in 1655 is capricious.

Much less easy to explain is a letter from one Daniel O'Neill, Groom of the Bedchamber and soon to be emissary and trouble-shooter for Charles II, written to the King on 8 March 1654, and ostensibly dealing with money matters. Suddenly, there is a tantalising reference included in the most matter-of-fact manner :

> . . . if he [Ormonde] had been here when he was expected, which was two moneths ago, in all likely hood you might have been at home with your wife and children now peaceably.

Wife and children? Could this be Lucy, who by now had a daughter as well as a son? The King never acknowledged paternity of Lucy's second child, born after he ceased to have anything to do with her, so the plural is mystifying whatever interpretation may be placed upon it. For my part, I can only surmise that, since the rest of O'Neill's letter uses pseudonyms and codes, presumably in order to befuddle interceptors who would soon gather who was providing the exiled Charles Stuart with money from England, then this bewildering reference to wife and children must be an elaborate code message, the key to which died with the two correspondents.

To return to Mr Gosfright. Lucy's uncle's brother apparently rebuked Lucy's mother, Elizabeth Walter, for abandoning her daughter and obliging her to lead an immoral life to support herself ('for leaving her daughter abroad in an ill way of liveing'). Mrs Walter told Gosfright that he had made a serious mistake, 'for her said daughter was married to the King'. What this does is to confirm, yet again, that Lucy and her relations put it about that a marriage had taken place, which is hardly surprising.

Much more substantial evidence comes into play when we look at the version which assigns the performance of the marriage ceremony to Bishop Cosin, Protestant chaplain attached to the exiled Court of Queen Henrietta Maria in 1648–49. This, too, is inconclusive, but the story has the merit of lasting power; 300 years later it is still believed by Lucy's descendants, and one must admit that it is the only presentation of the marriage theory which is plausible.

According to this account, Bishop Cosin married Charles and Lucy in 1648, and pocketed the marriage certificate, or some such document recording the occasion, rightly presuming that it would be more difficult for Charles to be restored to his throne if the public had a prostitute to look forward to as Queen. In 1660, Cosin was made Bishop of Durham, having previously heard the death-bed confession of Lucy Walter, who had revealed the truth about her life and made Cosin promise that the details would remain secret until after the death of the King. Unfortunately, Cosin predeceased Charles, dying in 1672 and leaving his heirs the guardians of whatever documents and confidences Lucy entrusted to him. Cosin's son-in-law Sir Gilbert Gerard inherited the certificate in a so-called Black Box, which, when the controversy spilled over from an amusing *canard* to a weighty affair of State, became the subject of a full-scale enquiry in 1680. 'They are endeavouring to get witnesses to swear the King was married to the Duke of Monmouth's mother.'

Secretary of State Jenkins heard evidence from anyone who had spread, listened to, or heard talk of, rumours concerning the marriage. In particular, he summoned William Disney, an attorney who was the very first to investigate the matter, and also George Gosfright and Margaret Gosfright (she had remarried and was now called Mrs Sambourne). Alas, the depositions of these two Gosfrights, who were in a better position than anyone to know the truth, subsequently disappeared. The result of the enquiry was to declare that the Black Box story was a malicious invention by enemies of the Crown, who sought to justify the treasonable aspirations of the Duke of Monmouth. But the Black Box would not be forgotten so easily.

Robert Ferguson, known as the Plotter, and something of a brave journalist dedicated to the exposure of humbug, published an anonymous pamphlet entitled *A Letter to a Person of Honour concerning the Black Box*, which firmly castigated Jenkins's enquiry as a long waste of time. Perhaps Ferguson sympathised with the Duke of Monmouth's cause, but his style is so eloquent and persuasive as to reveal the acute mind of an honest intelligence that would not stoop to base tomfoolery. The enquiry, he wrote, had been channelled in the wrong direction; instead of questioning people about the existence or otherwise of a Black Box, Secretary Jenkins should have investigated the supposed marriage of Mrs Barlow and Charles II; the box itself was a red herring:

> . . . all the examinations relating to this business would have been confined to those who were beyond sea with the king, when this marriage is supposed to have happened. But all this seems to have been industriously waved; and in the room of these, a few persons have been brought before, and interrogated by the council, who could never be supposed to have heard otherwise of it, than by way of vulgar tattle. And as I dare boldly affirm that there is no one person, who is accustomed to the fellowship of the town, who has not heard of such a marriage, so it is uncontroulably known that there was, in Oliver's time, a letter intercepted from the King to the said lady, then in the Tower, superscribed, To his wife.

What then became of the Black Box and its terrible contents? Gerard gave it to the Duke of Monmouth's descendants, who are the Dukes of Buccleuch, and it lay undiscovered for over 200 years amongst the Buccleuch archives. Then, in the time of the 5th Duke of Buccleuch, something was most certainly discovered, for there are three separate accounts of what happened which, though differing in detail, independently support one another. In 1905 Sir Frederick Barnwell wrote:

> A good many years ago Sir Bernard Burke, whom I knew very well, told me that the Duke of Abercorn had told him that he had heard from the late Duke of Buccleuch that one day, looking through papers in the muniment room at Dalkeith, he came across the marriage certificate of Charles II to Lucy Walter, that after considering the matter for some time he decided to destroy it, and thereon threw it into the fire, and it was burned.

Six years later, Lord Mersey entered a similar version in his diary:

In 1879 the Historical Manuscripts Commission had gone to
Montagu House in Whitehall to examine the muniments there, by
permission of the then Duke of Buccleuch. Delving into a corner of
a dark room, they found an old black box, and inside it the marriage
certificate of Charles II and Lucy Walters, mother of the Duke of
Monmouth. As in those days there was no Royal Marriage Act, and
as by common law a rightful Sovereign cannot be attainted, the
position apparently was that the Duke of Monmouth had been, the
then Duke of Buccleuch was, the real King of England. On this being
explained to the Duke, he said, 'That might cause a lot of trouble,'
and put the document in the fire.

The last word on the mysterious box should rest with the family and
descendants, some of whom have never been in any doubt that a document existed and was destroyed. A handwritten unemotional statement
was found among the family papers a few years ago, the authenticity of
which is secure, though the writer be anonymous; it was first published
in Lord George Scott's book on his ancestress:

> The certificate of marriage was found by Henry, Duke of Buccleuch
> and President Hope amongst some old papers at Dalkeith, and the
> Duke thought best to burn it. It does not seem clear whether it was
> the original or a copy of one at Liège where they were married by
> the then Archbishop of Canterbury . . . it is said Charles II would
> have acknowledged the Duke of Monmouth as his heir, if it had
> not been prevented by James II. And it is said that James never left
> him on his death-bed for fear he should then do it.

The historian Matthew Bloxham made a private search into the
archives, and satisfied himself that something had been concealed:

> My investigations confirm more and more the conclusion I have long
> ago arrived at, that there was a marriage, and that all direct evidence
> of it was destroyed, and that now inferential evidence only is to be
> obtained.

In other words, all those who have looked into the Buccleuch papers
emerge with a sober conviction, unalloyed with proselytising hysteria,
that Lucy Walter has been a maligned woman. The least they may

demand is an equally sober acceptance of their views, in spite of their being contrary to the great bulk of official opinion on the subject.

Whatever Charles II would not reveal about his early relations with Lucy Walter, he never seriously entertained the intention of legitimising their son. The decision was all the more difficult for him because he loved the boy dearly, and would have welcomed a son to inherit his throne and kingdom; Charles and his subjects would have been equally delighted. But Charles had a deep respect for the due process of proper descent, and would do nothing to inhibit the right of his brother James to inherit the throne. One is bound to deduce that, in Charles's view, there was no legitimate son to challenge that right. He said he would sooner see his son hanged at Tyburn than legitimise him.

Deduction is not entirely necessary, for the King did make categorical pronouncements denying that there was any truth at all in the rumours, when they became too loud and dangerous to be ignored. No other monarch has ever had to deny by public proclamation that he was a bigamist:

There being a false and malicious report industriously spread abroad by some who are neither friends to me nor to the Duke of Monmouth, as if I should have been either contracted or married to his mother; and though I am most confident that this idle story cannot have any effect in this age, yet I thought it my duty in relation to the succession of the Crown, and that future ages may not have any further pretence to give disturbance upon that score, or any other of this nature, to declare, as I do declare, in the presence of Almighty God, that I never was married nor gave contract to any woman whatsoever, but to my wife Queen Catherine, to whom I am now married. In witness whereof, I sett my hand, at Whitehall, the sixth day of January, 1678.   Charles R.

The rumours, however, would not be so readily smothered. Even as the King was writing, one Richard Forder of Houghton in le Spring, who had been Steward to Bishop Cosin and had served the Bishop at the time when he was said to have performed the marriage ceremony, was being very fluent in disclosing his version of events:

. . . had severall times declar'd in Public company, that to his knowledge ye Duke of Monmouth was ye lawfull Heire of ye Crowne of England : for he was present at ye marriage of ye Grace's Mother to ye King, a competent time before ye birth of ye Duke of Monmouth; of which he was, to ye discharge of a good conscience, ready to make affadavit, befor legall authority.

And so one is reduced to conjecture. Charles *could* have married Lucy. The King was legally free to marry whom he chose. In exile, young, passionate and suggestible, he may easily have succumbed to romance. He was of marrying age (fourteen for boys, twelve for girls), there was nothing in law to prevent him. His brother the Duke of York married Ann Hyde, the waiting-maid to the Princess of Orange. Or perhaps there was no real marriage, but a promise, a kind of contract declaring future intentions. It is safe to say we shall never know.

                    *   *   *

Now let us return to the tumble of events in Lucy's private affairs which followed the return of the King to Paris after his celebrated escape from the Battle of Worcester (this was the occasion when Charles was concealed in a hollow oak-tree while Cromwell's men passed beneath). Utterly penniless, wearing the same shirt for weeks, he found his mother peculiarly unsympathetic. She said she had no money to give him for shirts, and if he proposed taking his meals with her, he would be expected to pay for them. It was Cardinal de Retz who came to the rescue, borrowing a substantial sum from a friend, which he gave to Charles's then Jack-of-all-trades, Lord Taafe. This Irish nobleman acted as the King's chamberlain, equerry, messenger. For the moment, the money problem was alleviated.

As for Lucy, she was with Henrietta Maria's household, accompanied by her two-year-old son, and a new addition to the brood, a little daughter. Charles was anxious to see his son; it is not established whether he knew he would find a daughter as well, which is unlikely as she had been conceived and born during his absence in England. The father of the girl was none other than the same Lord Taafe.

Anyone else might have been thrown sideways by such a kaleidoscope of news – demanding gratitude for loyal service on the one hand, and fury at theft of a mistress on the other. But the King had already by this time fallen prey to the attractions of Lady Shannon, and was by temperament bound to treat the whole matter with nonchalance. (Five years later, Taafe suggested passing one of his mistresses on to Charles.) Lucy was much less taciturn. She 'used in vain all her little arts' to recover favour with Charles, promising to relinquish her scandalous way of life. The child was christened Mary, possibly in honour of Henrietta Maria, and with customary generosity was financially supported by Charles, which has led some to suppose that *he* was the father, though he never acknowledged her. One of Cromwell's spies reported back to England that 'Madam Barlow' bore Charles Stuart two children, but there is no other contemporary reference to support the assertion, apart from the exceedingly ambiguous coded letter of Daniel O'Neill, quoted earlier.

When Lord George Scott set about tracing the fate of this Mary, he discovered a piece of information fascinating in its implications. Mary married first a man called Sarsfield, and secondly a Mr Fanshawe. As Mrs Fanshawe she is on record as having performed an act of healing for the disease known as the King's Evil. In fact the disease was scrofula, but it was popularly called the King's Evil because it had long been widely believed, in those days of medical ignorance, that the only effective cure for it was a touch from the hand of the King, or, sometimes, of another person of royal blood. That the belief was extensive is illustrated by the number of times Charles II was called upon to exercise his powers; he is said to have 'touched' 92,000 people altogether, which represents twenty persons a day for the whole of his reign. The ceremony involved was fairly elaborate and solemn. The King would sit on his throne, in full regalia, a rich canopy above his head. Doctors would lead their patients one by one to the throne, where they would kneel as the chaplain, also resplendent, intoned the words, 'He put his hands upon them and healed them', whereupon the King stroked the face of the afflicted with both hands at once. Afterwards, each patient approached the throne a second time, and the King hung a gold coin on a blue ribbon about his neck as the chaplain said, 'This is the true Light who came into the world.'

Scott's discovery showed that a nineteen-year-old boy called Jonathan Trott, 'afflicted with a continual running of the most noysom matter in his Neck, accompanied often with so great Tumours and swellings about his Throat, as almost chocked him', was brought for cure before Lucy's daughter Mary Fanshawe, who, proceeding to stroke the young man with her hands, delivered him miraculously from the disease. Scott is perfectly right to conclude from this that at least some of the public believed Mary Fanshawe to be the King's daughter. More than that, however, it would be foolhardy to imply.

Lucy, meanwhile, was further endangering her reputation on the

Continent. In Brussels now, she captured the attention of the elderly, benign Sir Henry de Vic, Charles's representative in that city, so much so, that Sir Henry and Lucy travelled to Cologne in 1654 to seek the King's permission for a marriage between them. The Queen of Bohemia, Charles I's sister, wrote, 'I have the reason of Sir Henry de Vic's journey to Cologne : since it is doting time for the King's ould Ministers of State.' Anyway, Charles refused his permission, and instead gave Sir Henry a reprimand for having left his post in Brussels. (This is yet another contradiction in Lucy's story; if she wanted the world to believe she was married to the King, why on earth was she seeking his sanction to marry someone else?)

In spite of such a contretemps, Charles continued to provide financially for Lucy, at a time when it cannot have been easy for his hard-pressed Court in exile to spare a sou. The King himself was reduced to patching his clothes and repairing his worn-out shoes as best he could, and having to make do with cast-offs. He was dependent upon the goodwill of friends and allies for the food he ate. To his sister he wrote asking if she could spare a jewel or two that he may pawn, while Hyde admitted that he found the situation acutely depressing. 'I am weary sufficient of this place', he wrote from Brussels on 5 September 1657, 'having looked over the state of the debts, and finding that every bit of meat, every drop of drink, all the fire and all the candle that hath been spent since the King's coming hither is entirely owed for, and how to get credit for a week or more is no easy matter.' That Charles stretched his resources to send Lucy an allowance speaks less of her hold over him, I think, than of his concern for the welfare of his son. It was in Cologne, whence she had repaired with the intention of marrying Henry de Vic, that Charles dated the pension warrant assigning a huge sum for her upkeep :

Wee do by these presents of our especial grace give and grant unto Mrs Lucy Barlow, an annuity or yearly pension of five thousand livres to be paid to her or her Assignes in the City of Antwerp, or in such other convenient place as she shall desire, at four several payments or equal portions : the first payment to begin from the first of July 1654, and so to continue from three months to three months during her life, with assurance to better the same when it shall please God to restore us to our Kingdoms. Given under our sign manuel, at our Court at Collogn, this 21 day of January, 1655. And in the sixth year of our reign. By his Majestie's command.

Of course, it was moonshine to expect anything like this allowance to be forthcoming, but Lucy did receive £400 a year until she damaged her reputation so much that the King turned against her. Charles no doubt intended the money to be spent on the education of his son, amongst other things, and cannot have been pleased to hear that Lucy was 'living in great state, as much as the highest ladies of all England'. Just as Lucy Walter was the only mistress really to engage the King's passionate involvement, so was she the only one finally to be discarded and abandoned. One is bound to admit that she brought catastrophe upon herself.

By February 1656, Lucy had taken a new lover, Tom Howard, with whom she was living in The Hague. His rôle in the collapse of her fortunes is complex. The Princess Royal, tired of Lucy's monstrous behaviour and embarrassed by her drain on the purse, is supposed to have engaged Howard to drive a wedge between King and former mistress. If this be so, it certainly worked. But it also transpired later that Howard was a double agent, a spy in the employ of Cromwell, sent to gather whatever dirt he could which might reduce the King's persistent popularity. Add to this the fact that he may well have known Lucy since she was a little girl, and the entanglements become solid knots. Tom Howard was brother to the third Earl of Suffolk, and the Princess Royal's Master of the Horse. As a member of the ubiquitous Howard family, he was very distantly related to Lucy Walter, who was descended from the Howards on her mother's side. He was also something of a scoundrel.

When the King heard that Mrs Barlow was living with Howard, he despatched Daniel O'Neill to investigate. O'Neill (also a scoundrel) discovered such horrors that even he was alarmed, and advised the King to 'necessitate' her as the only means of bringing her to heel; she would have to be starved into decent behaviour. Apparently, she had been leading such a promiscuous life that her conduct was the talk of all the world, and since everyone knew that she was the mother of the King's child, her shame reflected on him. O'Neill found a vivid phrase to express his alarm: 'every idle action of hers brings your Majesty upon the stage'. There were tales of abortions, attempts at infanticide, the neglect of the boy, who was growing up illiterate and presumably a witness to these scenes of debauchery, even a murderous attack by Lucy on her maid Anne Hill. I quote O'Neill's letters in full, retaining the contemporary spelling:

B

I have hiterto forborne giving your majestie any account of your commands concerning Mrs Barloe, because those that I employed to hir, brought mee assurances from hir, she would obey your majestie's commands. Of late I am tould she intends nothing else, and that she is assured from Collen* your majestie would not have hir son from hir. I am much troubled to see the prejudice hir being here does your majestie; for every idle action of hers brings your majestie uppon the stage; I am noe less ashamed to have soe much importuned your majestie to have believed hir worthy of your care. When I have the honour to wayt uppon your majestie, I shall tell you what I have from a midwyf to this toune, and one of hir mayds, which shee had not the discretion to use well after knoweing so much of hir secrets.

That was from The Hague on 8 February 1656. A week later, O'Neill was able to be more precise :

Before I took the liberty to writ anything to your majestie of Mrs Barloe, I did sufficiently informe myself of the truth of what I writ, since I had the opportunity to save her from publick scandall att least. Hir mayd, whom she would have killed by thrusting a bodkin into hir eare ass she was asleep, would have accused hir of that, of miscarrying of two children by phissick, and of the infamous manner of hir living with Mr Howard; but I have prevented the mischiefs partly with threats, butt more with 100 gilders I am to give hir mayd. Hir last miscarriage was since Mr Howard went, ass the midwyf says to one, that I imploy to hir. Doctor Rufus has given hir phissick, but it was *allwayes* after her miscarrying; and though hee knew anything, it would be indiscreet to tell it. Therefore I would not attempt him, and the rather, that I was sufficiently assured by those, that were neerer. Though I have saved hir for this tyme, it's not lykly shee'le escap when I am gon; for onely the consideratione of your majestie has held Monsieur Heenuleit and Monsieur Nertwick, not to have hir banished this toune and country for an infamous person, and by sound of drum. Therefore it were well if your majestie will owen that chyld, to send hir your positive command to deliver him unto whom your Majestie will appoint. I know it from one, who has read my Lord Taaf's letter to hir of the 11th by this late post,

* Cologne.

that hee tells hir, your majestie has noething more in consideration than hir sufferings; and that the next monny you can gett or borrow, shall be sent to supply hir. Whyle your majestie incourages any to speake this language, shee'le never obey what you will have. The onely way is to necessitat hir, if your majestie can think hir worth your care.

Lord Taafe had obviously tried to reason with Lucy, but O'Neill realised she would not respond to sympathetic treatment, and would have to be subdued by hardship.

Lucy's way of life inevitably gave rise to gossip. There was an especially wicked lampoon entitled *Jacob Scott* which came out some thirty years later, after the deaths of Monmouth and Charles II, depicting Lucy as little short of a nymphomaniac. According to this publication, Robert Sidney is supposed to have declared that Monmouth was his son, and worse still, Prodgers indiscreetly claimed to have had something to do with the birth; 'he believed that he had at least for an hour helped to bring Monmouth into being'. As for Lucy, 'from day to day she got a new lover either for pleasure or for variety'. One cannot resist feeling sorry for Lucy, thus traduced and slandered after her own pitiful death. Unwise she may have been, but no one deserves to be remembered only for her faults. That, alas, is precisely the lot of Lucy Walter.

The King was much distressed by what he had been told of his son's condition. Quite apart from his being present in a house which appeared to resemble a brothel, the boy's education was being shamefully neglected. Now seven years old, he had assumed the beauty which he inherited from his mother and which Samuel Cooper captured forever in his celebrated miniature. 'The Beauty and Make of his Person and the dignity of his bearing and carriage even whilst an infant plainly discover'd the greatness of his Birth and the largeness of his soul.' Unfortunately, 'Master Jacky' was virtually illiterate. He had been taught nothing at all. 'He cannot be safe from his mother's intrigues wheresoever he is. It is a great pitty so pretty a child should be in such hands as hitherto have neglected to teach him to read or tell twenty though he hath a great deal of wit and a great desire to learn.'

Henceforth, Charles's concern for his former lover's welfare was entirely swamped by his determination to wrench his son from her control. There had already been one hair-raising occasion when an attempt had been made to kidnap Lucy's son when he was still a baby, but Cromwell's spies had been the culprits then. Lucy had set out to visit her boy, who was being cared for by a nurse in Schiedam. Accompanying her was a 'gentleman', who, when the party stopped for a rest en route, asked to be excused for a while. Lucy waited and waited, and realising that the man had decamped, she found someone else to escort her, and rode full speed to Schiedam. There she discovered both baby and nurse had gone, at which she not unnaturally grew hysterical. She 'rent her apparel, tore the hair from off her head, and with whole shours of tears bewailed the greatness of her loss'. Immediately she had sensed the child had been kidnapped in order to be shipped off to England, she had secured fresh horses and had rushed to the coast, where she created another scene, holding out a handful of gold and pleading for assistance. A crowd gathered round her, causing the Mayor to take her into shelter where she would cause less disturbance. He arranged for the town to be searched, but it was ten days before the child was found, at Loosduinen, where apparently he had been kept in hiding all this time. From that day, the mother kept a much closer eye upon strangers.

Thus when Charles went to see Lucy in Holland in 1656, spending a day and a night with her and trying to persuade her, no doubt, to release their son to his care, she would hear none of it. What Charles did not know was that Lucy would shortly make the surprise move of journeying to England herself, after an absence of nearly ten years. She did not get the reception she bargained for.

Lucy arrived in London on 7 June 1656, having been preceded by her maid Anne Hill, who rather surprisingly was still in her service despite the fact that her mistress had tried to do away with her. Lucy travelled with her brother Justus Walter, her two children, and Tom Howard. The little group took lodgings above a barber's shop near Somerset House, she posing as the widow of a Dutch captain, and it was not long before they were discovered by Cromwell's men and forthwith arrested. Lucy did not know that Howard was a Cromwellian spy – it was obviously he who disclosed her identity and whereabouts to his employers, possibly even he who engineered the visit in the first place.

When the soldiers came to take Lucy away, a neighbour recalled that she had jewels in her possession, and a paper 'containing something relating to a marriage, a dowry, a pension or maintenance from His Majesty'. This was most likely the pension warrant quoted earlier, purporting to give Lucy 5000 livres a year. It was confiscated, and later published in the newspaper *Mercurius Politicus* to show royalist sympathisers in England how Charles Stuart squandered their savings on harlots.

Lucy, under suspicion of being a spy, was incarcerated in the Coldharbour and Lanthorn Towers in the Tower of London, and underwent a thorough examination by the Privy Council. Questioned by the Lieutenant of the Tower, Colonel Barkstead, Lucy admitted her identity but lied about everything else. She had come to England to look after her mother's affairs, she said, she had not seen Charles Stuart for two years, and although she had conceived a child by him, that child was now dead. The two children she had with her were by her Dutch husband, also dead. For once, Lucy was very cool.

Tom Howard declared that he also had not seen the King for well over a year. He bumped into Mrs Barlow on board ship; it was purely a chance meeting. As Howard was playing a double game, it did not much matter what he said; his story was pitifully lame. Justus Walter did not fare any better – he produced his pass for Italy, and said that having encountered his sister by accident, he decided to accompany her to England instead.

It was the servant Anne Hill's evidence which did Lucy the most harm. Indeed, an impartial reader is bound to suspect that the girl was half-witted, bungling her story, contradicting her mistress, giving the game away in blithe innocence. Questioned on 26 June 1656, Anne Hill testified that she had been a servant to 'Lady Walter' for seven months, and that she knew one of the lady's children was fathered by Charles Stuart, who continued to maintain her 'in a costly and high manner'. Pressed ₁or further information, Anne Hill blurted out that she had heard her mistress say several times that 'Charles Stuart would quickly have England'. Had the lady seen anything of Charles Stuart recently? Oh yes, they were a day and a night together only the other week!

The interrogators brought back Anne for another session on 2 July and she proceeded obligingly to elaborate. Had Lady Walter ever been married to a Dutch person? No, said Anne, she had never heard anything about a husband in Holland, or anywhere else for that matter, but she was quite sure her lady's children belonged to Charles Stuart, although she could not help noticing that Thomas Howard also 'did much frequent her company there'. Her lady and Mr Howard 'lived but closely in their lodgings, yet very plentifully in their clothes and diet, and had a coach to attend them continually from week to week'.

Lucy spent two weeks in prison, and was released with a great deal of ignominious publicity. It served Cromwell's interest to discredit the King and at the same time display his own magnanimity. He wrote the warrant in his own hand for the release of 'one that goes by the name of Lucy Barlow', taking full opportunity to pour scorn on the heir apparent and his father, 'what a pious charitable Prince!', who spent the money collected for him on his concubines. 'Order is taken forthwith to send away his Lady of pleasure and the young Heir and set them on Shoar in Flanders which is no ordinary curtesie.' And so Lucy and her children were banished into exile.

The next month found Lucy in Brussels. As it happened, Charles was there at the same time, taking leave from his current liaison with Catherine Pegge, and while there is no evidence that he and Lucy encountered each other, it would be very strange if they had not. Hyde was uncommonly anxious lest their proximity might create more unwelcome fuss. To the Marquess of Ormonde he wrote, 'There is much talk here of a certain lady who is at Brussels, and I assure you very shrewd discourses of it, which will quickly get into England. I pray you let her go to some other place.' Ormonde replied, 'The lady has now her son and heir with her, to make up the cry.' Evidently, she would not be moved.

Lucy was now abandoned and threatened on all sides, a lonely desperate woman. The affair with Tom Howard ended unpleasantly. He appears suddenly to have deserted her, whereupon she took up with another (unnamed) young man. Lucy provoked her new lover to challenge Howard, who refused to get involved, but was nevertheless stabbed by his rival and, dangerously wounded, fled for shelter into a nearby church. In a subsequent lawsuit, he tried to extract from Lucy some pertinent documents which, if they fell into the wrong hands, might ruin him. Hyde related the stabbing incident to Digby in lighthearted vein. 'You may be merry concerning Mrs Barlow, but I assure you I cannot' was Digby's ominous reply.

Scandal followed Mrs Barlow wherever she went, and her very existence was proving an increasing embarrassment to the Court. It became imperative that the King should remove his son from her custody without delay. With this in mind, he arranged for her to be lodged at the house of one of his trusted agents, Sir Arthur Slingsby, and secretly instructed Slingsby to find some urgent but discreet means to prise Master Jacky out of her hands.

Unfortunately, Slingsby, who had a queer idea of discretion, approached the problem with the clumsiness of an unversed novice. As Lucy owed him for her board and lodging, he made a formal complaint against her and tried to have her arrested for debt. When the officers came to carry her off to prison, she grabbed hold of her eight-year-old son and, clasping him to her bosom, ran into the street, weeping, shouting, screaming for help. The ensuing uproar was so pitiful that Lucy soon had the whole street on her side, beating off the shameless officers and, in a body, protecting a defenceless mother against what they saw as a barbaric attempt to humiliate her. Lucy was quite an actress, it is true, and this was not the first time she had managed to stir up a sensational scene, but on this occasion she was entirely blameless and very much the victim of pragmatic, unsentimental political designs. Slingsby and his officers were completely taken aback by the belligerence of the opposition, and in justification the wretched Slingsby compounded his mistake by loudly proclaiming that he was acting on the King's behalf and with His Majesty's knowledge. This made matters worse, dragged Charles into disrepute, and almost provoked a riot. The Governor of Brussels, Alonzo de Cardeñas, was forced to intervene, and his secretary, Giles Mottet, wrote an indignant account of the affair to the Marquess of Ormonde:

> I am so much ashamed of the proceeding of Monsieur Slingsby and all his family, against Madam Barlow and her child, that I am loath to relate the particulars thereof to your excellency. . . . My Lord Ambassador has written to the King about it being forced thereunto *by the clamour of the people* who found this action most barbarous, abominable, and most unnatural; the worst of all is, that Sir Arthur doth report and say to all, that the King hath given him order for it. . . .

Slingsby's endeavours had achieved the very opposite of their objective. Lucy now had the people on her side, and her son in yet closer custody than before. Arrangements were made for them both to leave Slingsby's house and establish themselves with another royalist, Lord Castlehaven, subject to Charles's approval. The King could do nothing but submit to the pressure of events; it would be unwise to offend the Spanish over such a delicate issue as the honour of a lady.

Ormonde replied to Mottet in a tone designed to absolve the King from any brutal intent:

[the King] is pleased to acknowledge that he gave order to Sir Arthur Slingsby in a quiet and silent way, if it could be, to get the child out of the Mother's hands, with purposes of advantage to them both, but he never understood that it should be attempted with that noise and scandal that hath happened.

The King, said Ormonde, would be grateful for Ambassador Cardeñas' help in the execution of his plans, which, if they were thwarted, would revert to the detriment of both mother and child, whom the King would finally abandon to seek their own way in the world. Ormonde used language which was elegant yet firm :

besides the obligation it will be to the King, it will also be a great charity to the child, and in the conclusion to the Mother, if she shall now at length retire herself to such a way of living as may redeem in some measure the reproach her past ways have brought upon her. If she consents not to this she will add to all her former follies a most unnatural one in reference to her child, who by her obstinacy will be exposed to all the misery and reproach that must attend her, when neither of them is any further cared for or owned by His Majesty; but that on the contrary he will take any good office done to her as an injury to him, and as a supporting of her in mad disobedience to his pleasure. . . .

Lucy's defenders suggest that all her sorry reputation rests on the evidence of enemies, such as James II, but here is corroboration from a hitherto friendly and dispassionate source, which later refers to 'those wild and disgraceful courses she hath taken'. Charles had finally lost patience with her, and wanted to be rid of the burden once and for all.

Giles Mottet then went himself to see Lucy and tried to persuade her to give up the boy. This she still refused to do, but said she would live with her son in any house in Brussels the King cared to suggest, except of course Slingsby's, and always subject to her approval, if the King would kindly pay for the upkeep of them both. Lucy knew that she had the support of the indignant crowd, and furthermore that Cardeñas had been rebuked for allowing the *fracas* to occur. A domestic squabble had grown into a diplomatic incident. The Council of Brabant issued a formal complaint against Slingsby for 'interruption of justice'. For his part, Slingsby was outraged to find himself the villain of the piece, and vented his indignation in a letter to the King. He had been brought to ruin by having to keep Mrs Barlow, he said, and he thought it perfectly fair that he should want his money. He threatened to bring an action against Cardeñas if he did not get satisfaction.

All this might have been hot air, but Slingsby did introduce a new element into the drama which showed that the welfare of little James was not the only concern of those advising the King. He had been conferring with Daniel O'Neill, who pointed out that the best service one could render King Charles would be 'to get certain papers and letters out of her hands that concern your Majesty'. Lucy had turned to the offensive, and threatened that if she did not get her pension, she would 'post up all your Majesty's letters to her'.

The letters and papers most likely referred to compromising statements made in the heat of passion, perhaps even a promise of betrothal. That they included the famous marriage certificate is not impossible. Hester Chapman has pointed out that if Lucy had had such a document, she would have taken it to London with her (she had had no intention of coming back so soon), and Cromwell would have discovered it when he confiscated her other papers; he could not have resisted publishing such a *trouvaille*, which would have made the Restoration very questionable. But the same argument would apply to love letters or *billets-doux*, which could have been published with equal detriment to the Royalist cause. At any rate, the letters and papers have disappeared, and with them the reason behind Lucy's blackmail.

The King made another attempt at abduction. He sent Prodgers to Brussels with instructions to spirit the boy out of his mother's presence while her back was turned. Lucy was not so easily fooled a second time; she followed them out of the house, made another public fuss, and retrieved James within moments. Ambassador Cardeñas was now mightily sick of the sordid affair. He was as anxious as Charles to see the back of the awkward Lucy.

Suddenly, and for reasons which are unexplained, Lucy gave in to pressure in January 1658. Perhaps she was weary of the effort and too ill to pursue it any further (she only had months to live). At least she secured an increased pension, some of which was advanced eagerly by Cardeñas, and she remained in Brussels for another two months, having first surrendered James to the will of his father.

By April, the King had placed his son in the care of William Crofts, who was thereupon elevated to the peerage as Baron Crofts of Little Saxham, Suffolk. James would henceforth be known as 'James Crofts' until he himself would be made a duke at the age of thirteen. Thomas Ross was appointed tutor, although the boy spent much of his time among the Jansenists at the Port-Royal school just outside Paris.

Lucy never saw her son again. She followed him to Paris where she lingered, virtually friendless, for some months. King Charles, whose generosity of heart makes him one of our most attractive monarchs, would not let her starve. He told his cup-bearer, William Erskine, to look after her, while keeping her no doubt at a severe and safe distance. The King told Erskine that he had never had any intention of marrying Mrs Barlow.

Erskine himself, though he enters the story at the very end to take the most perfunctory bow, is not without interest. He was a wise and learned man, later to be appointed Master of Charterhouse, and he had in 1658 been a loyal servant to the King in exile for a number of years. He impinges upon Lucy's fate even after her death, in a most curious way. He could not have foreseen that his own niece, Lady Ann Scott, would five years later marry James Crofts, and become Duchess of Monmouth and Buccleuch.

Lucy died in the last quarter of 1658, 'of a disease incident to her profession'. Towards the end, she repented of her dissolute life and confided her secrets to Bishop Cosin. Evelyn says she died 'miserably' and miserable indeed it was to be discarded, persecuted, full of remorse and misgivings, and to know that her life's span was about to run out. Erskine looked after her burial, probably in the Huguenot Cemetery at Saint-Germain, Paris (since obliterated by development), and one of her aunts, Mrs Busfield, was recognised next of kin to 'Lucy Walter, alias Barlow, spinster'. She was about twenty-eight years old.

It was easy for the women in Charles II's life to take advantage of his inherent benevolence. He could not bear to see a lady unhappy, and that he was forced eventually to overcome his generous nature and treat Lucy with harshness is the most eloquent testimony of her behaviour. The details of her life rest on the careful weighing of probabilities, but there is enough to infer that she was a sensual, alluring woman who, once these assets ceased to attract, betrayed the weakness of her character. There was something in the Walter genes which made for poor judgement and wrong decisions. Had she been content to remain in the background and not advertise her woes, she would have been better treated. One longs to know the content of those letters which Charles had written to her and which she threatened to spread all over Brussels, but without them, the depth of Charles's feeling for her cannot be invoked in her defence. She is variously described as 'a very ill woman', or 'handsome, with little wit and some cunning'. Certain it is that, of all the King's mistresses, she is the one who was potentially the most harmful to his prospects and caused him the most embarrassment.

Their son the Duke of Monmouth inherited his mother's beauty and her instability. Of all Charles's children, he was the one to receive the most devoted attention, yet he was ultimately the one to disappoint the King most bitterly. Long after her death, Charles would be daily reminded of Lucy's character, and would have good cause to rue the day that he met her.

*   *   *

SOURCES FOR CHAPTER ONE

An Historical Account of the Heroick Life and Magnanimous Actions of the most illustrious Protestant Prince, James, Duke of Monmouth (1683)
Baronne D'AULNOY, *Memoirs of the Court of England in 1675*
Robert BAILLIE, *Letters and Journals* (1842)
British Museum, Additional Manuscripts 28094, Folio 71
Arthur BRYANT, *Charles II* (1931)
Sir Richard BULSTRODE, *Memoirs and Reflections upon the reigns and governments of Charles I and II* (1721)
Hester CHAPMAN, *The Tragedy of Charles II in the years 1630–1660* (1964)
Clarendon State Papers
The Complete Peerage
A. I. DASENT, *Private Life of Charles II* (1927)
Dictionary of National Biography
John EVELYN, *Diary*
Allan FEA, *King Monmouth* (1902)
Fortnightly Review, 1909 (for Andrew Lang article on James de la Cloche)
Gentleman's Magazine, 1866
C. H. HARTMANN, *Charles II and Madame* (1934)
Letter to a Person of Honour concerning the King's Disavowing his having been married to the Duke of Monmouth's Mother (1680)
Letters, Speeches and Declarations of King Charles II (1935)

Lewis MELVILLE, *Mr Crofts, the King's Bastard* (1929)
Memoirs of James 11, ed. Macpherson
Memoirs of the Princess Sophia, Electress of Hanover
Mercurius Politicus
Mrs NEPEAN, *On the Left of a Throne* (1914)
Elizabeth D'OYLEY, *James, Duke of Monmouth* (1938)
Samuel PEPYS, *Diary*
The Perplex'd Prince (1682)
Leopold von RANKE, *History of England* (1875)
P. F. William RYAN, *Stuart Life and Manners* (1912)
Lord George SCOTT, *Lucy Walter, Wife or Mistress?* (1947)
J. F. D. SMYTH–STUART, *Destiny and Fortitude* (1808)
Survey of London, Vol. VI (Greater London Council)
Thurloe State Papers
E. WALFORD, *Old and New London*, Vol. III
Violet WYNDHAM, *The Protestant Duke* (1976)

CHAPTER TWO

Barbara Villiers

The death of Lucy Walter went completely unnoticed in England, where the promise of far greater events was already whispered in the streets and in the coffee-houses. The same year saw the funeral of Oliver Cromwell, the 'joyfullest funeral I ever saw', wrote Evelyn, 'for there were none that cried but dogs'. It took more than another year for the rumblings of royalist triumph to reach their crescendo, but when they did, the explosion was as sudden as it was overwhelming.

On 11 February 1660, General Monk demanded the dissolution of the Rump and the establishment of a Free Parliament, and marched into the City to inform the Mayor and Aldermen of his action. The streets were lined with watchers, but that evening, when every man realised what Monk's action signified, there were bonfires all over London, thirty-one of them in a single street, and on each a rump was roasting; butchers and shop-keepers in the Strand burst into spontaneous revelry, all the church bells pealed and clanged in noisy celebration, 'the common joy was everywhere to be seen . . . indeed it was past imagination, both the greatness and the suddenness of it'.

After the execution of Charles I, his statue outside the Exchange had been torn down, and over the empty niche had been inscribed the words *'Exit Tyrannus, Regum Ultimus'* (The tyrant is gone, the last of the kings). Now there appeared an anonymous workman, obedient to nothing more nor less than his own impulse, who set up a ladder by the niche, climbed it with a pot of paint in his hand, and proceeded carefully to efface the terrible words. Having done so, he threw his cap in the air and cried *'God Bless King Charles the Second'*, at which everyone who had watched him joined in and shouted with him.

The entire country appeared to go mad. As soon as it was known that Charles had been invited to return to his kingdom, and that he had promised to devote himself to the welfare of his people, there erupted such a contagious manifestation of joy as the nation had never before seen. People sank to their knees in the street to drink the King's health, bells rang everywhere, happiness was not only audible but tangible. Lady Derby was filled with wonder. 'The change is so great,' she wrote, 'that I can hardly believe it. This passes human wisdom, and in all humility, we ought to recognise in it the hand of the Eternal; it is beyond our understanding.'

On 14 May Charles II left Breda to reclaim his kingdom. He was accompanied by the Dukes of York and Gloucester, his sister Mary and her son William of Orange. On the morning of 23 May the *Naseby*, afterwards rechristened the *Royal Charles*, took the King on board, and 50,000 people waited at the waterside to cheer him. He spent the afternoon pacing up and down the deck, and entertaining his courtiers with reminiscences of his escape from Worcester nine years before. Then they sailed for England, and anchored off Dover on 25 May. More crowds were waiting on shore to greet him. At first they were silent, as the tall, dark, slim man set foot on English soil, and knelt to thank God for his return, but when Monk placed his sword in Charles's hand and shouted *God Save the King*, the whole multitude took up the cry. It was a moment impossible to forget.

From Dover he rode to Canterbury, where the bells of the cathedral rang as bells were ringing in every little church he passed. Still more crowds thronged the streets. To his beloved sister Henriette the King wrote, 'My head is so prodigiously dazed by the acclamations of the people, and by quantities of business that I know not whether I am writing sense or no.'

All the way from Canterbury to Rochester and on to London, the crowds grew more and more dense, with common folk and landowners mingling to share their excitement, perched in trees and standing on hillsides. Many had come from miles around to be present at what they prayed and believed was a sign of salvation. On 29 May, the King's thirtieth birthday, the company approached Blackheath, where 120,000 subjects were waiting. It seemed, wrote Clarendon, 'as if the whole kingdom had been gathered there'.

So ecstatic was the general expression of thankfulness that flowers were strewn in the streets, wine and ale flowed in the rivers and fountains, tapestries hung from windows; there were morris dancers, drums, trumpets, the glitter and sparkle of resplendent uniforms, the upward thrust of polished triumphant swords. Through the Old Kent Road, people cheered from balconies, over London Bridge and into the City, where the streets were so packed that it was impossible to budge. John Evelyn was standing in the Strand, and was so overcome that he was moved to hyperbole. 'It was the Lord's doing,' he wrote, 'and such a restoration was never mentioned in any history, ancient or modern, since the return of the Jews from the Babylonish captivity.' It was certainly an event unique in the history of England, and a transfer from commonwealth to monarchy without a drop of blood being shed.

The King was naturally proud and happy. At moments it all seemed like an impossible dream after years of humiliation, and one can well believe that he spoke from the heart when he answered the oration of the Speaker of the House of Commons in the Banqueting Hall with the words, 'Whatsoever may concern the good of this people I shall be as ready to grant as you shall be to ask.' But he was also exhausted, and although now a King in fact as well as by inheritance, he was still the same sensual man. That night, he spent his private hours in the arms of a new mistress, Barbara Palmer.

*   *   *

Lucy Walter had answered the passionate needs of Charles's youth. Barbara Palmer was to be the most tenacious love companion of his maturity. Love is perhaps too tender a word to describe the nature of their tempestuous liaison, but she aroused desire to such an overwhelming degree that she came to exert a power over the King which caused her eventually to be despised by the people and cost Charles some of the popularity which had been so gratefully given him. It was not only the strength of her libido which afforded her such a pernicious influence, but the toughness of her personality. She was the most difficult and the most tiresome woman Charles ever encountered, and her demands upon his attention were such that at times he appeared to be her slave. In order to understand how her influence should be so potent, it is important to remember that she was born Barbara Villiers, and was every inch a member of that extraordinary ubiquitous Villiers clan which has made its mark on the affairs of England over the centuries, and whose ghosts still echo their peculiar power today. The Villiers family was characterised by beauty, ambition, single-mindedness, and invincible determination to see their designs to fruition. To this end they would use flattery, intrigue, or bloody-mindedness; in short, they were successful courtiers.

The Villiers had come to England with the Norman Conquest and had been granted estates in Nottinghamshire, Leicestershire and Lancashire. The author of their astounding prominence was Sir George Villiers, Barbara's great-grandfather, who was Sheriff of Leicestershire in 1591, and father of the infamous George Villiers, 1st Duke of Buckingham and favourite of James I. It was he who advanced the name of Villiers to giddy heights and at the same time brought the reputation attached to that name to such deplorable depths. The 2nd Duke of Buckingham, a crony of Charles II and one of the men held responsible for introducing him to a life of dissipation in Paris, was therefore Barbara's cousin. One must assume that it was he who first brought Barbara and Charles together.

Some measure of the tenacity of the Villiers genes may be appreciated when one considers the number of resourceful people who have carried them in the blood. The Dukes of Marlborough and Sir Winston Churchill are descended from Elizabeth Villiers; the Dukes of Atholl and Hamilton from Susan Villiers – both girls were daughters of Sir George and great-aunts of Barbara. There is Villiers blood in the Cecil family (the Marquesses of Salisbury), in the Russell family (Lord John Russell and his grandson Bertrand Russell as well as the Dukes of Bedford), and even in Queen Elizabeth II. Barbara herself is an ancestress of Lord Castlereagh, Lord Melbourne, and Sir Anthony Eden (Lord Avon). The achievements of Sir George Villiers lie not so much in his own life as in the legacy of personality proclaimed by subsequent generations; no less than thirteen Prime Ministers can trace their line straight to him. No wonder, then, that Barbara Villiers proved to be the most enduring of Charles's mistresses, retaining her hold over him long after he would have wished. She was, quite simply, stronger than the King.

Barbara was born in 1641 in the parish of St Margaret's, Westminster. Her father was William Villiers, Viscount Grandison, a staunch royalist who had fought at the battle of Edgehill and who had died from wounds received at the siege of Bristol. His friend Clarendon* wrote of him in supremely eulogistic vein : he was

> so great a lover of justice and integrity that no example, necessity, or even the barbarities of this war could make him swerve from the most precise rules of it; and of that rare piety and devotion that the court or camp could not show a more faultless person, or to whose example young men might more reasonably conform themselves . . . his affection, zeal, and obedience to the King was such as became a branch of that family.

---

* Edward Hyde of pre-Restoration years had been ennobled as Earl of Clarendon.

It was perhaps fortunate for him that he did not live to observe the nature of his daughter's fame. She was not yet two years old when he died.

Her mother Mary Bayning (daughter of Viscount Bayning) married for the second time another Villiers, Charles, Earl of Anglesey, who, notwithstanding his nobility, was a relatively poor man. The first mention of Barbara is at her stepfather's house in London, where she appeared 'in a very plain country dress', aged fifteen. It is assumed that she had lived in poverty in the country and had been brought to London to try her luck closer to the sources of power, pending a restoration of the monarchy, for which her kinsmen worked and hoped. Her family had particularly suffered from the reluctance of debtors to redeem large sums owing to Grandison and secured by mortgages on estates which had since been sequestrated by Cromwell. It is fascinating that one such debt, of £10,000, had been owing for twenty-six years by the Earl of Cleveland, bearing a name the infant Barbara would one day take for herself. Her childhood had been dominated by the atmosphere of war and the material effects of deprivation. She had learnt to be pragmatic and had been tutored in the virtues of the royalist cause. With the name of Villiers, she could not long remain in the cold; it was inevitable that she should be brought into favour as soon as the Stuarts were again ascendant.

But first, Barbara had some early lessons in the luscious delights of flirtation. Her mother and stepfather cannot have watched over her too closely, for even as a girl, we find her 'the object of diverse young gentlemen's affections' and involved very soon in a clandestine affair with Lord Chesterfield.

This Lord Chesterfield, grandfather of the 4th Earl of Chesterfield who was to write such glorious *Letters to his Son*, was twenty-three when he came into Barbara's life, and already a widower. Curiously enough, he may well have come across Lucy Walter in Holland or Paris, for he spent some of his adolescent years at the Court of Princess Mary (to whom his grandmother had been governess) and at the Court of Queen Henrietta Maria. Whatever the case, by the time he returned to England, he had a sorry reputation as an insatiable reprobate. He admitted that he would sleep with any woman provided that she was not old or ugly. At fifteen, Barbara Villiers was neither, and within six months of Chesterfield's arrival in London, the affair was under way, nurtured by romantic flattery on his side which was so treacly one marvels how she could have believed it.

Is it not a strange magick in love [he wrote when a journey to Derby-shire had separated him from her side] which gives so powerfull a charme to the least of your cruel words, that they indanger to kill a man at a hundred miles distance; but why doe I complain of so pleasant a death, or repine at those sufferings which I would not change for a diadem? No, Madame, the idea I have of your per-fections is too glorious to be shadowed either by absence or time; and if I should never more see the sun, yet I should not cease from admiring the light.

Subsequent correspondence shows that the lovers met often in secret, and that young Barbara's emotions were aroused at least so far as to make her a prey to jealousy. 'I am never so well pleased as when I am with you', she wrote, 'though I find you are better when you are with other ladyes.' Poor girl! There is no evidence that she ever again allowed herself to feel such heartache as long as she lived; rather did she resolve always to have the upper hand. With Chesterfield, however, she saw that the only way was to be available whenever he wanted her. Despite the formality of the language, her next letter is nothing less than an invitation to bed :

It is ever my ill fortune to be disappointed of what I most desire, for this afternoon I did promis to myselfe the satisfaction of your company; but I feare I am disappointed, which I assure you is no small affliction to me; but I hope the faits may yet be so kind as to let me see you at about five a clock; if you will be at your private lodgings at Lincoln's Inn Fields, I will endeavour to come.

Again, she wrote to him a joint letter with Lady Anne Hamilton, daughter of the Duke of Hamilton, telling the rake that she and Anne were 'just now abed together contriving how to have your company this afternoon'. Clearly, Barbara was obsessed with Chesterfield, and prepared to accept his other *amours.* 'My life is never pleasant to me but when I am with you or talking of you', she wrote.

The picture of two adolescent girls hatching plots to effect a rendez-vous with a known dissolute accords with the gossip which flew around London after Barbara became famous as the King's mistress, and which Pepys recorded in his *Diary* with little regard for modesty. Barbara, he tells us, was 'a little lecherous girl when she was young, and used to rub her thing with her fingers or against the end of forms'. How potent is the emotion of shame even after 300 years, and how we may blush on Barbara's behalf at such intimate revelations. But that she would herself blush, I seriously doubt, for, as we shall see, one of the boldest characteristics of the Court of Charles II was its utter wantonness; chastity and refinement in morals were not given much encouragement.

In 1659 Barbara married Roger Palmer, a man whom posterity has dismissed as one of nature's cuckolds, unlikely to be remembered for any worth of his own. This is not entirely merited. Palmer was born at Dorney Court in Buckinghamshire in 1634 (and was therefore seven years Barbara's senior), the son of a well-to-do, respected country knight. Educated at Eton and King's College, Cambridge, his career demonstrates that he was an accomplished mathemetician and scholar as well as a diplomat, and the author of a number of erudite books. History has lost sight of his own achievements, overwhelmed as they are by his rôle as the inadvertent father of his wife's numerous offspring, with most of which he had nothing whatever to do. Yet, as for his own behaviour, 'there is a singular absence of scandal about him, in an age when scandal left few indeed untouched'.

A curious distinction had befallen the Palmer family in 1489 when Lady Alice Palmer gave birth to triplets, who took a total of three weeks to appear, the first on 7 June, the second a week later on 14 June, and the third a week after that on 21 June. At the time of the Stuarts, the Palmers were noted loyalists. Sir James Palmer, Roger's father, was made a Gentleman of the Bedchamber to James I, and afterwards became an intimate friend of Charles I. The Palmers to this day still live at Dorney Court, and the village has a pub, the *Palmer Arms*, which suggests their erstwhile importance.

Roger was admitted a student at the Inner Temple in 1656, but not called to the Bar. Some time in the next three years he met Barbara Villiers, then living near St Paul's, and notwithstanding her continuing affair with Lord Chesterfield, he fell in love with her and determined to marry her. Barbara's reputation was already sufficiently black to alarm Roger's father, who did everything he could to warn his son against so dangerous a match. 'If you persist in marrying that woman', he said, 'I predict that you will live to be the most miserable man in the world.' His words went unheeded.

The marriage took place on 14 April 1659, at St Gregory's Church by St Paul's, when Barbara was eighteen years old. Roger tried to keep his bride in the country away from temptation and brought her but rarely to town, which deprivation excited all her resentment. Whenever she could manage to slip away, she went to Chesterfield, who could not really have cared what she did. Her husband, she told him, was being difficult, 'and is in an ill humour because he does not wish anyone else but him to set eyes upon me'. Flirtation was not a pastime Roger was prepared to allow, and he would have been beside himself had he known that Barbara was writing to Chesterfield that she was 'ready and willing to go all over the world with you, and I will obey your commands'. She was already bored with Roger; yet he remained unaware of her duplicity.

Two unrelated events in 1660 put an end to the affair with Lord Chesterfield. Barbara fell a victim to the smallpox which was then so common, and though it did not impair her beauty, it turned the noble Lord's fitful ardour to ice. Then he was engaged in a quarrel in Kensington, which ended with his murdering his opponent. He fled to the Continent, sought a pardon from Charles, and was with him at the glorious landing at Dover on 26 May.

Meanwhile, the time was approaching for Barbara's momentous meeting with the King, which took place probably in Holland in the early part of 1660. Roger and Barbara Palmer are said to have gone to the Continent to offer their support, and in Roger's case, to offer the sum of £1000 in return for which he would expect preferment after the Restoration. What he actually received was much less welcome – the humiliation of a discarded husband. Roger was obliged to return to London before 25 April, to take up his duties as Burgess for Windsor, to which he had recently been elected. Barbara might have stayed behind and cemented her friendship with the King, or she might have returned with Roger. At all events, she was not with the mighty procession which entered London on 29 May, but she was in the King's bed at the end of that day, which can only mean that they both knew what they wanted beforehand. Charles must already have been infatuated. Roger Palmer was so innocent of the affair, not suspecting for one moment that his wife was unfaithful, that he risked becoming a figure of fun. Thanking him for his financial support, the King rather mischievously wrote, 'You have more title than one to my kindness.'

Pepys first noticed Barbara's presence on 13 July, when he was working late into the night writing letters at the house of Sir Edward Montagu in King Street, Westminster. Next door, formerly the residence of the regicide Sir Edward Whalley, now lived Mr and Mrs Palmer.

Pepys was disturbed by the sound of a great party in progress, with 'great doings of Musique', and he noted in his journal that the King and Duke were there 'with Madam Palmer, a pretty woman that they have a fancy to make her husband a cuckold'.

By October it was manifest that Barbara had been insinuated into Court circles, her purpose no longer disguised. Pepys observed her talking with the Duke of York 'very wantonly through the hangings that parts the King's closet and the closet where the ladies sit' during a sermon at Whitehall chapel, and a few months later the diarist is slightly less circumspect, remarking that 'the King doth discover a great deal of Familiarity' with Mrs Palmer.

Barbara was at this time in the full bloom of her beauty, which was so extraordinary that, in spite of everything, there is not one contemporary opinion to denigrate it. Reresby called her 'the finest woman of her age', and Boyer wrote that she was 'by far the handsomest of all King Charles's mistresses, and, taking her person every way, perhaps the finest woman in England in her time'. Pepys himself, never slow to admit his full-blooded appreciation of female beauty, pays frequent tribute to her attractions. At the theatre, 'I sat before Mrs Palmer, the King's mistress, and filled my eyes with her, which much pleased me', he wrote, and later mused how strange it was that 'for her beauty I am willing to conster* all this to the best and to pity her wherein it is to her hurt, though I know well enough she is a whore'. Even though Pepys occasionally finds other women more becoming and speaks disparagingly of Barbara's beauty fading, he confesses years later that he dreams of her. The best dream he ever had, he says, was one in which he had Barbara in his arms 'and was admitted to use all the dalliance I desired with her'; if we could have such dreams in our graves, he concludes, he would not fear death half so much.

The great painter Lely paid the most lasting and sincere compliment to the beauty of Barbara Palmer by painting her portrait so often and so superlatively well that her looks are better known to us now than those of any of her rivals. He wanted to paint her so often because he found that it was impossible for his brush to do justice to its subject, and he must always try again. He used to say that it was 'beyond the compass of art to give this lady her due, as to her sweetness and exquisite beauty'. We can only assume he was right, for to us she appears to have a dazzling, immediate kind of appeal which is less fine than the subtler attractions of, say, Louise de Kéroualle.

* construe.

As for King Charles, at thirty, he was now a compelling masculine man in his maturity, though with some isolated grey hairs which led to his adoption of the periwig, then the prevailing fashion and originally an affectation of the roundheads, who wanted at all costs to avoid comparison with cavalier dandies and their luxuriant locks. Charles in a wig was irresistibly commanding.

Charles and Barbara had little in common apart from their lust, which was then pronounced a healthy and vigorous trait; in many cases it was neither, but that did not matter. A lascivious nature was part of the whole man, and the Restoration period was characterised by a jubilant, hedonistic desire to live life to the full and to celebrate the available delights. These included music, dancing, conversation, drink, good weather, and good love-making. A man of pleasure, capable of enjoying the diversions which the good life offered, was called a 'goodfellow', and he was to be found as much in the taverns as in the theatres – there was no distinction which made the one acceptable and the other degrading to a man of taste. He could enjoy and appreciate Shakespeare or the ancients, speak with authority on the virtue of idealism in art, drink to excess, never bathe, urinate in the gutter, flatulate gleefully, go to bed with his servants, and still be considered a 'goodfellow'. London was full of taverns which slopped over with ale and gossip, and where you could find an easy bed-mate. Gossip was the principal method by which news travelled, there being no newspapers in the sense that we understand, and so the taverns, and St James's Park, and the alleys around Whitehall, were the arterial channels of information. It was there that the progress of the King's affair with Barbara Palmer was observed, there that with dismay he was seen to evolve from a goodfellow to a prisoner of his sexual nature, the pleasures of life gradually taking the first place above all else. 'He is at the command of any woman like a slave', reflected Pepys, and 'cannot command himself in the presence of a woman he likes.'

So the Court mirrored the character of the King, and teetered on the thin line between hedonism and debauchery. 'I find that there is nothing almost but bawdry at Court from top to bottom', said Pepys, who was adept at condemning the sin and condoning the sinner, especially if he were in the mood himself. 'It is the effect of idleness and having nothing else to imploy their great spirits upon.' The prudish John Evelyn was even more censorious, though he kept his worst lamentations for private use, and it is in Pepys's diary, rather than Evelyn's, that we discover he 'cries out against it, and calls it bitchering', because the King and the Duke of York followed ladies like dogs on heat. The entire Court grew more and more loose, with 'nobody looking after business but every man his lust and gain', and the King and Court so indulging in gaming and whoring, 'and the most abominable vices that ever were in the world'. For once Pepys does not elaborate. A quick inventory would reveal that Lady Chesterfield flirted with both James Hamilton and the Duke of York, 'the most reckless ogler of his day', who had just discarded Jane Middleton, who was now pursued by Henry Jermyn when he was not paying attention to Barbara Palmer.

It is against this background that the behaviour of Barbara Palmer must be seen, and the censure which she suffered must be measured. When it was common knowledge that the Duke of York, the King's brother, regularly climbed out of his wife's bed, having satisfied her, to climb into the bed of another who was waiting for him, it was hypocritical to regard Barbara as the very incarnation of vice, and even to avoid mentioning her name, as Clarendon did.

Charles was fond of children. Indeed, he would need to be, as he was eventually to father at least fourteen. When the Duke of Buckingham said that Charles was 'father of his people', he added *sotto voce*, 'well, of a good many of them.'

One of them was born on 25 February 1661, rather less than nine months after the King's first night back in England. This was Barbara's daughter Anne, immediately called Anne Palmer, but with a choice of three possible fathers. Roger Palmer, still innocent, had no doubt that the child was his; Barbara said that it was the King's, and he eventually acknowledged paternity thirteen years later; the general opinion was that Lord Chesterfield was the lucky man. All three of them had opportunity, it is true, but on balance Anne was most likely to be Barbara's one and only legitimate child. The King accepted paternity in order to placate his by then exacting mistress and to make easier the girl's marriage to Lord Dacre. Roger was not deflected by this from regarding Anne as his daughter; he ever showed affection towards her, took her to live with him at Dorney Court, and at the end of his life was to make her his trustee and chief beneficiary under his will. For the moment, however, the confusion surrounding her birth was used by Barbara as a lever with which to ensconce herself more securely in Court circles and so make the King more and more dependent upon her company.

Not everyone at Court welcomed her. An arrogant manner and

imperious ways brought her many enemies, fired by envy, disapproval, or fear of her potential influence. Chancellor Clarendon could not bring himself to mention Mrs Palmer by name, referring to her, if he could not avoid it, as 'that lady'. This was all the more painful an insult since Clarendon had been such a close friend and admirer of Barbara's father Lord Grandison and might have been expected to be her ally. On the contrary, he was implacably hostile to her growing influence and did everything he could to destroy it. Unfortunately for him, Barbara was equal to the struggle. She fought him not only with spirit, but ultimately with venom, and was, as we shall see, finally victorious.

Others were alarmed that the King was spending so much time with his mistress and, what was more important, paying so much heed to her opinion. Her presence at Court created dissension and the splitting of factions. The Dowager Duchess of Richmond had a fierce argument with Barbara one day, telling her that she hoped she would end up the same way as Jane Shore, Edward IV's mistress who died in poverty and whose body was thrown on a dunghill. Ladies began to treat her slightingly (in many cases, it must be admitted, without the comfort of superior virtue), and even outside the walls of Whitehall, Barbara was not safe from insult. There was an occasion when three masked men, well-dressed, accosted her in St James's Park, reminded her again that Jane Shore ended her life despised and abandoned, and berated her for some minutes with disgusting language. Barbara was terrified, and fainted as soon as she was back in her apartments. The King ordered the gates of the Park to be closed, and had a few vagabonds brought in, but the culprits were never discovered, probably because they came from within Court circles.

Public concern was seriously aroused by Barbara Palmer's infiltration into the King's most intimate circle, and when Evelyn called her 'the curse of our nation' he was probably closer to public feeling than Pepys, who gazed lustfully after her.

Charles's indifference to public opinion (or perhaps his ignorance of it) was demonstrated in blatant form at the end of 1661. He bestowed a title on Roger Palmer so that Mrs Palmer could enjoy the privileges of higher rank, and her children benefit from being semi-blood royal. In other words, Barbara's position as mistress was to be given official recognition. On 16 October the King sent a note to William Morrice, one of his Secretaries of State, saying:

Prepare a warrant for Mr Roger Palmer to be an Irish Earle, to him and his heirs of his body gotten on Barbara Palmer, his now wife, with the date blank.

P.S. Let me have it as soon as you can.

Everyone knew, of course, why the warrant should be limited in this way. Barbara was again pregnant, and not even Roger Palmer could doubt who the father was this time. It was Charles's intention that the title should be denied the Palmers, and that the real beneficiary should be Roger's wife. Palmer was humiliated. Though he had sought preferment for the support he had given the royalist cause, he was disgusted at the manner of and by the reasons for his ennoblement. It did not get through without difficulty. Clarendon was determined not to let anything pass which bore 'her' name. Consequently, the plan was held up, until Charles made it clear yet again that he wanted an Irish title for Mr Palmer; the advantage of this was that it would not have to come before the Lord Chancellor of England, but would be sent to Ireland for the Great Seal and thus kept secret from Clarendon. One can well imagine Barbara scheming with the King how best to make her a 'lady'. The King sent another note to his Secretary of State on 8 November:

Prepare a warrant for Mr Roger Palmer to be barron of Limbericke and Earl of Castlemaine, in the same forme as the last was, and let me have it before dinner.

Henceforth Barbara was to be known as 'my lady Castlemaine', a title which, to her surprise and horror, did little to ingratiate her into the hearts of the people, who recognised the injury done to Roger. For his part, though he lived into and beyond the reign of James II, he never took his seat in the Irish House of Lords, and scarcely ever used his title.

Barbara's second child, and the King's first son by her, was born in the Spring of 1662, and known at first as Charles Palmer. Shortly before the birth, the King and Barbara were seen cavorting together and weighing each other amid much laughter, because of course she weighed the more. This was while the rest of the country was preparing to welcome the King's bride, Catherine of Braganza.

The child was baptised at St Margaret's, Westminster, on 18 June, and was the prelude to a furious row between Roger and his wife. He, now a devout Roman Catholic, insisted on the baptism being performed by a priest. Barbara then had the child baptised again by a Minister, with the King as witness, and solemnly promised that it had not already been baptised. As a result of this, the Palmers (or the Castlemaines as we should now call them) decided to part. Barbara stalked out of the house in King Street with everything she could lay her hands on, every plate, every knife and fork, leaving Roger nothing but virtually bare floors. He then went to France in high dudgeon, refusing to continue the argument, and allowing Barbara to return to the house triumphant.

Barbara had now become so bold that she was prepared to take on anyone, and felt sure she could secure the obedience of the King in the fulfilment of any of her desires. The most supreme test was about to challenge her, for the King was to be married, and his mistress must needs take a secondary place. That was not at all how my lady Castle-maine saw the matter; she knew that if she were humbled now, she would find it difficult to reassert her authority. She would have to make it plain once and for all who was the most important woman in the King's life. There was too much to lose.

*   *   *

The choice of a wife for King Charles was dictated by reasons of state and finance. The marriage portion offered by Catherine of Braganza, Infanta of Portugal, was almost twice as much as any King of England had ever received from a Consort, besides which the additional advantages of territorial gain and the mastery of trade routes made the proposal irresistible. One of the results of this marriage, and of the treaty signed with Portugal in 1661, was the transfer of power in Bombay from Portugal to England. This was the foundation of the British presence in India, and eventually led to the vast colonial expansion there in the nineteenth century.

So much for reasons of state. On a personal level, it would have been difficult to find any princess less temperamentally suited to adapt herself to the libertine Court of Charles II. She was sweet and kind and agreeably mannered, but pious to a degree which bordered on the insane, and was bound to irritate the self-indulgent Charles. She had been brought up in such closely confined circumstances that she had hardly been outside her palace more than ten times in her life, and that only to pray. On hearing that she was to be Queen of England, she went to visit the shrines of two saints in the city, and promptly withdrew again to her sheltered abode. Of course, there were positive sides to this piety. Catherine seemed imbued with holiness, there was a purity and simplicity in her understanding of human motive, a freshness and innocence in her behaviour, and integrity in her actions. She was governed by conscience and devotion to duty, both born of a deeply Catholic love of God. All these were negative qualities when it came to dealing with the unscrupulous Lady Castlemaine. Fate could not have devised a more brutal encounter than the throwing together of these two women.

Even Catherine's appearance stood in heavy contrast to the kind of arrogant beauty which always ensnared King Charles. She was short and unremarkable, with a protruding tooth and a 'swarthy' complexion, typical of Mediterranean ladies. This is not to say that she did not possess a certain prettiness; goodness of heart conferred its own attraction.

The fleet bringing Catherine and her retinue to England sailed on 25 April 1662, and consisted of fourteen men-of-war. As it approached Portsmouth in May, bonfires were lit in celebration outside every door in London, it seemed, except for Lady Castlemaine's in King Street. Inside, the King dined and played with her every night (she was eight and a half months pregnant with the King's son Charles 'Palmer'), until it was time for him to journey to Portsmouth and welcome his bride. Barbara was seen to be 'disconsolate' at this parting.

The King was taken aback at the first sight of the Queen. She had led such a retired existence that she was dressed in fashions which had not been seen in England since the time of Queen Elizabeth, and which looked distinctly odd. Evelyn called them 'monstrous'. All her ladies were dressed in like manner, and the *démodé* aspect which the group presented, did not augur well. To make matters worse, she had been advised that to surrender her way of dress in order to accommodate the English taste would be detrimental to the dignity of Portugal. So a certain stubbornness was felt from the first.

Still, the King was pleasantly surprised by her demeanour.

Her face is not so exact as to be called a beauty [he told Clarendon], though her eyes are excellent good, and not anything in her face that in the least degree can shock one. On the contrary, she has as much agreeableness in her looks as ever I saw; and if I have any skill in physiognomy, which I think I have, she must be as good a woman as ever was born. Her conversation, as much as I can perceive, is very good; for she has wit enough and a most agreeable voice. You would much wonder to see how well we are acquainted already. In a word, I think myself very happy.

As Charles did not speak Portuguese, nor Catherine English, his appreciation of her conversation must have been limited. He added a remark, ominous in the circumstances, that 'it was happy for the honour of the nation that I was not put to the consummation of the marriage last night, for I was so sleepy', not only as a result of the journey, as he claimed, but for having come straight from the bed of the luscious Castlemaine.

The day after her arrival at Portsmouth, Catherine was married to Charles II, first in a private ceremony in her bedroom, according to the Roman Catholic rites on which she insisted, and then publicly by the Bishop of London. The ribbons on her wedding dress were cut to pieces, so that everyone present should have a fragment as souvenir. From Portsmouth the royal couple went to Hampton Court, while Barbara languished in King Street waiting for the imminent birth of her son. Desperately anxious to consolidate her right, she proposed going to Hampton Court for the birth, but this amazingly indelicate idea was rejected by the King, who was sufficiently sensitive not to wish to subject his wife to such cruel embarrassment. It says much for Barbara's power over him that she even suggested it. Catherine made a good impression at Hampton Court by her discretion and dutiful behaviour which, said Pepys, 'will put Madam Castlemaines nose out of Joynt'. Not for long.

Unexpectedly, and unwittingly, Barbara's allies in her schemes to reassert her authority were Queen Catherine's ladies in attendance. They were all ugly, old and proud, over-protective towards Catherine, and disdainful towards their English hosts. They refused even to attempt to learn English, and maintained their Portuguese dress in the face of all entreaties (Catherine at least tried to please her husband by wearing English fashions). They were also bigoted and prudish; they made it clear that they would not sleep in any bed that had been occupied by a man, and did not take kindly to some of the more extrovert habits of the English, who would cheerfully urinate when and where the need came upon them. 'They complained that they cannot stir abroad without seeing in every corner great beastly English pricks battering against every wall', wrote Chesterfield.

King Charles would not tolerate this for long, nor would he consent that his wife should be in the control of narrow-minded foreigners. It became imperative that the appointment of English ladies to the Queen's bedchamber should be advanced. The only name so far put forward had been the Countess of Suffolk; now it was time to present a full list to the Queen and entice her away from her convent-bred attitudes. She still heard Mass every day, sapping all her energy at devotional exercises. This would not do, and the ambassador, Francisco de Mello, who was also Catherine's godfather, gently advised her that she must be seen to join in Court festivities and that her duties henceforth would lie in pleasing Charles. One way in which she would be dutiful would be to show delight at the choice of ladies the King had assigned to her bed-chamber.

At the top of the list was Lady Castlemaine, the King's mistress. The Queen fainted with shock.

Barbara had pleaded with the King to give her this public demon-stration of loyalty, now that she had been abandoned by her husband, and Charles had weakly assented. What the King did not know was that the fame of Barbara Palmer had been heard in Portugal, and the Queen, Catherine's mother, had instructed her daughter never to allow Barbara's name to be mentioned in her presence. Catherine had thus far carefully avoided making any allusion to Barbara's existence. Now she was to be faced with her husband's sexual betrayal every day of her life, by being forced to live in close harmony with his lover. Furious, she immediately struck the name from the list, and told Charles that he *must* allow her this privilege, or he could send her back to Portugal without further ado. Charles was not used to having thrust at him an ultimatum; he did not expect his wife to have a will of her own, and was much taken aback by the demonstration. At first, he tried to placate her; his affair with Lady Castlemaine belonged to the past, he said, he would not need her now that he had Catherine, his wife would be everything to him, and he would promise to discard Barbara from that day forth. It was a promise he never intended to keep.

A few days later, Charles intruded his mistress into the Queen's presence, without giving her any warning. There were other ladies to be presented, and although Catherine knew all about Lady Castlemaine, she had never seen her and would not recognise her. Nor was she familiar with the sound of English names, so that when this attractive stranger approached her, the Queen received her graciously and allowed Barbara to kiss her hand. One of the Portuguese ladies leaned forward and enlightened the Queen. Catherine changed colour, tears welled up in her eyes as soon as she realised the full horror of the insult; she tried to control herself and proceed with the presentation, but could endure the hurt no longer. Blood poured from her nostrils, and she had to be carried from the room in a fit.

What no one had considered was that Catherine did not only have her pride to protect, but her love. She had fallen totally and irrevocably in love with her husband.

Charles was either unaware of or indifferent to the strength of his wife's emotion. For the moment all he could see was that she had defied him, and this excited all the fury of his kingly authority. He demanded compliance; she burst into tears. He decided to delegate the unpleasant task to another.

Clarendon was summoned. In a long interview with the King he took Catherine's part, pointing out that the affront was more than a lady of Catherine's modesty could be expected to withstand. The King told Clarendon that if he gave way, the country would think him too weak to exact obedience from his wife, and he would be a laughing-stock. Moreover, Lady Castlemaine would be humbled, and that would never do. (It did not occur to him, apparently, that the country was already sick of his weakness in the face of Castlemaine's demands, which made him look far more ridiculous than sympathetic consideration for his wife's feelings would have done.) Now that Lord Castlemaine had left his wife, the King continued, it was his duty, as the author of her shame, to redress the injury done to her reputation by securing a place of honour for her at the Court. He promised that if only the Queen would stop making a fuss about Barbara, he would never again press any other appointment without her approbation, or make further demands on her tolerance. With this casserole of inconsequence and hypocrisy, he sent Clarendon off to the Queen with the commission to remonstrate with her and bring her round to decent submission.

Hearing that Clarendon's sympathies persisted in the Queen's favour, Charles added an illogical threat to his arguments; if Catherine did not quickly cease her objections to having her husband's mistress constantly in her presence, her husband would feel free to multiply the number of mistresses to whose embraces he would turn in future. Catherine was being asked to settle for the evil she knew, or risk others as yet unknown. Clarendon went uneasily about his task of persuasion, for he felt private outrage against the King's attitude.

In a letter to Clarendon which repeated the substance of their interview, Charles made it quite clear that he was determined to brook no opposition. Having desired Clarendon to warn Sir Alan Broderick 'not to meddle any more with what concerns my lady Castlemaine', he went on sternly to admonish Clarendon himself :

> Now I am entered on this matter, I think it very necessary to give you a little good councell in it, least you may think that, by making a further stirr in the businesse, you may deverte me from my resolution, which all the world shall never do : and I wish I may be unhappy in this world and the world to come, if I faile in the least degree what I have resolved; which is, of making my Lady Castlemaine of my wives bedchamber : and whosoever I find use any endeavour to hinder this resolution of mine (except it be only by myselfe), I will be his enemy to the last moment of my life. You know how true a friend I have been to you. If you will oblige me eternally, make this businesse as easy as you can, of what opinion soever you are of; for I am resolved to go through with this matter, lett what will come of it.

With the image of King Charles's bristling anger still fresh in his mind, Clarendon went about his loathsome task of bending the meek little Queen to His Majesty's pleasure, after her first (and almost her only) expression of will. Poor Catherine again burst into tears at Clarendon's first words, causing him to withdraw in some embarrassment; he would talk with her again, he said, when she was better composed.

The next day, the interview continued. Catherine said that the Chancellor was one of the few friends she had in England, and she hoped he would not now abandon her to wickedness. Gingerly, Clarendon began to tell her that which she did not wish to hear. Her education, he said, had not prepared her well for the world, had given her none of the insights into the follies of mankind with which we all, nowadays, had to arm ourselves. Had she been better instructed, ventured Clarendon, she would have observed many instances of human behaviour in her own country, which, by comparison, would make her present position much more tolerable. The implications of this circumspect verbiage made the Queen blush, but she was able nonetheless to come straight to the point. She did not expect, she said, 'she should have found the King engaged in his affections to another lady'. While Catherine thus reasoned like a woman in love, Clarendon manoeuvred his way through the emotional undergrowth like a wily politician; honest directness confronted unwholesome expediency. Surely the

Queen did not imagine that Charles could have remained celibate all this time, pending the arrival of a wife whom he had never seen? It was only natural that he should have sought release. But that was the past; his affections were now turned wholly to the Queen, and for her own sake she should not enquire into the past nor trouble herself with the history of her husband's *amours* before he met her; that would be fruitless and unhappy.

It looked as if Clarendon would win the day. Queen Catherine begged forgiveness for her intransigence, thanked the King for his graciousness and Clarendon for his careful explanations; she would be dutiful and obedient in future.

Now was the time for Clarendon to suggest how she might show her new resolve. One likes to think that he trembled slightly as he opened his mouth to speak. She had only, he said, to welcome Lady Castlemaine as a Lady of the Bedchamber, and all would be well.

At this, Catherine began to shout and gesticulate with rage. The King must hate her to wish humiliation upon her in this way; she would not stand for it; she would pack her bags and take the next boat to Portugal. Gently, Clarendon reminded her that she was not free to do anything or go anywhere without the King's leave, and 'she had not the disposal of her own person'. She had better not talk any more of Portugal, but try to see how she could best adapt herself to her situation with the least trouble to all concerned. Better to accede to the King's wishes, said Clarendon, and be sluggish in executing them, than to defy him outright. So pragmatic politics would emerge victorious, and the pious Catherine would take some elementary lessons in hypocrisy. But her Latin temperament would not allow submission so easily. Clarendon advised the King to let the matter rest for a few days; he, however, terrified lest his authority as King should appear to be diluted by a mere woman, insisted on instant obedience. There followed a meeting between husband and wife which quickly developed into a full-scale shouting match. He accused her of stubbornness and perversity, she called him a tyrant and unfeeling. Right, said Charles, you will learn where your duty lies, and I shall send all your Portuguese ladies straight back where they came from. The quarrel was so loud and passionate that everyone heard what was going on, and everyone noticed also that the next day the royal couple hardly looked at each other, so determined was each not to climb down.

Paradoxically, it was this furious argument at Hampton Court, when Charles and Catherine had been married only two months, that marked the turning-point in the development of his affection for her. Charles, though he did not perhaps realise it himself, was growing more and more fond of his wife. He liked her, and so the passion of the exchange had other causes besides his desire to see his authority carried. Charles was not such a tyrant where women were concerned; he was soft and indulgent. He needed to satisfy Barbara, but the price of losing Catherine's affection would be too high. He talked about nothing else for days afterwards, which alone was an indication how important it was to him, and always what irritated most was Catherine's constant threat to go back to Portugal. Barbara would have been shocked to discover that she had unwittingly advanced the King's affection for his wife.

Catherine spent many days crying alone in her bedroom, or presenting a good face in company with the King, though still ignoring him and feigning indifference. Clarendon tried again to counsel her, not very tactfully; she had better give in to the inevitable, was the gist of his advice. She thought the King's command was as unattractive in him as it was dishonourable towards her, but a King's command, if it cannot be resisted, can be despised. She would never consent to the appointment of Lady Castlemaine; if the appointment were honoured without her consent, so be it. The appointment was made.

Agnes Strickland describes Catherine at this point in her marriage as 'friendless, neglected, and almost broken-hearted'. Charles had not bothered to declare his affection for her. She saw only that his will prevailed, while her sufferings went apparently unnoticed. She felt slighted and isolated. With dignity, she withdrew to her rooms more often than not, and while the merry-making proceeded within earshot, she consoled herself with discussions and endless cups of tea. (Tea had only recently been introduced in England, and Catherine of Braganza has the credit of making it popular; she was the first tea-drinking Queen.)

On 23 August, Charles brought his Queen to London, in a spectacular royal procession by water from Hampton Court. Both our diarists were there to witness the event, which Evelyn described as 'the most magnificent triumph that ever floated on the Thames, considering the innumerable boats and vessels, dressed with all imaginable pomp', which, he said, surpassed anything the Venetians could muster. There were thousands of barges, canopies, glittering costumes, all the paraphernalia of majesty. Typically, it is Pepys who brings us the more personal picture. He noticed Lady Castlemaine standing nearby at the

C

waterside (she had yet to take up her position at Court full time, and was not therefore in the procession), where he 'glutted' himself with looking on her. Roger Castlemaine was there too, tactfully covering for his wife's new motherhood, and their nurse was holding the infant Charles. 'Methought it was strange to see her Lord and her upon the same place', says Pepys, 'walking up and down without taking notice one of another.' Roger raised his hat once, and Barbara graciously acknowledged, after which they occasionally took the baby from the nurse's arms, separately, never together, and fondled it, all the time ignoring each other. Suddenly, one of the scaffolds collapsed on the throng of ordinary folk standing below, and of all the grand ladies present, Barbara alone rushed down to see if anyone had been hurt. Finding that a child had been injured slightly, she took care of it, which, said Pepys, 'methought was so noble'. This is the one instance we have of a generous impulse on the part of Barbara, to set against a veritable mountain of discreditable anecdotes; it would be proper for us to assume, as this was the only incident witnessed by Pepys, there were others which he was not there to record. Yet Barbara is said to have treated her own son Charles so badly that he suffered all his life from mental retardation. (It was shortly after this that the King finally allowed Roger to go off to Europe.)

At Whitehall, Barbara assumed her duties with the Queen's retinue, and poor Catherine had to suffer the mortification of seeing her Lady of the Bedchamber more popular than herself, of hearing fun and laughter everywhere at Court except when she herself was in sight, whereupon gloom descended; and of observing that even her own servants curried favour with Lady Castlemaine and showed her more respect than they did their own mistress, because everyone knew that Barbara had more influence with the King. For the next three months, Charles spent every evening with Barbara, while the Queen sat sadly at home. Pepys says, 'the Queene hath little or no company come to her, which I know also to be very true – and am sorry to see it'.

In the circumstances, there was only one thing for Catherine to do, and that was to capitulate. For months she bore everything in silence, comporting herself with a dignity which won her many admirers, until one day she was overcome with loneliness, and to the surprise of all, began to chat merrily with Barbara and to show her all the outward signs of familiarity and friendly confidence. Barbara was seen to wait upon the Queen at chapel, in spite of her not being a Catholic. The fact was that Catherine was so much in love with her husband, she could not bear to displease him. If it would cheer him up to see his lover accepted by his wife, and if he would accordingly amend his treament of his wife, then she would oblige him in this. She was perfectly aware what she was doing; Clarendon may have taught her some lessons in pragmatism after all. Though she appeared to welcome Barbara's familiarity, she remained true to herself. There was an occasion when Barbara discovered the Queen in the midst of a lengthy session with her dresser, and commiserated with her. 'I wonder', she said, 'your Majesty can have the patience to sit so long a-dressing.' 'Oh', replied the Queen, 'I have so much reason to use patience, that I can very well bear with it.'

The King had promised Catherine that Barbara would never be permitted to live at Court, so long as Catherine continued to treat her with the same regard as she treated all other ladies. The Queen did her best to conform, but she underestimated Lady Castlemaine's obstinacy. Barbara's affair with the King had, in spite of everything, been pursued with some small discretion; now, she would settle for nothing less than open and public acknowledgement of her position. This would best be achieved by her having rooms at Whitehall, and any promises the King had made to the contrary would naturally have to be disregarded. Barbara now behaved with the insolence of victory; the King's marriage had, after all, made no difference.

Somebody told the Queen that Lady Castlemaine had 'enchanted' the King, which, figuratively, was perfectly true, as all were able to observe. Catherine, unfamiliar with the language of love, interpreted the word literally, and concluded that Barbara was a sorceress who had bewitched her husband. She took the matter very seriously, looking upon Charles with such tender concern for the danger he was in, and entreating him to be wary, that he could not at first understand her meaning. He may well have smiled with amusement when he realised the cause of his wife's anxiety, but guilt he felt none.

In truth, it would only require slight exaggeration to uphold the conviction that Charles was indeed 'enchanted', for there seemed no limit to Barbara Castlemaine's influence. She took exception to some disrespectful remarks of Lady Gerard, in attendance upon the Queen, and had her dismissed forthwith. She then turned to extending her power to the appointment of the King's ministers. She persuaded Charles to dispense with elder statesmen, and replace them with her own creatures on the pretext that young blood was needed to cope with the modern world. Thus 1662 saw the departure of the dutiful and loyal Sir Edward Nicholas, whose letters told us so much about Lucy Walter, and his place as Secretary of State was taken by Sir Henry Bennet (later Earl of Arlington). Sir Charles Berkeley was brought in to take the Privy Purse. Both were in Barbara's debt, and obedient to her commands. (Bennet's daughter would eventually marry one of Barbara's sons, and start the line of the Dukes of Grafton.)

Pepys voiced the alarm which was generally felt at these appointments. 'Lady Castlemaines interest at Court encreases and is more and greater then the Queenes. That she hath brought in Sir H. Bennet and Sir Ch. Barkeley; but that the Queene is a most good lady and takes all with the greatest meekness that may be.'

A week later, Pepys is so uneasy that he forgets his earlier promise to forgive the luscious Barbara anything and is moved to write, 'the King's dalliance with my lady Castlemaine being public every day, to his great reproach. And his favouring of none at Court so much as those that are the confidants of his pleasure as Sir H. Bennet and Sir Ch. Barkely – which good God put it into his heart to mend – before he makes himself too much contemned by his people for it.'

There was not much point in Charles's protesting, as he often did, that he resented any suggestion of his being governed by his mistresses; Barbara was for the moment patently the boss. Of all the King's advisers, the one who had most to fear, who knew that Barbara hated him and would use all her arts to get rid of him, was Clarendon. This winter of 1662–63 saw the beginning of the decline of Clarendon's influence, brought about directly by Barbara, the first act in a drama which would culminate in his ignominious departure.

Meanwhile, Charles was indulging his lust with increasing abandon. He would dine with Barbara four or five times a week, often not returning to his wife's bed until the following morning, and making no attempt to disguise his movements. Openly, he would walk from Barbara's lodgings to the palace, causing even the sentries to comment upon it. For three months at the beginning of 1663 he did not dine with the Queen once, which distressed her more than she was able to express, in the light of his easy promises not to have anything more to do with Barbara. By April, the mistress had achieved one of her cherished objects; she now had a room at Whitehall next to the King's own quarters. Though Charles was ever more fond of his wife, she could not begin to compete with Barbara in wit and gaiety; her upbringing and her persistent piety made her no match for the sparkling amusement which Barbara afforded, the reckless fun, the practical jokes, the youthful exuberance of a woman whose energies were devoted to the pursuit of pleasure. However much she tried to join in, Catherine was, by comparison, hopelessly dull.

More than that, Barbara was able to answer Charles's sexual needs with greater stamina and more invention than any other woman he knew, or was to know. The secret of her hold over him was at least in part attributable to her agility between the sheets, in which she was so expert as to imprison the King in a wild infatuation and dismiss all other thoughts from his mind save how to get back to bed with her.

My Lady Castlemayne rules him [wrote Pepys], who hath all the tricks of Aretin* that are to be practised to give pleasure – in which he is too able, having a large ——; but that which is the unhappiness is that, as the Italian proverb says, *Cazzo dritto non vuolt consiglio.*† If any of the Sober counsellors give him good advice and move him to anything that is to his good and honour, the other part, which are his counsellors of pleasure, take him when he is with my Lady Castlemayne and in a humour of delight and then persuade him that he ought not to hear or listen to the advice of those old dotards. . . .

In a celebrated verse, Rochester dared to give voice to the prevailing opinion :

> Nor are his high Desires above his Strength;
> His sceptre and his —— are of a length.
> And she that plays with one, may sway the other,
> And make him little wiser than his Brother.

Nobody could say that Barbara was a shy woman. Though still only twenty-two, she had enough experience to keep Charles entertained with novelties at every encounter, and she had no truck with modesty or demure refusals. What a startling, and, one supposes, refreshing contrast with the innocent Catherine. If only, said some, Barbara was as good within as she was fair without.

Samuel Pepys appreciated Barbara's attractions more than most, for though his conscience bade him sometimes shake his head and express some disapproval, he was himself sufficiently lascivious to envy the

---

* Pietro Aretino, whose erotic writings made him a kind of sixteenth- and seventeenth-century pornographer.

† A man with an erection is in no need of advice.

King's good fortune. One of his informants was Sarah, maid to his employer Lord Sandwich, and on at least one occasion he was so excited by tales of Lady Castlemaine that he made a pass at Sarah herself. 'I went up to her and played and talked with her and, God forgive me, did feel her', he told his diary, adding, 'which I am much ashamed of, but I did no more, though I had so much a mind to it that I spent in my breeches.'

Most amazing of all, even in this Court given over to sexual licence, was the number of Barbara's other lovers. Charles, it seems, did not demand fidelity from her all the time, for he must have known that he was not the only man to share her bed. Captain Ferrers and Will Howe once looked through her window and watched her go to bed while Sir Charles Berkeley was in the room. Berkeley was used by the King as his go-between in relations with Barbara, and he sometimes took advantage of his mission to taste of Barbara's delights. Another rival was James Hamilton, a Groom of the Bedchamber to the King, soon to be joined by Lord Sandwich and Henry Jermyn. In later years, there would be so many competitors for the notorious lady that the most diligent researcher loses count.

In the autumn of 1662, James Crofts, the King's thirteen-year-old son by Lucy Walter, was in London, and was quickly the darling of the Court, by reason of his extreme beauty and the King's evident fondness for him. Poor Catherine had now to deal not only with her husband's mistress, but with the offspring of a former mistress as well, and in asking her to accept all at once, Charles was expecting much from her. When the insatiable Barbara began to show more than attentive interest in her unofficial step-son, the King was at last shaken from his complacency. Pepys noticed that the boy 'doth hang much upon my lady Castlemayne and is alway with her', and saw all four *dramatis personae* riding in one coach together – the King, the Queen, Barbara, and young James. Two months later, when the child had been created Duke of Monmouth and already had a mistress of his own, we find him dancing with Barbara at a great Court ball. It was said that the King hastened Monmouth's marriage to the Countess of Buccleuch in order to rescue him from Barbara's attentions, though from what we know of her it is doubtful whether that would have put a rein on her designs, had they been serious.

The first sign of a crack in Barbara's formidable power came with the sudden, unforeseen appearance of a rival. At the beginning of 1663 there arrived from Paris a charming fifteen-year-old girl called

Frances Stuart, to join the Court as Maid of Honour to Queen Catherine. Grand-daughter of Lord Blantyre, and a kinswoman of the King, this girl was so ravishing that, when everything else is forgotten about her, she is still known to history as '*la belle Stuart*', and we are every day reminded of her beauty because she was the model for Britannia on our copper coins, designed by Philip de Rothier. The King's sister Henrietta of Orléans recommended her as 'the prettiest girl in the world and one of the best fitted of any I know to adorn a Court'.

Frances captivated the King in one move. In almost every respect she was the antithesis of the reigning mistress, Lady Castlemaine. If Barbara was voluptuous, Frances was pretty; against Barbara's wit and conversation, Frances was decidedly artless and immature, not to say stupid; Barbara was ambitious, Frances had no interest in politics and made no attempt to meddle; Barbara was constantly available, but Frances Stuart was so virtuous that she was to inflame Charles's ardour by her very refusals. He said he hoped one day to see her 'old and willing'.

By the beginning of February, Frances was already so well established at Court that games were being devised for her entertainment; she had lamentably poor taste, and was never happier than when passing the hours in childish diversions – perhaps her age can excuse her. Far from being put out by the arrival of this delightful poppet, Barbara quickly perceived that she must be friends with her, if she were not to arouse the King's anger. She invited Frances to all her evenings, made sure she was present at festivities organised for the King, and indulged her predilection for frolic. At one of the very first of these evenings, Barbara devised a game whereby she and Frances would pretend to be man and wife. They went through a mock marriage ceremony, with rings exchanged and priest officiating, went to bed and flung the stockings in traditional manner. All this of course was presented before a ribald audience. Frances thought it was great fun. When the King arrived, Lady Castlemaine, who had played the part of the husband, ceded her place to him, but Frances still would not allow the amusement to develop beyond a game. She must have been infuriating; Charles was not at all used to frustration.

Frances was often told that she had the best pair of legs at Court. Giggling with vanity, she would obligingly lift up her skirts to confirm the report. It was said that she was so childishly vain that a clever man could get all her clothes off her before she realised what was happening, simply by complimenting other women on their legs, their neck, their bosom, and so on.

If Barbara thought that her treating Frances as a bosom friend would ingratiate her with the King, she was soon disillusioned. By July it was clear that she had fallen from favour, and was seen less in the King's company. Whenever she appeared in public, it was noticed that fewer people paid attention to her, and she herself went about with a fearsome scowl.

The reason for her ill-temper was of course obvious. Pepys expressed the general view when he remarked that Frances Stuart was 'the greatest beauty I ever saw I think in my life; and if ever woman can, doth exceed my lady Castlemayne . . . nor do I wonder if the King changes, which I verily believe is the reason for his coldness to my lady Castlemayne'. Pepys was still dreaming about *la belle Stuart* when he went to bed that night, staring at the ceiling and imagining himself 'sporting' with her. The King went so far as to declare that he would not visit Barbara again unless she would guarantee that Frances should be present. Since Barbara's other interest in promoting the new affair was to deflect attention from her own with Jermyn, the entanglements of love life in 1663 were such that everyone had to be careful what he said from day to day, and gingerly to pick his way through a dangerous web of tactfulness. The whole business was complicated still further by reports that the King was, at last, declaring his affection for his wife.

Before the end of the year, Charles was so infatuated with Miss Stuart that 'he gets into corners and will be with her half an hour together, kissing her to the observation of all the world . . . but yet it is thought that this new wench is so subtle, that she lets him do not anything more then is safe to her'. As for Barbara, she had to content herself for the time being with an occasional conversational intimacy.

There were two important events in 1663 which contributed to temper the King's passion for Barbara, apart that is from the irritating delectability of little Frances. In the first place, Barbara had been pregnant most of the year, and secondly the Queen had suffered a serious illness which had served to remind the King, as such catastrophes generally do, that in spite of his manifold infidelities he did in fact love her.

Barbara's second son was born, according to the records, on 20 September 1663. Called at first Henry Palmer (although Roger had been out of England for over a year), the baby arrived in circumstances steeped in ambiguity. The King and Queen were in Oxford that week, and Pepys heard that Barbara went to join them there on 22 September, which would have been impossible unless Barbara had had the physical constitution of an acrobat. Pepys also avers that she had miscarried, a piece of gossip which, though inaccurate, at least confirms that there was some mystery about this particular *accouchement*. Charles hesitated for a long time before owning the boy, which lent weight to the scandalous stories imputing paternity to Charles Berkeley. The King seemed to accept that the origin of Barbara's children was as certain as the odds which determine a lottery, but he was nonetheless ready to recognise them as his natural offspring. With Henry he was more slow. Eventually, he would be convinced that the boy was his, would treat him with manifest affection, load him with honours and titles. His direct descendant is the present Duke of Grafton.

Far more significant in the long term was the Queen's mysterious and dangerous illness in October, which developed rapidly into a raging fever so virulent that there were fears she would not recover. The King's reaction was astonishing. Overcome with tenderness, and perhaps some sincere remorse, he wept bitterly by her bedside for hours on end. Catherine, thinking she was about to die, declared that the only thing she would regret losing in this world was her husband, whose concern for her touched her so deeply. She well knew, she said, that she did not possess charms enough to deserve him, but she was consoled by the thought that her death would enable him to find a Consort who was more pleasing to him, and who would surely be better able to give him an heir. This was too much for Charles, who bathed her hands in his tears, and begged her 'to live for his sake'.

The fever dragged on for the rest of the month, causing the Queen to descend into a delirium which affected her brain. Pathetically, she imagined that she had given birth to a son, and told Charles how sorry she was that he had turned out to be so ugly. Charles reassured her, saying that on the contrary it was a very pretty boy she had given him. 'If it be like you', she said, 'it is a fine boy indeed, and I would be well pleased with it.'

If only Catherine had been able to produce an heir to the throne, her personal story would have been less tragic. But it was becoming obvious, despite frequent rumours of pregnancy and miscarriage, and, we may assume, many an effort by the King, that she was barren.

While the illness lasted, it was openly bruited that the Queen's death might be no bad thing at all, for the succession to the throne would be more secure if the King were to marry again. The scatterbrained Frances

Stuart was seriously proposed by a committee of statesmen as the next Queen of England.

Notwithstanding the endearments the King uttered by his wife's bed, he was not disposed to forego his pleasures, and even while she lay close to death, he paid daily visits to Frances and Barbara. Barbara was now reasserting some of her old authority, for, while Frances was undeniably prettier, Barbara was far and away the better company. On balance, it would be unfair to ascribe all her attractions to her strength of lust; for the King's involvement to have lasted so long, beyond the term of his other affairs at the time, and in spite of the number of hers, she must have been an agreeable companion as well as a sensual bed-mate. Too little of her conversation has come down to us to permit of a proper judgement, and almost all the indications we have are to her detriment, but the King obviously looked to her for solace as well as amusement. In short, they grew to know each other very well.

When the Queen recovered, she was again faced with the truth of her sorry childless condition, and had once more to swallow her hurt at the spectacle of her husband's continued dalliance. She sometimes surprised the King with Frances in her own dressing-room, and took to enquiring whether he were there alone before daring to go in.

Frances, this 'innocent, raw girl', managed to keep the King's interest alive throughout the following year, obliging Barbara to resort to bold stratagems in order to demonstrate that she was not to be left in the bottom drawer. At the theatre one evening, she ostentatiously rose from her box and went, without invitation, to join the King in his, sitting at his right between him and the Duke of York. It was a carefully timed assertion of right.

Whenever Barbara was on the defensive, she responded with a display of power. Nobody understood better than she that most people judge according to what they can see, so she made it her business, if Frances appeared to be in the ascendant, to out-dazzle her with jewels. Many a time she was wearing more jewels than the Queen and Miss Stuart together. As usual, of course, she went too far, turning what could have been her advantage into a damaging mark against her. When, according to custom, all the peers of the realm gave the King rich presents of silver at the New Year, Barbara appropriated them for herself, after which the custom was wisely dropped.

Greed was one of Barbara's least attractive characteristics. When one considers that she shamelessly raided the Privy Purse, through the agency of friends whom she had placed in positions of power, in order to pay her ever-increasing debts; that she squandered what she acquired either in gambling or in reckless spending on her favourites; that she was constantly asking for greater and greater grants of land and more disguised sources of income, it is no wonder that she gained a reputation for rapacity. According to one estimate, she devoured more than half a million pounds, which was deplorable by any standards, and moved Burnet to describe her as 'enormously vicious and ravenous'. The greater part of her plunder was in the future, when, as the King gradually grew tired of her, she was to squeeze him dry as a reward for her promises not to bother him. The marvel of it was that Charles allowed himself to be used in this way, for Barbara's vainglory reflected ill upon him at a time when he sorely needed the support of the country.

Barbara's political influence, too, continued unabated. It was she who rendered impotent the mission of Louis XIV's ambassadors sent to negotiate a peace between England and Holland. (At the great battle of Southwold Bay, her *protégé* and occasional lover Charles Berkeley was killed, his brains spattered all over the Duke of York; it would be in character for Barbara Castlemaine to direct the affairs of nations in a spirit of emotional pique and bad-tempered vengeance.) Even more insulting, the night the Dutch burnt the English fleet, Charles supped with Barbara at the house of his daughter-in-law, Duchess of Monmouth, and all three of them wasted their time chasing a moth around the room and giggling the night away. The King appeared to all the world to be quite mad, neglecting his duties and his honour in the service of insane sexual passion. As Thomas Povey, a Treasurer at Court, told Pepys, 'the King hath taken ten times more care and pains making friends between my lady Castlemayne and Mrs Stewart when they have fallen out, then ever he did to save his kingdom'.

It was more than ever apparent that Charles was a paradoxical character. His extreme susceptibility to women must be admitted a failing, and yet however insensitive he appeared to the humiliation he inflicted upon the Queen, he was not inconsiderate by his own estimate. He saw no inconsistency in the rampant infidelity of his married life, and his tender fondness as a husband. In his own lights he was kind to Catherine, often saying that she was one of the best women in the world, and springing to her defence if any courtier was so unwise as to misinterpret his behaviour and risk a disrespectful reference to her. On one occasion, she felt ill during the night when he was in bed with her. He got up to fetch her a basin, but she was sick in the sheets before he returned. Not until he had himself cleaned and dried her, and changed the sheets, did he call her women to help, and repaired to his own room, even then returning three times to see how she was before he finally went to sleep.

Charles passionately wanted a son and heir, and well knew that his subjects shared that desire. When a country squire told him that if he would produce a Prince of Wales he would make his people the happiest on earth, he replied, 'I'll promise you I'll do my best.' But he would entertain no thoughts of divorcing Catherine, however often the proposal was made.

The King was just as energetic in his pursuit of innocent pleasures as he was in the satisfaction of his libido. He kept open house at Whitehall, affording access to people of all descriptions who came countrywide to see him and kiss his hands, so much so that he scarcely had time to himself. He was alone early in the morning, rising at five to walk in the park or boat on the Thames, sometimes after a night of revelry which went on until two or three in the morning. When he walked, taking great strides and pausing only to look at the ducks, people would happily come up and join him, running to keep up with him, and exchange jokes. He could be a carefree and endearing companion, and his personality was the root of the easy-going, 'merry' atmosphere of his Court. But there was still time, *pace* Pepys who tells us so often that he neglected 'business', for daily consultations with ministers and long hours of work. On occasion, he would relax after work by donning a disguise and venturing south of the river to play chess with local people in one of the many taverns. The disguise was rarely successful; Charles II was one of the most easily recognisable monarchs.

Nor was he by any means a philistine. Charles appreciated the fine arts, music, beautiful objects, handsome books. He was an enthusiastic patron of the great portrait painters of the age, and his wife a keen suporter of Italian musicians. There were times when he was surprised with his books, browsing through them and handling them with the love which only a bibliophile can feel. All this alongside the man's rejoicing in the coarseness of the age, the hideous cock-fighting, the frequency of duels, the drunkenness and loutish pugnacity, the indifference to proper sanitation, appears to us another confirmation of paradox. But in Restoration England, all were facets of the whole man, the 'good-fellow'. When the King's son, the Duke of Monmouth, was responsible for slitting a man's nose with a knife in settlement of a quarrel (it happened often), Charles was not outraged.

* * *

Barbara's fourth child and second daughter, Charlotte Fitzroy, was born in September 1664; no need for the surname 'Palmer' to be introduced this time – Roger had not set foot in England for two years. Charles happily recognised Charlotte as his own, as he did the fifth child, George, born at Merton College, Oxford in December 1665, whither the Court had removed to escape the dangers of the Plague. The Oxford scholars were not at all pleased with the invasion, which necessitated turning fellows and undergraduates out of their rooms, and for what? 'There is no other plague here but the infection of love', wrote Denis de Repas.

Barbara was looked upon with scorn at Oxford, where her status as a whore was proclaimed without adornment. Pepys said, recording that she was ill yet again, that she was doubtless 'slipping her filly', and it was language like this which followed Barbara in the university, where polite hypocrisy was not considered a virtue. The boy George was given the name Palmer, rather absurdly, but also registered *Filius naturalis regis Carolis II*. Some students made clear to Barbara what they thought of her by pinning on her door some insulting words, in the spirit of what we should nowadays call *graffiti*. 'Hanc Caesarc pressam a fluctu defendit onus', read the notice. 'The reason why she is not duck'd? Because by Caesar she is fuck'd.'

Her husband Roger was briefly in England that year, where he discovered his household had grown by two children since his departure. This cannot have been an altogether overwhelming surprise. He had taken the trouble to protect himself against Barbara's extravagance in his absence by obtaining a bond from Lords Grandison and Sandwich in the sum of £10,000, to indemnify him 'from all and every manner of debts' incurred by his wife; quite properly, if the King was to enjoy her company, the King could foot the bill.

Another reason for Roger's visit was in connection with his written work. In 1666 he wrote *An Account of the Present War between the Venetians and the Turks with the State of Candia*, followed by a history of the Dutch naval war, which he wrote in French. His most important work was, however, *The Catholic Apology*, a highly articulate and persuasive piece of proselytising, all the more remarkable for its courage at a time of supposed Popish menace. Roger might also have taken the opportunity to visit the Court; his family had recently presented to King Charles the first pineapple to be grown in England, produced by the gardener at Dorney Court.

There is no reason to think that Lord and Lady Castlemaine met during this visit of Roger's, although they now had slightly more in common than previously. Barbara had become a convert to Catholicism, and announced the matter publicly. The Queen was none too pleased to gain such a disreputable disciple, and she made it obvious that she would expect the King to ban his mistress from attending Mass. Charles's reply showed the kind of gentle wit which makes all his sins forgiveable; 'as for the souls of ladies, I never meddle with *those*'. Stillingfleet, later Bishop of Norwich, was even more sarcastic. 'If the Church of Rome has got by her no more than the Church of England has lost', said he, 'the Matter is not much.' In time, Barbara's Catholicism was to cause her much bother, and lead to her dismissal from the post as Lady of the Bedchamber in accordance with the provisions of the Test Act of 1672.

Still respectability eluded Barbara, always supposing that she wanted it. She was, after all, a woman of noble birth, and it must have been galling even to her to be forever pursued by scurrilous gossip. She complained to the King when Harry Killigrew, son of the dramatist Tom Killigrew, put it about that she had played with herself as a child, but that too backfired, because she ought in justice have first complained to the Duke of York, in whose household Killigrew was employed. 'Happy-humoured Killigrew, soul of mirth and all delight' was just one of the many iconoclastic wits and wags about the Court who treated Lady Castlemaine's life-style as a subject for jest.

Then there was the telling frequency with which Barbara consulted Dr Frazier, the King's most trusted medical adviser. Frazier himself was discreet, otherwise he would not have held his position, but everyone knew that part of his function, in the manner of many a friendly doctor, was to repair the effects of promiscuity at Court. Pepys tells us that Frazier had influence with the ladies 'in helping to slip their calves when there is occasion, and with the great men in curing of their claps'.

Was it for some such reason that Barbara was less seen in 1666, the year of the Great Fire of London, when she was said to be living the life of a retired nun? John Evelyn was predictably delighted, for he saw the Plague and the Fire as judgements from Heaven against 'our prodigious ingratitude, burning lusts, dissolute Court, profane and abominable lives'.

Nevertheless, in 1667, Barbara was again all-powerful, and several events occurred to demonstrate in spectacular fashion the extent of the control she had accumulated over seven years. She was hardly instrumental in the first of these surprises, though she was the one to gain by it. The rival Frances Stuart suddenly eloped with her cousin the Duke of Richmond, who was also a relation of the King's, putting an abrupt stop to the frivolity of the King's private conduct. Charles was truly vexed by this unexpected slap in the face, which came about, at least in part, owing to his continued attempts to seduce Frances. The relationship had reached a point beyond which it could not progress without Frances making herself a fully-fledged whore, and this it seems she would not do. Barbara, of course, was delighted. That Charles's fondness for *la belle Stuart* managed to survive this *contretemps* was made evident the following year, when Frances fell ill with smallpox at her palatial quarters in Somerset House. Charles paid her several visits, and on her recovery had her appointed a Lady to the Queen's Bedchamber; Catherine, who knew she could rely upon Frances's virtue, did not object. One Sunday, the King was so transported by a sudden access of desire to see her, that he abruptly cancelled appointments, got into a small boat with a single pair of oars, and rowed himself alone down the Thames to Somerset House, where, finding the gate closed he climbed over the wall. Charles contrived to ally easy promiscuity with a strange kind of attachment to his loves.

Ever since Barbara had placed her puppets at the source of power among the King's closest advisers, his old and faithful friend Clarendon, who had shared the most difficult years of his life and had served him selflessly, was left with comparatively little to do. Barbara was waiting for the opportunity to exact full revenge upon the man whom she hated, and get rid of him once and for all. The chance came with the signing of the Treaty of Breda (which brought peace to England, France and Holland), ratified before Parliament could be summoned. Clarendon was blamed for having prevented Parliament from being assembled, and an outcry ensued, fanned by Barbara and her henchmen.

The King was persuaded that Clarendon had to go. He summoned the old man to a private conference, at which Clarendon was foolish enough to speak out against Lady Castlemaine's pernicious influence in the nation's affairs. This enraged the King, who walked out, leaving the Chancellor disconsolate and confused. He then left as well, observed from a window by Barbara in her nightclothes, unashamedly gloating

over the man's abasement. Pepys remarked 'this business of my Lord
Chancellors was certainly designed in my Lady Castlemaine's chamber'.
Two days later, the King sent to collect the seal of office from Claren-
don's hands, and summarily dismissed him; he left England on 3
December, never to return. The one man who might still thwart
Barbara's constant indulgence of greed was now out of the way, by her
own agency.

The origin of the most fearsome quarrel between Charles and his
imperious mistress was ostensibly her embarrassing defence of her
relation, the Duke of Buckingham. Buckingham had twice been in
disgrace recently, and was stripped of all his offices and imprisoned
in the Tower of London for his vociferous attacks against the King.
Barbara took it upon herself to intervene and not ask, but tell Charles to
release Buckingham. The King flew into a mighty rage, called Barbara
a whore and a jade who meddled in matters that did not concern her.
Undaunted, she yelled back at him, telling him what a fool he was
to entrust his affairs to idiots who did not know what they were doing,
while his true friends he clapped into prison. They did not speak for
about four days after this display, but Charles weakly relented, and
allowed Buckingham to be released without trial.

Emboldened by success, Barbara next attempted an even more out-
rageous demand. She was again pregnant, this time by the notorious
rake Henry Jermyn, whose affair with Lady Falmouth had driven
Barbara into a jealous frenzy. Undeterred by Charles's certain knowledge that the child could not be his, she resolved to force him to
acknowledge it and add it to the list (this was her sixth pregnancy). She
would have her child christened in Whitehall chapel, she said, or by
God she would bring it to Court and dash its brains out before the
King's face.

The King declared that he had not 'lain with' Barbara in the past
months, and could not therefore have paternity ascribed to him this
time. Barbara so bullied him that she would not even allow him to
choose which of her bastards he would accept as his own. 'God damn
me! But you shall own it!' she screamed. We owe to one of Pepys's
gloriously indiscreet informers the basis of the King's certainty in this
instance; it was because 'for a good while the King's greatest pleasure
hath been with his fingers, being able to do no more'.

So the farce continued, Charles furious that his mistress had gone
off with Henry Jermyn, Barbara furious that Jermyn had turned his
affection to Lady Falmouth. 'So they are all mad', mused Pepys, 'and

Charles II, by Sir Peter Lely

Lucy Walter, with a miniature of the Duke of Monmouth (Kneller)

The Duke of Monmouth (Huysmans)

Barbara Villiers: detail from a portrait by Lely

Barbara Villiers, Duchess of Cleveland, in old age
(Kneller)

Chiswick Parish Church, where Barbara, Duchess of Cleveland is buried.

Holbein Gate at the palace of
Whitehall

Frances Theresa Stuart
afterwards Duchess of
Richmond, as Minerva
(Lely)

Nell Gwynn (Verelst)

79, Pall Mall, the home of Nell Gwynn

Covent Garden Piazza, at about 1660

The 1st Duke of St Albans and Lord James Beauclerk,
children of Nell Gwynn and Charles II, from a
painting by C. Netscher

Louise de Kéroualle, when she first came to England
(Gascar)

Louise de Kéroualle, Duchess of Portsmouth,
(Mignard)

Moll Davis (Lely Studio)

Duchesse Mazarin, by Sir Godfrey Kneller

thus the kingdom is governed.' Amidst all this, Dr Creeton preached a sermon before the King, the theme of which was the sins of the Court and the terrible iniquity of adultery.

The last act in this little drama made the King an object of derision in his own Court, so that people openly commented upon his being made a fool of by the raging shrew who obsessed him. Having threatened to publish his letters (Lucy Walter had tried the same tactic), Barbara made the King get on his knees in front of her and beg her forgiveness, told him that she did not care whose child she bore so long as he would recognise it, and made him promise not to offend her in this manner again. She threatened to 'bring all his bastards to his closet-door, and hath nearly hector'd him out of his wits'.

Typically, Charles would consent to such a show in order to secure immediate peace and quiet, but in the end he would not give Barbara the satisfaction she sought. He waited for her to calm down and find other outlets for her bad temper. No more was heard of the baby in question.

*   *   *

From now on, there was abundant talk of the King wanting to rid himself of a woman who had developed into a termagant. Once he banished her from Court after an exhibition of insolence which it was impossible to ignore. After three days, she sent for her things, but was told that she would have to come and get them; as soon as they were face to face, the King relented, and all was well again, at least for the time being. It was said that she might go and live in France, but her demands for compliance were so high, in financial terms, that the plan was temporarily shelved. Besides, the King was by now not a little afraid of the furore she would create. Pepys said that he was 'as weary of her as is possible, and would give anything to remove her; but he is so weak in his passion that he dare not do it'. Barbara's power over the King was as strong as ever, not so much as a lover, for she scorned him, but, again in Pepys's words, 'as a tyrant to command him'.

Like lovers who have fought beyond the point of reconciliation, they then proceeded to out-do one another in infidelity. Charles took a fancy to Moll Davis, an actress of uncertain origin, who danced like a dream, but was otherwise 'the most impertinent slut in the world'. Mary Davis had been a milkmaid, the daughter of a Wiltshire blacksmith's wife, but she was commonly thought to be the illegitimate daughter of the Earl of Berkshire, one of the Howard family. The King took her as a mistress, characteristically lavishing gifts upon her. He bought her a ring worth £700, which, like the chorus girl that she was, she proudly displayed to all and sundry, and he set her up in a house in Suffolk Street.

Barbara looked like all the furies while this was going on. She watched sullenly when Moll gave her little performance at Court, while the Queen, knowing her to be the King's whore, walked out in disgust. At a performance of *Macbeth*, Barbara noticed the King look up to bid greeting to someone in a box above; when she also looked to see who it was, and her eyes met Moll Davis, she blushed like fire.

Another actress, Nell Gwynn, also came upon the scene at about this time, but her story belongs to another chapter. One of Nell's previous lovers had been the actor Charles Hart, a great-nephew of Shakespeare. Barbara's revenge upon the King was to take the form in which she was most practised; she promptly became Hart's mistress, and was shortly making every show of being passionately in love with him.

Consorting with such people, Barbara made herself the object of yet more abuse. A petition was published addressed to 'the most splendid, illustrious, and eminent lady of pleasure, the Countess of Castlemaine', which purported to be written by the poor prostitutes of the city and sought redress for the wrongs they suffered, which Barbara, being one of their number, would be best able to secure. She was 'horribly vexed'.

It is difficult to credit, but Charles was still all too ready to bestow favours upon Barbara, if only to keep her at a distance. He removed her from the immediate vicinity of Whitehall, and provided for her a sumptuous home at Berkshire House, standing in its own grounds not far from St James's Palace. Cruelly, this had been the home of the disgraced Chancellor, Lord Clarendon. Here she lived for a while with three of her children, until her debts made it necessary for her to sell, all unconscious of the insult to the nation which this ungrateful act implied, retaining for herself only part of the grounds in which to build another house. She also managed to extract from the King a pension of £4700 a year, from Post Office revenues, a shameful deal which was hardly concealed by the grant being made out in the names of her uncles, Lord Grandison and Edward Villiers.

Her taste in lovers sank to new depths when she took up with a rope dancer called Jacob Hall, acting on the surely sarcastic recommendation of Charles himself. Hall was a handsome man of robust physique, one whom the ladies regarded as an agreeable fusion of Hercules and

Apollo, but not at all the kind of paramour for a lady of rank. Barbara went so far as to have her portrait painted with Hall, and to pay him a salary, presumably taken from the Post Office income. The contest in lovers' pique presented an unedifying spectacle of wilful degradation, but Barbara was past caring what the world thought.

If gossip of the day is to be believed, she even took a fancy to the running footman who accompanied her coach, and forced the poor man to have a bath with her. One of the lampoons which gleefully recorded Barbara's indiscretions snatched at this latest absurdity with delight:

> She through her lackey's drawers, as he ran,
> Discern's love's cause, and a new flame began . . .
> Full forty men a day have swiv'd the whore,
> Yet like a bitch she wags her tail for more.

In the British Museum there lies a document which gives a dispassionate and amusing account of Barbara's most horrid exploit, frankly too awful to be believed, yet seemingly derived from an eye-witness to the incident. Lord Coleraine tells the story. The body of Bishop Robert Braybrook had been dug up and found to be in a remarkable state of preservation (he died in 1440). The skeleton was almost intact save for some damage inflicted by the pick-axes. One day, 'a lady as she seem'd to be of great quality, being attended there with a gentleman and two or three gentlewomen, desired to see this Body and to be left alone by it for a while'. The lady was Barbara. When she left, the horrified witness noticed that the carcass 'served like a Turkish eunuch, and dismembered of as much of the Privity as the lady could get into her mouth to bite (for want of a circumcising penknife to cut)'. We are told that it was a very tough bit to remove, *vix major uncia singula vel tribus longior,** 'and though some ladys of late have got Bishopricks for others, yet I have not heard of any but this that got one for herself . . . Bishop Braybrook was thus more despoil'd by a kind lady in a quarter of an hour, than by the Teeth of Time for almost three centureys of years.'

One cannot be entirely astonished at her impudence, for it was justified by events. In 1670, Charles bestowed fresh titles upon the Countess, making her Baroness Nonsuch, Countess of Southampton, and Duchess of Cleveland. The story that her part of the bargain con-

* Scarcely greater than a single inch, nor made longer by rubbing.

sisted only in her promising to give up Henry Jermyn once and for all, and to cease making unkind remarks about the King's other mistresses, has been dismissed as too ridiculous to be true, but after such a career as has been here described, does it really seem so absurd? Anyway, the patent of creation directed that the titles should pass to her 'first' and 'second' sons, by which were intended Charles and George, who were respectively first and third to be born. The second, Henry (later Duke of Grafton), was still not recognised by the King. The arrangement also included more money, to enable Barbara to live like a Duchess, and the grant of Nonsuch House, one of the most beautiful residences in England, a favourite haunt of Elizabeth I. Barbara, however, was more concerned for the moment to dignify the new house she was building, with her exalted rank; she called it Cleveland House, and though it no longer exists, its echo is heard in the names of Cleveland Row and Cleveland Square in Westminster.

The creation of the title Duchess of Cleveland threw Evelyn into a speechless fit, and even after all these years aroused the normally sedate editors of the *Complete Peerage* to a passionate footnote, reminding us that the title was

> conferred as actual wages of her prostitution and one which had stunk in the nostrils of the nation during the forty years she enjoyed it [she died in 1709]; one, too, which had not been redeemed from the slur thus attached to it by any merit of her successors, of whom the one was a fool and the other a nonentity.

As for Nonsuch House, Barbara plundered it and sold the contents, neglecting it to such a perverse extent that it fell into decay and completely disappeared, to be discovered by archaeologists only in the twentieth century.

Meanwhile, ever more enormous sums of money were granted to the new Duchess to supply her ravenous needs, until from one source and another she was receiving up to £30,000 a year in addition to the settlement of her debts; this after the King had met and turned all his attention to Louise de Kéroualle. On one day, Barbara was seen wearing £40,000 worth of jewellery, and on another she lost £20,000 gambling. Of all the rancour she understandably aroused, the bitterest comment was made by the Duke of Ormonde, who said that his dearest wish was that he might live to see her old.

*   *   *

We are approaching the end of Barbara Villiers's residence in England, and her exit from the life of Charles II. But before she retreats into the wings, there are more lovers who must be mentioned, if only because their identity brings as much surprise as that of any of their predecessors. One was the famous dramatist Wycherley, whose first play, *Love in a Wood*, Barbara had seen at Drury Lane Theatre. The following day, she and Wycherley met in Pall Mall, as they were driving their carriages in opposite directions. Barbara shouted something coarse to the dramatist, to which he replied in like fashion, then ordered his coach to turn around and catch her up. That evening, Barbara saw the play a second time, and a very special friendship ensued. By introducing him at Court, she was instrumental in launching his career, and when he published *Love in a Wood*, he dedicated it to 'Her Grace the Duchess of Cleveland'. She was still a beauty, though past her best, at the age of thirty.*

The second man in her life at this time was none other than John Churchill, the great Duke of Marlborough. Churchill was then twenty-one years old and extremely attractive. Beauty and charm in equal measure made him quite irresistible, and Barbara was temperamentally incapable of resistance. The meeting took place by chance, it was said, at Cleveland House, when Barbara caught sight of the handsome young Ensign and immediately flushed with interest. She asked who he was and demanded an introduction. (This does not ring true, for Churchill was her own second cousin once removed, and she might well be supposed to have known of his existence. The governess to Barbara's children, Mrs Godfrey, was Churchill's aunt.) It was not long before they were engaged on a full-blooded affair, which was conducted with Barbara's customary indiscretion and publicity. The King, of course, knew what was going on, and was angry only because Barbara made such an unbecoming display of it. Tipped off by the Duke of Buckingham, he once discovered the two of them in bed together, and young Churchill had to make a hurried and undignified exit through the window.

It is generally accepted that Barbara's infatuated generosity towards her lover was the foundation of Churchill's subsequent fortune. He already showed signs of that meanness which was to make him notorious; love of money was the most obvious trait of his character. Barbara made him a gift of £5000, which, instead of gambling away like so many other young men about the Court, he prudently invested

* Years before, she had helped establish Dryden by her enthusiastic patronage.

to provide himself with an annuity of £500. A little later, when Barbara found herself short and needed twenty guineas to play with, she asked him very civilly for a small loan, which he turned down out of hand. So when the King commented upon Churchill's romantic embroilment with the gentle cynical reproof, 'I forgive you, for you do it for your bread', he was well aware that Churchill's motives contained no small part of greed.

The affair lasted more or less until Churchill married Sarah Jennings four years later and began the line of Dukes of Marlborough which has given us the great Sir Winston. In the interim, Barbara gave birth to Churchill's daughter, Barbara, in July 1672, only two weeks before Louise de Kéroualle bore the King's son. This time, there was not even a whisper that the King should take responsibility for the child. Barbara grew up to resemble her mother; when she was but eighteen, she gave birth to a bastard child, the son of the Earl of Arran, later Duke of Hamilton – he was murdered in the course of a duel in Hyde Park in 1712. The child of this union, Charles Hamilton, was raised by his grandmother the Duchess of Cleveland, while the mother, Barbara, was packed off to spend the rest of her life as a nun in the convent of Pontoise.

*   *   *

In 1672, Barbara's grandmother, Dame Barbara Villiers, died, leaving the Duchess a risible legacy of £50 with which to buy a mourning ring; evidently she assumed Barbara had enough already. In the same year, her son Henry was finally recognised by the King as 'our second naturall son by ye Lady Barbara', and given the titles Baron Sudbury, Viscount Ipswich and Earl of Euston. The titles were chosen in celebration of the boy's betrothal, two weeks earlier, to Isabella Bennet, daughter of Barbara's old friend Henry Bennet, now Earl of Arlington. Arlington lived at Euston Hall, a splendid estate near Thetford in Norfolk, still the residence of Barbara's descendants through this second son. Henry and Isabella were respectively nine and five years old when their marriage took place, in a sumptuous ceremony at which no expense was spared, offering yet further proof that the King was by now happy to accept the boy as his.*

* The marriage was repeated in 1679, when the children were of age legally to consent.

The wedding of the first son, Charles Fitzroy, to the seven-year-old Mary Wood in the previous year, was by comparison a dull affair. Mary was the daughter of Sir Henry Wood, a clerk of the Green Cloth, and not perhaps of sufficiently distinguished a family to warrant an ostentatious revel. But she was rich, and Barbara was determined to have her. With typical lack of scruple, the Duchess had kidnapped the child and kept her forcibly and illegally until she was assured that the marriage would take place and the dowry conveyed immediately. To Lady Chester, who remonstrated against such arrogant behaviour, Barbara retorted, 'I wonder that so inconsiderable a Person as you will contend with a Lady of my Quality.' This did not prevent her, a few years later, from intriguing to secure an even richer wife for her son in the great heiress Elizabeth Percy, sole possessor of the vast Percy estates left by her father the Earl of Northumberland. Barbara arrogantly assumed that legal obstacles were not difficulties which need stand in her way, and she would simply have the earlier marriage annulled. She was, however, out-manoeuvred by the girl's relations. (Poor Lady Elizabeth was pursued by every fortune-hunter, and found herself married no less than three times by the age of sixteen.)*

In 1674 the two eldest daughters were married. Anne, aged thirteen, and Charlotte, aged nine. Anne was given to Thomas Lennard, 15th Lord Dacre, afterwards Earl of Sussex, in a ceremony at which not only was the King present, but two of his older bastards, the Duke of Monmouth (by Lucy Walter) and 'Don Carlos' (by Catherine Pegge). The dowry she received from the King amounted to £20,000.

Charlotte was betrothed to the Earl of Litchfield, but stayed with her mother for another three years before the marriage was consummated. In view of the largely denigratory accounts we have of Barbara's other children, it is worth recording that Charlotte grew up to be a model of virtue and sobriety, unlike her mother in every respect. She and Lichfield were destined to live out a happy marriage, distinguished by its modesty and constancy.

Barbara's influence at Court was now entirely eclipsed by the reigning *maîtresse en titre*, Louise de Kéroualle, and to a lesser extent by the King's jolly relationship with Nell Gwynn. Nell was more common

* This whole business is confused. Some say that Barbara intrigued for Elizabeth Percy to marry her second son Henry, and then transferred the attempt to her third son George (upon whom was bestowed the title of Northumberland); she was never intended for Charles, the first son.

than the high-born Barbara, and Louise more refined in taste, but to Barbara must regrettably belong the honour of being the most vulgar woman to play a part in Charles II's life.

Nevertheless, she retained sufficient spirit successfully to demand the highest rank for her sons when Louise's bastard was made Duke of Richmond at the age of three. Charles, Henry and George Fitzroy were swiftly endowed with the titles Duke of Southampton, Duke of Grafton, and Duke of Northumberland respectively;* of these, only the second continues in line (the Duke of Northumberland now living at Alnwick is of a later creation, and does not count Barbara's son among his ancestors).

Her education of the children was not much admired. She quarrelled with Lord Arlington, father-in-law of the second boy (Duke of Grafton, Earl of Euston, etc.), who wanted to take responsibility himself for the young man's education, having little faith in her contention that she could teach him everything he needed to know. When she did employ a tutor for the other boys, she made herself so obnoxious to him that he gave up the job in despair. This was Mr Edward Bernard, a fellow of St John's College, Oxford, who was 'so affronted and abused by that insolent woman that he hath been forced to quit that imployment'.

For years the King had been trying to despatch Barbara out of England where she could embarrass him no more. In 1676, she finally went to live in Paris, followed shortly by her daughter Anne, Lady Sussex, who at fifteen had just given birth to her first child, and had promptly deserted her husband. Also with her was the youngest daughter Barbara Fitzroy (fathered by Churchill). Even in Paris, however, the Duchess of Cleveland was to prove a most troublesome memory to the King. Some remarkable letters were exchanged between them which show the King's amazing inability entirely to be rid of her, as well as the vestiges of her power in his counsels.

In Paris, Barbara proceeded to enjoy herself as she had done for twenty years in London : she took a number of lovers. The most talked-of affair was with the English Ambassador, Ralph Montagu (though the Archbishop of Paris was said to have preceded him). Montagu would have cause deeply to regret that he ever allowed himself a romantic attachment to the lady. Things first began to go wrong when she quit his bed to favour the Marquis de Châtillon. Montagu's response was twofold, and both prongs of his jealous revenge were extraordinarily silly. He first wrote and told the King of Barbara's intrigue with

* The Northumberland title was not quite so swift, being granted in 1683.

Châtillon, knowing full well that Charles no longer cared whom she slept with but did mind if she brought shame upon the English, which she was clearly doing. Secondly, he repaid her infidelity by seducing her daughter Anne, Countess of Sussex.

Barbara, a seasoned strategist, was more than a match for Montagu. She went to London briefly in 1678, and told Charles what a lamentable and disloyal ambassador Montagu was (in this she was quite right); and on her return, and her discovery that Montagu had debauched her daughter Anne, she wrote long letters to the King, two of which survive, uniquely revealing and personal in the annals of royal correspondence. They brought about Montagu's ruin. In the extracts which follow, I have corrected the spelling, which was never accurate in the seventeenth century, and variable even with educated persons. In Barbara's case, it was sometimes confusing.

Now all I have to say for myself [she wrote] is, that you know, as to love, one is not mistress of oneself, and that you ought not to be offended with me, since all things of that nature is at an end with you and I; so that I could do you no prejudice. Nor will you, I hope, follow the advice of that ill man, who in his heart, I know, hates you, and were it not for his interest would ruin you too if he could. For he has neither conscience nor honour, and has several times told me that, in his heart he despised you and your brother; and that for his part he wished with all his heart that the Parliament would send you both to travel, for you were a dull governable fool, and the Duke a wilful fool. So that it was yet better to have you than him, but that you always chose a greater beast than yourself to govern you.

She was horrified, she said, at her daughter's familiarity with Montagu, and begged the King to prise her out of his clutches. Her own conduct had been irreproachable, except for the occasional fling, and she hoped Charles would not heed the ambassador's malice in this regard. Barbara makes a comment in her defence which tells much of the loose morals of the day:

all the world knew, that now all things of gallantry were at an end with you and I; that being so, and so public, [the King of France] did not see why you should be offended at my loving anybody. That it was a thing so common nowadays to have a gallantry, that he did not wonder at anything of this nature.

Barbara talks of her daughter Anne as if there were never any doubt that the King was her father (as we have seen, she was just as likely Roger Palmer's daughter, and Roger certainly thought so), and she quotes back to Charles something he had said to her in conversation :

Madam, all that I ask of you, for your own sake, is, live so for the future as to make the least noise you can, and I care not who you love.

This sounds so much like King Charles, that it must surely be authentic, and so like Barbara Villiers to ignore the advice.

This was Barbara's last great victory. Montagu* was struck from the Privy Council and replaced as ambassador by the Earl of Sunderland.

Little is heard of Barbara in the concluding years of Charles II's reign, apart from the beginning of an affair with a disgraceful actor, highwayman, and scoundrel called Cardonell Goodman, whose nickname 'Scum' gives some indication of his character, and who was found guilty of conspiring to poison Barbara's sons the Dukes of Grafton and Northumberland. Chance brought her to England in time for the King's own death in 1685. Six days before his final and fatal convulsion, Barbara was playing at basset with him and two other mistresses, much to the outraged consternation of John Evelyn, to whose account we owe the vivid picture of dissipation. Evelyn also records that one of the King's dying requests was that his brother should be kind to the Duchess of Cleveland. As Evelyn hated her, it must have hurt him to dip his pen and write her name on an occasion which he found as sad as did anyone, but he is the only chronicler who mentions that Charles uttered her name on his death-bed. In spite of everything, Barbara and Charles had been friends united by a common sense of fun, hundreds of shared confidences, and an unabashed pleasure in sexual enjoyment.

The faults of Barbara Villiers have been dwelt upon by all who have written about her, because they were colourful and because they are immediately accessible to any readers of Samuel Pepys. Ambition, ostentation, violent temper, greed, lack of principle, profligacy, vulgarity, all must be admitted essential to her character. Her qualities are less easy to discern. Apart from her obvious beauty, for which she cannot

* He later became Duke of Montagu, and married the mad Duchess of Albermarle, who thought she was the Empress of China and obliged the eager Duke to crawl on his hands and knees before her.

really claim credit, she was a lively and intelligent companion, refreshingly impatient of humbug, and always available.

When Charles II died, Barbara was still heavily involved with the totally amoral actor 'Scum' Goodman, despite his having been found guilty of trying to poison two of her children. His best parts on stage were Julius Caesar and Alexander the Great, performances of which he would delay until *la Cleveland* deigned to appear in the audience. 'Is my Duchess come?' he was heard to shout from the stage. In 1686 she is supposed to have had a child by him, whom the wags christened 'Goodman Cleveland', but nothing more was heard of this offspring. They were still close companions in 1687, when Goodman witnessed a deed by which Barbara granted her son Henry the reversion of her interest in the manor of Woking. Goodman retired from the stage in 1688, and years later, having embraced the Jacobite cause, was arrested for causing a riot and sent to Newgate Prison. He finally emigrated to France, where one report has him in irons in the Bastille, and died there in 1699.

Barbara, meanwhile, did little as she grew older to repair her infamous reputation. There was talk of liaisons with servants and of her falling into the hands of gamesters. This 'second Messaline' slipped gradually into a poor and wretched old age, although she did manage to retain her pension from Post Office revenues, granted by Charles II, under the three successive reigns of James, William and Anne, and in 1705 there is news of her kissing Queen Anne's hand at Court.

Barbara Villiers would not leave this life without a final noisy assault upon convention which, had there been newspapers as we understand them today, would have made headlines the world over. She was the innocent party in a scandalous trial for bigamy at the Old Bailey.

At the age of sixty-four, Barbara flung herself into a relationship the only discernible motive for which was lust. The object of her atentions was Robert Feilding, a reprobate ten years her junior, whom everyone knew to be both unscrupulous and violent. His most obvious distinctions were handsome features, so superior to those of any of his contemporaries that he was nicknamed 'Beau' Feilding. Alas, his good looks were allied to a vanity which considered all praise inadequate and which rendered suspect his undoubted charm. The Feildings were descended from Hapsburgs and as such could claim to be Counts of the Empire. Beau accordingly had the spread eagle emblazoned on his coach, and dressed his footmen in yellow liveries with black sashes and black plumed hats. His pretension went so far as to have his tea brought in by beat of drum. Though well provided with money derived mostly from a clever marriage (he was by this time a widower), he so squandered his wealth that he was reduced to a resource which might nowadays be called 'selling his body' to ladies who were only too keen to buy it. Notorious for public squabbles, he was once wounded in a brawl at the theatre, and bared his chest to show the ladies his wounds.

In 1705, Beau was desperate for a rich wife. The Duchess of Cleveland, he thought, might fill the role. On meeting her, he said, 'Madam, it is not only that Nature has made us the two most accomplished of each sex and pointed to us to obey her dictates in becoming one; but that there is also an ambition in following the mighty persons you have favoured.' Barbara seems to have been well pleased with this speech, for she married him on 25 November of that year. Six months later, in May 1706, she made the horrifying discovery that her husband had married another woman on 9 November 1705, only two weeks before he went through the ceremony with her. Someone wrote, 'The Duchess of Cleveland is given over by her physicians', which is not altogether surprising.

Beau Feilding was tried for bigamy at the Old Bailey. In the course of the trial it emerged that in the first of the two marriages the previous November, he had been duped by those whom he had sought to use. Casting around for a suitable heiress, he alighted upon a widow named Mrs Deleau, whom he had never met. He looked up the will of her late husband and found that she was worth £60,000. So he bribed a go-between to effect a meeting, secure in the belief that Mrs Deleau would require only one look at him to throw herself into his arms. But the go-between, pocketing the £500 reward, introduced him to another lady, Mary Wadsworth, passing her off as Mrs Deleau. Feilding was so taken with the lady (and with her supposed fortune) that he averred he would marry her that same day. She demurred at such haste; twice more she sought to delay, until the fevered Beau, on 9 November, locked her in while he went to fetch a priest. That evening, indeed, they were married, and there were witnesses to confirm that the newly-weds consummated their union in bed, not just once, but on several subsequent occasions. Calling his wife the Countess of Feilding, Beau professed undying love on his knees. Then he married the Duchess of Cleveland and behaved in similar fashion with her.

Nowhere in the trial is there a clue as to how Beau thought he could get away with such monstrous duplicity. What was clear was his uncontrollable anger when he found out that his wife was not the former

Mrs Deleau, worth £60,000, but the former Mary Wadsworth, worth a few pennies. He went straight to the go-between who had fooled him, a woman named Mrs Villars, and threatened that he would slit her nose if she dared reveal the Wadsworth marriage, and that he would get two black men to tear her limb from limb.

Mrs Villars was so frightened that she approached the 2nd Duke of Grafton, grandson to the Duchess of Cleveland, spilled the beans and implored protection. In such a way did Barbara discover she had married a bigamist.

Feilding was found guilty and sentenced, in the manner of the day, to be burnt in the hand. Queen Anne exercised clemency and pardoned him, so the sentence was never effected, whereupon the irate Beau fell upon Barbara, threatened and beat her, and tried to make off with as much of her property as he could. Her grandson Grafton intervened to have Feilding confined in Newgate Prison for his grandmother's protection.

Strangely enough, Feilding was finally reconciled with the legal wife he had married by mistake, Mary Wadsworth, and died on 12 May 1712.

Barbara spent her last few years in Chiswick, at a house on Chiswick Mall known today as Walpole House, with the illegitimate son of one of her illegitimate daughters; this was young Charles Hamilton, one of the few in her family to do her credit. The Duke of Grafton, also, was kind to her. Having rescued her from the clutches of Feilding, he did not punish or berate her, but showed real devotion. She died at Chiswick on 9 October 1709, at the age of sixty-eight, dropsy having swollen her body to a vast bulk and destroyed all vestige of her beauty. Her funeral took place at Chiswick Parish Church, the coffin borne by six noblemen. Her ghost is said to haunt Walpole House.

*   *   *

SOURCES FOR CHAPTER TWO

Osmond AIRY, *Charles II* (1904)
Allen ANDREWS, *The Royal Whore* (1971)
Philip BLOOMFIELD, *Uncommon People* (1955)
British Museum, *Landsdowne MSS.*, 1236, Folio 124 (for Charles II's letter to Clarendon from Portsmouth, giving his first impressions of Catherine of Braganza).

British Museum, *Harley MSS.*, 7006, Folio 171, and Add. MSS 21,505 (Royal autographs), for Barbara's letters to King Charles from Paris.

British Museum, *Stowe MSS.*, 154, Folio 16, for Charles II's letter to Clarendon 'not to meddle any more with what concerns my lady Castlemaine' and her appointment to the Queen's bedchamber.

Arthur BRYANT, *King Charles II* (1931)

Clarendon State Papers

The Complete Peerage

Dictionary of National Biography

John EVELYN, *Diary*

Bernard FALK, *The Royal Fitzroys* (1950)

Margaret GILMOUR, *The Great Lady* (1944)

HAMILTON, *Memoirs of the Comte de Grammont*

C. H. HARTMANN, *La Bell Stuart* (1924)

T. HEARNE, *Reliquiae Hearnianae* (1857)

J. OLDMIXON, *History of England during the Reigns of the Stuarts* (1730)

Samuel PEPYS, *Diary*

T. W. E. ROCHE, *A Pineapple for the King* (1971)

The Earl of ROCHESTER, *Collected Works,* ed. Hayward

Philip SERGEANT, *My Lady Castlemaine* (1912)

G. STEINMANN, *A Memoir of the Duchess of Cleveland* (1871)

Agnes STRICKLAND, *Lives of the Queens of England* (1845), Vol. VIII

John TIMBS, *The Romance of London,* 2 Vols.

E. WALFORD, *Old and New London* (1908), Vol. VI

H. WALPOLE, *Correspondence*

H. Noel WILLIAMS, *Rival Sultanas* (1915)

CHAPTER THREE
Nell Gwynn

It was part of the charm of King Charles II that he was easily imposed upon, that he was soft and malleable in the hands of a clever woman, and liable to trust too readily promises born of passion. That he grew furious if anyone suggested his mistresses controlled him only added to the charm, because his protests were risibly superfluous in the light of Barbara Castlemaine's all too obvious influence. In order to find respite from her constant bad temper, and also to show the gossips that he could be independent of her if he chose, the King took to spending more and more time in simple pleasures, chatting, walking, boating, and relaxing with his dogs (of a breed still known as King Charles spaniels). These dogs slept in his bedroom and sometimes gave birth on his bed, which caused consternation among those who applauded debauch but despised procreation. Still, Charles was not concerned; he took the dogs with him on rambles, and was good-natured about passers-by wishing to pet them. One of the dogs bit the finger of an eager loyalist who dared approach too close, and forgot himself long enough to yell, 'God bless your Majesty, but God damn your dogs!' Charles apparently appreciated the humour of the situation, and was not offended.

On occasion, so weary was he of 'business' and of dealing with the demands of his mistresses, that Charles would repair to chapel, and there promptly fall asleep during the sermon. South was once heard to say to Lord Lauderdale, 'My lord, my lord, you snore so loud you will wake the King!' This is not to say, of course, that Charles's libidinous needs were in any way suppressed. 'God would not damn a man for a little irregular pleasure', he told Burnet, and to his sister Henrietta, the Duchesse d'Orléans, he confided, 'If you were as well acquainted with a little fantastical gentleman called Cupid as I am, you would neither wonder nor take ill any sudden changes which do happen in the affairs of his conducting.'

Browbeaten by Barbara's ceaseless tantrums and her irritating ambition to interfere in the affairs of State, the King needed more than anyone a nice, agreeable, amusing, attractive, uninhibited, and lustful young lady who would give him pleasure and good company without making life a problem. Was such a wench impossible to find? Did pretty girls always wish to meddle in matters that should not concern them, always allow their eyes to grow big with ambitious designs as soon as they realised they could take advantage of their position? Was there no one who would simply love him for himself?

The impossible did happen. In a cheeky Cockney actress called Nell Gwynn, who is still remembered as a popular heroine by every Englishman 300 years later, the King found the easiest and most cheerful sensual relationship of his life. Nell treated the King with neither obsequious respect, nor gross indelicacy, but always as a man and a lover. She was relaxing, and enormous fun to be with. Above all, she was mercifully free from ideas above her station: she did not want to know what it was like to be Queen. As an anonymous versifier put it, most vividly:

> Hard by Pall Mall lives a wench call'd Nell.
> King Charles the Second he kept her.
> She hath got a trick to handle his prick
> But never lays hands on his sceptre.
> All matters of state from her soul she does hate,
> And leave to the politic bitches.
> The whore's in the right, for 'tis her delight,
> To be scratching just where it itches.

Rochester's version is predictably more lewd, taking advantage of the King's distressing inability, already noted in connection with Barbara, to achieve visible expression of excitement:

> This you'd believe, had I but time to tell ye,
> The pain it costs to poor laborious *Nelly*,
> While she employs Hands, Fingers, Lips and Thighs
> E'er she can raise the *Member* she enjoys.

It was natural that such a beguiling creature as Nell Gwynn should be found in the theatre, and natural too that Charles should encounter her there. One of the King's first acts, within a few weeks of the Restoration, had been to re-establish the theatres after years of Puritan prohibition had effectively denied theatrical entertainment to a whole generation. Both the King and his brother the Duke of York were frequent visitors to the theatre, and it was fitting that the two buildings opened by King Charles should be called the King's Theatre, and the Duke's Theatre. All other theatrical companies in London and West-minster were suppressed when these two were founded, thus establish-ing a monopoly which could harness the best writing and acting talents of the day, although some other companies did perform in defiance of the order and with the tacit tolerance of the King. The Duke's Theatre played *Romeo and Juliet, Hamlet*, and *Macbeth* in the first year of its operation, while the King's Theatre tended to specialise more in comedy and light drama, often satirical and spicy. It is the King's Theatre which concerns us more, for it was here that Nell Gwynn made her fame as an actress, and it was here that she was first spied by the King.

Moreover, the King's Theatre stood on the site now occupied by the Theatre Royal, Drury Lane, and was in fact the first of four theatres to be built here. It might be called the original Drury Lane Theatre, in spite of its name, because it still exercises its right to present enter-tainment under a patent dated 25 April 1662, granted to Thomas Killigrew and signed by Charles II. It is one of only two theatres in London* which operates not by licence from the Lord Chamberlain or from a local authority, but by direct grant from the Crown. The original document is still in the possession of the lessees. There is a tradition which identifies one of the dressing-rooms at the Theatre Royal as Nell Gwynn's, but it is not verifiable; one can only marvel at the fact that parts of the walls and floor in this room date from the original building.

The theatre was built in 1662, and Killigrew presented his first entertainment there, *The Humorous Lieutenant*, by Beaumont and Fletcher, on 7 May 1663. Though small, the building was elegant and luxuriously appointed, with seats covered in green baize and gilt leather. The less expensive seats were, however, open to the elements. Performances usually began at three in the afternoon. The theatre may have been restored as a respectable entertainment, but the actors them-selves were still held in low regard, being treated for the most part as servants. Still worse, the actresses were considered fair game for enter-tainment after the performance, and backstage was sometimes scarcely disguised as an avenue to prostitution; Sir William Davenant, who ran the Duke's Theatre, gave board and lodging to his four principal

* The other is the Royal Opera House.

D

actresses at his own house, in order to protect them. With such a reputation, it was considered unseemly for ladies to attend the first night of a new play, unless they were masked. They could then conceal their blushes, occasioned both by the evident physical talents of the actresses and by the bawdiness of the dialogue.

Even the presence of women on stage was an innovation. Until then female parts had generally been played by men, but Charles II's patents to Killigrew and Davenant specified

> we do likewise permit and give leave that all women's parts to be acted in either of the said two companies for the time to come, may be performed by women, so long as these recreations, which, by reason of the abuses aforesaid were scandalous and offensive, may by such reformation be esteemed not only harmless delights but useful and instructive representations of human life to such of our good subjects as shall resort to the same.

This was a momentous clause for our theatre generally, and for Nell Gwynn especially, in the context of our story. Without it, she may not have been noticed by the King. On the other hand, even had she not become the King's mistress, Nell would still deserve an important place in the history of Restoration theatre.

Standing in the pit at the front of theatre, with their backs to the stage, were the 'orange girls', the equivalent of today's dispensers of ice-cream and chocolates. The orange girls carried baskets on their arms, laden with fruit and vine-leaves, and offered their goods with the cry, 'Oranges, will you have any oranges?' Chief among them was Mrs Mary Meggs, popularly known as 'Orange Moll', who was in charge of the girls and held her licence to sell fruit at the theatre for thirty-nine years. Orange Moll was a splendid character, chatty and irreverent, a law unto herself and very much a feature of the theatre. Gossip and banter were expected of her, and she demanded the same talents from her girls. An orange girl who was silent would not last long.

Shortly after the King's Theatre opened in 1663, Nell Gwynn, then a mere child of thirteen, was employed as one of the orange girls. Intimacy between the actors and the girls in the pit bore results, for Nell soon became the mistress of the leading actor, Charles Hart, who played Othello amongst other parts, and found herself mixing with the theatrical crowd. She made the transition from front of house to backstage over the next eighteen months, being trained in the actor's craft by Hart himself, and taught to dance by the King's favourite actor, John Lacy. By 1665 she was a leading actress.

Before we look at Nell's stage career, and enjoy her unique relationship with the King, possibly the most attractive friendship between monarch and subject in English history, we should first see who Nell was and where she came from.

This is by no means easy. Tradition is more persuasive than fact, and tradition says that Nell was born in a slum called Coal Yard Alley, just east of Drury Lane. This invites belief, because it reinforces the romantic notion of Nell as a child of the streets and a Cockney urchin who knew the Drury Lane area from birth. Besides, it is probably true; at least we know that she lived in Coal Yard Alley as a child, with her mother and her sister Rose, and since they were a totally destitute family, without the wherewithal to travel, it is more than likely that they had always been there. Her father was said to be a Welshman, Thomas Gwynne, who sold fruit. That also is quite possible. Other conflicting traditions ascribe Nell's birthplace to Hereford and Oxford, but there is less reason to believe them. Unmoved by the sceptics, the people of Hereford boast a Gwynne Street to celebrate Nell's supposed association with the city. The Oxford connection is yet more insubstantial. Thomas Gwynne, who had been a captain in the Royalist army but had, as they say, come down in the world, was thought to have died in a debtor's gaol in Oxford.

Nell was born in 1650, her mother's second daughter. Sister Rose, whose husband was a highwayman, was imprisoned for theft in Newgate in 1663, but managed to secure a reprieve before coming up for trial by reason of her connections in high places. She knew Harry Killigrew (who said such unkind things about Barbara Palmer's youthful experiments in sexual gratification) who, as Groom of the Bedchamber to the Duke of York, was able to use influence. Rose's letter from Newgate pleaded with Killigrew and the Duke's cupbearer, Browne, to rescue her from 'this woeful place of torment', with success. As Harry Killigrew's father was Thomas Killigrew, who had just been granted the patent for the King's Theatre Company, it must surely be Rose who introduced her younger sister to the Killigrews and started her on the path to enduring fame.

Before she joined the theatre as an orange girl, Nell had been a seller of fish on the streets, and a servant-girl in a brothel, both in the immediate vicinity of Drury Lane.* In the brothel her function was innocent

* Perhaps the brothel was run by her mother (*History Today*, June 1977).

enough, as far as is known, consisting in pouring drinks for the gentle-men between engagements.

That is about the total of our knowledge of Nell Gwynn's upbringing. It was not of a nature likely to make her prudish. But it did teach her how to look after herself, which she needed to do as her mother, constantly drunk on cheap brandy, was not much help; it also trained her in that caustic wit which was to make her rather more than an ordinary orange girl, as she flirted and jested with the audience, giving them something of a performance even before the curtain went up.

And of course she was delectable to look at. Quite small, with tiny feet which were then considered a mark of especial beauty, chestnut hair which more often than not hung loose, and hazel eyes, Nell Gwynn had the kind of quality which only French words can adequately describe – *gamine, mignonne, petite*. Samuel Pepys called her 'pretty witty Nell', and in one passage of his diary depicted her in her beauty and casual self-confidence so neatly that her character emerges as vividly as her presence. Pepys was watching the May-day festivities in London in 1667, when a fiddler pranced down the street followed by milk-maids dancing, with garlands on their pails, 'and saw pretty Nelly standing at her lodging door in Drury Lane in her mock-sleeves and bodice, looking upon one – she seemed a mightly pretty creature'.

Thanks to the portraits which were left to posterity, we also know that Nell Gwynn had a fine bosom, and since she tended to wear loose comfortable clothes rather than stiff formal garments, the natural grace of her body was constantly shown to advantage. Fortunately, she was not self-conscious about undressing, which was just as well, since actresses could not then expect privacy in their dressing-rooms. Pepys and his wife went backstage to see her, and found that she was 'dressing herself and was all unready; and is very pretty, prettier than I thought'. She was then seventeen years old. Pepys was again quite moved when he one day had the opportunity to kiss her, mentioning the pleasure in his diary more than once in the same paragraph.

There is a rhyme which pays tribute to the effect which Nell had upon all who saw her :

> And once Nell Gwynne, a frail young sprite,
>   Looked kindly when I met her;
> I shook my head, perhaps – but quite
>   Forgot to quite forget her.

Withal, she laughed easily, with an infectious merriness which took over her whole face so that her eyes were almost invisible.

Frail she may have appeared, owing to her small stature, but frail she certainly was not in her handling of colleagues, admirers and rivals. She had a ready, mocking wit, and a gay, sparkling sense of humour which often turned to sarcasm, but was used mischievously rather than wickedly. Never at a loss for something to say, and never meekly deferential, Nell had that self-assurance in her conversation and social behaviour which even now one still associates with certain theatrical ladies who make a reputation on their capacity for fast, engaging repartee, and are as a result forever surrounded by men. Pepys was present on one occasion when Nell and another actress, Rebecca Marshall, came off stage together; 'but Lord, their confidence', he exclaimed, 'and how many men do hover about them as soon as they come off the stage, and how confident they are in their talk'.

It is also not uncommon in the theatrical world for ladies to speak indelicately. Nell was typically rough, candid, and honest; her language could be quite foul, but no one was inclined to castigate her propensity for robust talk because, unlike Barbara Palmer's manufactured tantrums, in which the language was calculated to bear the maximum malice, Nell's outspokenness was essentially earthy, natural, and hearty, in all senses of the word. Bad language was part of her character – she would have been untrue to herself had she sought to control it. She talked lewdly, and roundly cursed the audience if it was a 'bad' house, just as many a respected actress does today. Her rival a few years hence, Louise de Kéroualle, who could hardly be expected to hold a dispassionate view, said that anyone could tell she had been a cheap seller of oranges by the way in which she swore. But Pepys was not so jaundiced. He saw her sitting in a box at the theatre, 'a bold merry slut', laughing both with and at people she recognised in the audience, in a completely free and warm-hearted manner. Her vitality did not recognise inhibition.

Other aspects of her personality, all good, emerge when Nell is in the company of Charles II. For the moment, the picture we have represents her character when she took the bold step up from the pit on to the stage at the King's Theatre. Her lover, Charles Hart, who was the manager of the theatre as well as its leading actor, was a great-nephew of William Shakespeare. He and Nell acting together became the darlings of the stage, their collaboration affording Nell her greatest successes. Her first appearance was at the end of 1664, but her first triumph was in the rôle of Lady Wealthy in a play called *The English Monsieur* by James Howard, a son of Lord Berkshire. It is a part of such iconoclastic humour that it was most likely written for her. Nell exceeded in comic parts, seducing the audience with the wit of her rejoinders, and presumably also by the sheer incongruity of an uncultured Cockney girl playing the stock haughty aristocratic ladies. In a 'mad' part, Pepys records, she was inimitable, as in *The Mad Couple* (also playing opposite Charles Hart), or as Celia in *The Humorous Lieutenant* by John Fletcher. Her greatest success was in a play called *The Mayden Queene*, by John Dryden (who wrote parts especially for Nell Gwynn). Pepys saw it several times, with growing enthusiasm. 'There is a comical part done by Nell, which is Florimell', he wrote on 2 March 1667, 'that I never can hope ever to see the like done again by man or woman'. She was required in one scene to appear in male clothes, and to dance a jig, both of which transported the diarist into hyperbole.

> So great a performance of a comical part was never, I believe, in the world before as Nell doth this, both as a mad girle and then, most and best of all, when she comes in as a young gallant; and hath the notions and carriage of a spark the most that ever I saw any man have.

How enchanting she might have been in *As You Like It*!

Tragic rôles, however, were not within Nell Gwynn's scope. 'I know you in your hearts, Hate serious parts – as I hate serious parts', she said in her epilogue to the audience after *The Duke of Lerma*, and no doubt they applauded wildly. They did not like to see their heroine take on something with which she could not cope. In Dryden's *The Indian Emperour*, for example, a play about the Spanish conquests, the leading female parts of Cyderia and Almeria were played by Nell Gwynn and Rebecca Marshall respectively. Pepys was most upset by what he saw. 'I find Nell come again', he wrote, 'which I am glad of, but was most infinitely displeased with her being put to act the Emperour's daughter; which is a great and serious part, which she doth most basely.' Three months later, Pepys saw the play again, and confirmed his opinion: 'Nell's ill speaking of a great part made me mad.' Again, as Samira in Robert Howard's *The Surprizall*, Nell could not rise to the demands of a heavy rôle. Hence her epilogue remarks in *The Duke of Lerma* (a play, incidentally, about kings and their mistresses, also written by Robert Howard), which were spoken with more than usual feeling.

At one performance of *The Mad Couple* (sometimes called *All Mistaken*), there was present in the audience a good-looking man in his late twenties, who was so inflamed by Nell Gwynn's bare thighs, frequently shown in the play as she rolled around the stage to escape amorous advances, that he resolved to have her as his mistress. The young man in question was not likely to suffer defeat, being a notorious rake and one of the most celebrated jokers of the age. He was Lord Buckhurst (Charles Sackville by name, later to be Earl of Dorset by inheritance and Earl of Middlesex by creation), a poet and man of letters, very highly respected in literary circles, and a man whom Walpole was moved to call 'the finest gentleman in the voluptuous Court of Charles II'.

Walpole's judgement only shows that he could not have known much about Lord Buckhurst, for apart from being a witty companion and a clever man, he was unwholesome, coarse, lubricious and brazenly lecherous. His boon companion in his excesses was Sir Charles Sedley, who shared all Buckhurst's characteristics – keen mind, sharp wit, brisk intelligence, bright company, and unbridled vulgarity. They made a colourful pair.

Five years before, Buckhurst and Sedley had been arrested for robbing and killing a tanner named Hoppy, probably for amusement after a too indulgent session in the tavern. Their high-spirited pranks over the years frequently landed them in trouble. They were once tried before Lord Chief Justice Foster for committing various acts of gross indecency in a public place. The place was a well-known and popular tavern – Oxford Kate's – in Bow Street, Covent Garden, which had a first-floor balcony overlooking the street. Buckhurst and Sedley, after drinking themselves into a stupor, summoned the strength to appear on the balcony, in broad daylight and before a growing assembly of the curious, and give an impromptu show. They stripped naked, and acted out all possible sexual positions that could be imagined, including buggery (which was then becoming a popular innovation, almost as common as in Italy). Pepys relates the scene without shame – it must have been very amusing as well as compulsively entertaining. As the incredulous crowd grew to about a thousand, the naked pair preached a mock sermon from the 'pulpit', saying that they were marketing a powder 'as should make all the cunts in town run after him'. Afterwards, Sedley took a glass of wine, 'and washed his prick in it and then drank it off; and then took another and drank the King's health'.

Chief Justice Foster administered a severe reprimand, calling them wicked wretches, and fining them £500 for causing a riot. But such irrepressible wags were not so easily put down; they were, after all, merely expressing the ideal of the 'goodfellow', writing their works of art in the morning, and descending to debauch in the afternoon. It strikes us now as absurdly incongruous that Sir Charles Sedley's writing was thought to be immortal, that Lord Buckhurst was credited with being the first man to perceive the genius of Milton's *Paradise Lost*, and that they both spent a night cavorting about the streets stark naked and ended up in a prison cell.

This, then, was the man who took a fancy to Nell Gwynn, and 'bought' her from Charles Hart, as a result of which she gave up her profession to go and live with Buckhurst at Epsom, with a reputed allowance of £100. It was rumoured that she would never act again. At Epsom, Nell lived with Buckhurst *and* Sedley (though only Buckhurst was said to be her lover), and the three of them had a riotous time together. Considering their character, it is small wonder that Pepys felt bound to say, 'Poor girl, I pity her', adding that her absence from the theatre was perhaps the more severe loss; he no doubt thought that Nelly could look after herself.

He proved right. Within a few weeks, Nelly was back, scorned by the rake who discarded her when he had had all he wanted of her; she was much the poorer, and despised by her former friend Hart. But it looks as if it was she who made the decision to leave Epsom and make the best of a bad business. As it turned out, Buckhurst, who was already M.P. for East Grinstead at the time of this escapade, was later appointed a Gentleman of the Bedchamber and is on the list of Nell's trustees; so they presumably patched up their quarrel and resumed some kind of friendship.

Anyway, Nelly did not have long to wait before her affections were engaged by the greatest lover of them all, the King himself. Charles had obviously seen Nell on stage many times, though we have no records of the occasions, and we know that as early as 1655 she and Rebecca Marshall had accompanied the King and Barbara Castlemaine to the theatre. It was, however, towards the end of 1667 that the King showed a more specific interest. He and the Duke of York found themselves sitting next to Nell at the theatre; she was in an adjacent box, as the guest of a Mr Villiers (of the same family as Barbara and the Duke of Buckingham), when the King introduced himself into the conversation, and insisted that he join them for supper afterwards. The Duke of York was brought along to occupy Villiers's attention while

Charles devoted himself to seducing Nelly. At the end of the meal, neither Charles nor his brother had any money with which to pay the bill, thus obliging the hapless Villiers to pay for all four of them, a questionable privilege in the circumstances. Nell's comment was typically impudent. 'Oddsfish', she exclaimed, 'but this is the poorest company that ever I was in before at a tavern.'

By the following January, Pepys reported that the King had sent 'several times' for Nelly, but Charles also was behaving typically in trying to juggle with the attractions of several women at the same time. He was deep in his involvement with Moll Davis (whom he seems temporarily to have abandoned in favour of Nell), and he was still coping with the persistent demands of Lady Castlemaine. There was in addition another actress on the scene, one Elizabeth Farley, who performed under the name of Mrs Weaver; she had been one of the King's bed companions some years before, but it is not clear whether or not she was again receiving attention at this time.

Until then, Nell had lived in lodgings above the Cock and Pie Tavern in Drury Lane, at the southern end, near the Strand. (It was pulled down in 1891, and had stood opposite Wych Street, a name still present in 'Aldwych'; Drury Lane itself had previously been called 'Via de Aldewyche'.) She now moved to Lincoln's Inn Fields, and it was there, on 8 May 1670, that her first son by King Charles was born.

Nell gradually abandoned the stage to become the King's mistress. Pregnancy, which was a burden borne by almost all the ladies who had any intimate relation with the virile Charles, was not a convenient state for an actress. Indeed, her last great part, Almahide in Dryden's play *The Conquest of Granada*, was so unsuitable for a pregnant woman that the production had to be postponed until after the birth of Nelly's son. Dryden makes a wry comment on the reasons for delay in his epilogue :

> Pity the virgins of each theatre;
> For at both houses 'twas a sickly year!
> And pity us, your servants, to whose cost
> In one such sickness nine whole months were lost.

Dryden means, of course, that Moll Davis, at the rival Duke's Theatre, was pregnant at the same time; her daughter by the King was called Mary Tudor, and married the Earl of Derwentwater.

Nell was lured back to the theatre briefly to play in a revival of Beau-

mont and Fletcher's *A King and No King*, but with the birth of her son
she virtually stepped out of the history of Restoration theatre to assume
her most enduring rôle, as part of the folklore of England.

In one of those neat coincidences which make the facts of history so
much more startling than the inventions of novelists, at the very time
Nell Gwynn was giving birth to the future Duke of St Albans, the King
was on his way to Dover to meet his sister Henrietta d'Orléans, in whose
service was a demure and enchanting French girl, Louise de Kéroualle.
No sooner did Charles set eyes upon Louise than he was once more
ensnared, and she it was who was destined to succeed Barbara Castlemaine as his 'official' mistress, or *maîtresse en titre*, and for many years
to be driven speechless with irritation at Nelly's impudent hold over
the King's affections. Even after Louise was given the highest rank,
and created Duchess of Portsmouth, still she could do nothing to
command the respect she thought she deserved from the cheeky little
actress. They were the most entertaining rivals, and Charles found
much amusement in playing them off one against the other. Nell, of
course, always emerged victorious, because she was unaffected, frank,
and honest, and had no time for humbug, whereas Louise was haughty,
proud and pompous. Moreover, Nell was completely devoid of jealousy,
and so did not imagine she had anything to lose by making fun of the
King's senior mistress. When Louise announced that she was a lady
of quality, Nell retorted that she should not then demean herself by
being a prostitute, and ought to die with shame. As for herself, said
Nell, she did not pretend to be anything else, she had borne the King's
son and was faithful to him, and what's more, she was quite sure that
the King was every bit as attached to her as he was to the arrogant
Duchess. And of course she was right. Louise could only seethe at the
impertinence.

Madame de Sévigné, writing to her daughter, gave a gloriously
descriptive picture of Nell's carefree treatment of the new arrival.
Louise, she said, was taken aback to find

> a young actress in her way, whom the King doats on; and she had
> it not in her power to withdraw him from her. He divides his care,
> his time, and his health between these two. The actress is as haughty
> as Mademoiselle; she insults her, she makes grimaces at her, she
> attacks her, she frequently steals the King from her, and boasts
> whenever he gives her the preference. She is young, indiscreet, con-
> fident, wild, and of an agreeable humour; she sings, she dances, she

acts her part with a good grace . . . this creature gets the upper hand, and discountenances and embarrasses the duchess extremely.

Shortly after the birth of her first son, and on the return of Charles from Dover to London, arrangements were made for Nell to move from humble lodgings in Lincoln's Inn Fields to a more substantial abode in Pall Mall, the new and stately avenue which had been laid out in 1661 on the site of the old pall mall alley. It was still an essentially rural area, lined with elm trees, and with haystacks not far away. In 1671 Nell Gwynn was again pregnant, and needed larger quarters, so she moved down the road to No. 79 Pall Mall, on the south side, with gardens backing on to St James's Park. This is the house which has always been associated with her, and where she lived for the rest of her life. Ironically, Moll Davis was to be a neighbour, as in 1673 she bought a house on the north side, at the entrance to St James's Square, at a cost of £1800.

Originally, Nell was granted a Crown lease, but having wisely and quite rightly pointed out that she gave her services to the King free (unlike most of her rapacious rivals), she claimed that she should have her house unencumbered. Secretary of State Sir Joseph Williamson reported in 1673 that 'Madame Gwinn complains she has no house yet'. In the end her reasoning prevailed, for the King granted the freehold of 79 Pall Mall to his confidential page, William Chiffinch, who in turn conveyed it to Nell's trustees. It has been conveyed free ever since, and though Nell's house was demolished in 1866, the present building on the site, occupied by the Eagle Star Insurance Company, is the only freehold on the south side of Pall Mall. The insurance company owes its good fortune to the charms of Nell Gwynn and the carnal appetites of King Charles II.

The Pall Mall house was conveniently situated to allow chats over the garden wall with the King, for which purpose a rise in the ground had been constructed so that Nell could climb on to the wall. It was here that John Evelyn, censorious as ever, observed 'a familiar discourse between the King and Mrs Nelly, as they called an impudent comedian, she looking out of her garden on a terrace at the top of the wall, and the King standing on the green walk under it'. Harmless enough, one might think, but Evelyn was the lone voice crying against the moral laxity of the age, a rôle one suspects he enjoyed a trifle too much, and any hint of pleasure always concealed for him a warren of vice.

Inside, Nell gave many 'merry' parties, both with and without King

Charles as principal guest. She loved music, yet another trait which
endeared her to the civilised and cultured monarch, and there was one
recorded occasion when Nell engaged the services of Harry Bowman,
a famous singer of the day, to entertain her guests. Both the King and
his brother were present. At the end of the performance, Charles congratulated Bowman and said how much he had enjoyed himself. 'Then,
sir,' said Nell, 'to show you do not speak like a courtier, I hope you
will make the performers a handsome present.' As usual, the King had
no money about him, and the Duke of York was not much better
equipped. 'Oddsfish!' cried Nell, to the amusement of all present, 'what
company am I got into.'

There were times, also, when she played basset at 79 Pall Mall,
though never to such excess as the Duchess of Cleveland. Basset was a
card game introduced from France, of Venetian origin, which relied
entirely upon chance. There were fifty-two cards, distributed between
five players, one of whom represented the bank. Enormous fortunes
could be lost in a few minutes. Rarely was anything won.

As Louise de Kéroualle consolidated her position at Court, so Nell
became more and more mischievous in deflating her. There was much
fun to be derived from watching the vulgar irrepressible little Cockney
lady constantly get the better of the disdainful foreigner, and the
London crowd, always an unfailing discerner of truth, unhesitatingly
took Nell's part. They distrusted Louise, whom they thought nothing
more nor less than a spy sent to intrigue against England (and they were
not far wrong), and joyfully contrived both to mispronounce her name
and reduce her status by referring to her as 'Mrs Carwell'. Nell herself,
taking advantage of Louise's slight cast in one eye, called her 'Squintabella'.

The people further disliked Louise by reason of her Catholicism,
which caused her to be known as the Popish Mistress. There was a
famous occasion, often retold, when Nell Gwynn's coach was mobbed
in Oxford, the crowd hurling insults at the occupant whom they
believed to be Louise. Nell quite calmly put her head out of the
window and said, 'Pray, good people, be civil; I am the *Protestant*
whore.'

Nell delighted in mocking the pretensions of the grand Frenchwoman. When the Chevalier de Rohan was executed, Louise went into
deep mourning not so much to show how deeply she was affected, but
to show she had a *right* to be upset. In fact, her gesture had a spurious
origin, for she was no relation to the Chevalier whatever. Nell realised

this. The next day, Nell appeared at Court dressed entirely in black. One of the courtiers enquired the reason. 'Why? Have you not heard,' said Nell, 'my loss in the death of the Cham of Tartary? I was exactly the same relation to the Cham of Tartary as the Duchess of Portsmouth was to the Chevalier de Rohan.'

The same ludicrous game was played when the King of Sweden died, and Louise again went into mourning. Nell followed suit when the King of Portugal died, and accosted Louise one day with the remark, 'Let us agree to divide the world; you shall have the kings of the north, and I the kings of the south.' The humiliation was too much for Louise, who frequently resorted to tears in her frustration, and besieged the King with complaints about Nell's insolence. The King was merely amused, and Nell, unperturbed, nicknamed her rival 'the weeping willow'.

It was not entirely a secret that Louise maintained an all-too-close conection with the French court, which aroused suspicion. While others murmured behind their hands, Nell Gwynn had no time for discreet meanderings and boldly said out loud what the rest of the court disguised in circumlocution. 'Why is it', she said to the French ambassador one day, 'that the King of France does not send presents to me, instead of to the "weeping willow" who has just gone out? I promise you that he would get more profit by doing so. The King is a thousand times more fond of me than of her. '

Correspondence between the French ambassador and his master indicates that he was well aware Nell Gwynn enjoyed a very close relationship with Charles, and that notice should be taken of what she said. She would have been most unsuitable as a spy, however, because she lacked the essential quality of discretion. She was, on the contrary, wildly and rapturously indiscreet, and might well have been unable to retain the King's affection had she been as circumspect and dishonest as the rest of the people around him. It is significant that Nell Gwynn is the only mistress of Charles II with whom there is absolutely no recorded instance of his having quarrelled. There can be little doubt but that she was right to tell the ambassador the King was more fond of her than of the official mistress.

Nell was refreshingly free from affectation, cheerful, uninhibited, and completely honest to herself. Charles went to her to escape from the pressures of his office or the chaotic mess of his private life. She responded to that cheeky side of his nature which enjoyed seeing the haughty and pretentious discomfited. He was always at heart a rascal, and Nell became his playmate. She could be relied upon to amuse and relax him.

Louise de Kéroualle was not the only woman to suffer from Nell's *penchant* for mischief. Barbara Castlemaine, too, came in for her share of ridicule. When Barbara made herself look silly by ostentatiously driving around in a coach drawn by eight horses, Nell hitched up her coach with eight oxen. The Duchess of Norfolk, who had indulged in a notorious affair with Sir John Germaine, apologised to Nell for having her hair out of order. Nell wondered why, after a night such as the Duchess had passed, her hair was not out of powder and curl too, and advanced the opinion that she expected to see Germaine crawl out 'like a drowned rat'.

Moll Davis was the victim of one of Nell's most inspired jokes. Hearing that Moll was due to share the King's bed one night, Nell invited her to eat, and mixed the sweetmeats which she offered with a drug called jalap, made from the roots of a Mexican plant and guaranteed to produce diarrhoea.

Fishing at Hampton Court with the King and the Prince of Neuberg, Nell played practical jokes upon them both. When the King felt at last a weight on his line, he yanked it in to find fried fish tied to the end of it. Nell said that ordinary fishermen could only aspire to catch their fish alive, but great kings must needs catch them ready for eating. Neuberg's haul from the water was a purse of gold and a miniature of the lady with whom he was known to be in love.

As we have already seen, Nell was free of false pride, and did not object to being called a whore; as she was unmarried, and bore the King two sons, that word, to her, was a perfectly proper and accurate description of her situation. Her admirers sometimes rose to her defence and were cordially thanked, but told not to bother. Mr Herbert, Lord Pembroke's brother, once caused a fight at the Duke's Theatre, with swords drawn, when someone used the word 'whore' with reference to Nell, and her own coachman got himself into a tumble for the same reason. 'Go to, you blockhead', she told him, 'if you want to risk your hide, do so in defence of the truth.' The coachman is said to have replied, 'You may not mind being called a whore, but I'll not be called a whore's coachman.' Another time, Nell was planning a party at 79 Pall Mall for the King's birthday, and Charles suggested that she might invite the Countess of Shrewsbury. This she declined to do, one imagines with a wink, saying, 'One whore at a time is enough for you, Sire.'

Nell was on sure ground, for she knew that she had less to reproach herself with than most. When 'Beck' Marshall picked a quarrel with her, reminding her that she had been Lord Buckhurst's whore, Nell replied that she had only one man at a time, whereas Beck managed to keep three or four in tow. This was absolutely true. Nell was the mistress of only three men, consecutively not simultaneously, which was remarkably conservative in Charles II's court. All three men were called Charles, which inspired Nell to call Charles Hart her 'Charles the first', Charles Sackville (Buckhurst) her 'Charles the second', and the King her 'Charles the third'. Buckhurst was supposed to have been given the earldom of Middlesex in return for yielding Nell to the King.

Once Nell was attached to the King, she remained faithful and loyal to him throughout. Flirtatious she might have been, but there was never any serious threat that she would go off with anyone else. The King found her fidelity a relief, never a burden, and he did not have to forgive her familiarity – he rejoiced in it. Meeting him in the fields at New-market, Nell was heard to say to him, 'Charles, I hope I shall have your company at night, shall I not?' Had he been unable to oblige, she would not have made a fuss, for she was neither jealous nor possessive. A touching insight into this curiously close relationship of King and Cockney is revealed in a letter which Nell addressed to the new King after Charles's death. After saying that she had loved Charles not for the benefit she might derive from the connection, but for himself, she continued (I have corrected the spelling):

> Had he lived, he told me before he died, that the world should see by what he did for me that he had both love and value for me . . . He was my friend and allowed me to tell him all my griefs and did like a friend advise me and told me who was my friend and who was not.

This, in Nell Gwynn's own words, is surely the most eloquent and graphic depiction of the two in private.

*   *   *

With the birth of Nelly's second son on Christmas Day 1671, her contribution to the extra-curricular nursery was complete. This boy, the only son of Charles II not to be given a peerage title of his own, was known as James Beauclerk (after his uncle James, Duke of York), and was destined to have a very brief life. He died in Paris at the age of

eight, 'of a sore leg'. The use of the surname 'Beauclerk' instead of the
more usual 'Fitzroy' might be taken to indicate that the sons of an
actress, though acknowledged by the King, should not be counted
among the most noble families in the land. This leads us into a consideration of the manner in which Nell's older son did eventually receive
his title.

Nell was not ambitious for herself, but even she showed signs of
irritation when the bastard sons of Barbara were all made dukes before
they were adolescent, when Catherine Pegge's son was made Earl of
Plymouth in 1675, and especially when Louise de Kéroualle's son broke
all records by being elevated to the highest rank as Duke of Richmond
at the age of three. 'Even Barbara's brats were not made dukes until
they were twelve or thirteen', said Nelly, 'but this French spy's son is
ennobled when little more than an infant in arms!'

It was too much. Nell determined to confront the King with his
neglect of her son's status. There are a variety of stories which purport
to account for the way in which she set about the task, but the most
characteristic of all is the one first told by Granger. When the King
visited 79 Pall Mall one day in 1676, Nell called to her boy saying,
'Come here, you little bastard, and say hello to your father!' The King,
fond of his son as he was of all his children, pleaded with her not to use
this word in reference to him, to which she retorted, 'Your Majesty has
given me no other name to call him by', which was of course quite
true; until then, he did not even have the surname Beauclerk. The ruse
was successful, for later that year Charles created the boy Baron Head-
ington and Earl of Burford, and in 1684, Duke of St Albans (he is the
ancestor of the present Duke).

According to other versions of the story, Nell is supposed to have
held the child out of the window and threatened to drop him to the
street below unless he was ennobled, whereupon the King, thinking
quickly which title was available, exclaimed 'God save the Earl of
Burford'; or that she held him head downwards over a river, with the
same effect. Whatever the case, it is quite certainly the most original
method for the creation of a noble family in the history of the peerage,
and one well in keeping with the boisterous personality of its progenitrix.

The title of Burford, in the county of Oxford, was probably chosen
because Charles already had in mind that his son should marry the
last heiress of the illustrious de Vere family, Earls of Oxford. Why 'St
Albans' was selected remains a mystery.

Young Burford was educated by the dramatist Thomas Otway, and sent to Paris at the age of twelve, where his French studies were in the hands of the Ambassador. Upon being created Duke of St Albans, he was also appointed Grand Falconer of England, a post still held by his descendant and still carrying the right to attend a coronation bearing a falcon perched on his wrist.

In 1682 Charles II laid the foundation stone of the Royal Hospital at Chelsea for wounded and disabled soldiers, a building which cherishes the tradition that it owes its existence to the good heart of Nell Gwynn. The story holds that one day a crippled old man came up to the window of Nelly's coach and begged for alms. She questioned him, and he explained that he was reduced to such pitiful circumstances by the wounds he had received in battles on behalf of the Royalists before the Restoration. Nell was so overcome with compassion, reflecting no doubt that her own father had himself suffered a similar fate for the same reasons, that she prevailed upon the King to establish a hospital that would care for old soldiers; there were many who had fought at Edge Hill, at Marston Moor, and at Worcester, whose lives were now rendered miserable as a result of injuries sustained. Nell's sense of justice excited her to plead their cause, and the King, who was himself sensible to the debt he owed his people, was not difficult to persuade. As his secret service payments show, he had never ceased to give generous financial support to the Penderell family, to whose loyalty and courage he owed his escape from Worcester; those who harshly castigate the money he squandered on mistresses should pause to consider his unseen payments to worthy folk who had supported him with their hearts and their valour. That he should respond to a suggestion from Nell to look after the old soldiers would be perfectly in character.

It was also perfectly in character for Nell to propose the idea. She was well known for her generous impulses, giving £100 for the relief of poor people made homeless by a disastrous fire in Wapping, and making a specific bequest in her will that money should be provided for the release of poor prisoners from debtors' gaols. (Her intentions were honoured, and the money was distributed every Christmas Day to the inmates of Whitecross Street prison.) When she saw a clergyman being dragged off to prison, she enquired the reason, and immediately paid up the amount owed when she discovered his offence was debt.

When plans were submitted for the Royal Hospital, Nell is said to have torn her handkerchief into four pieces and made a hollow square with them, thus inducing the King to double the area of the proposed building.

Alas, there is no proof of any of this. It was actually Sir Stephen Fox, paymaster-general of the forces, who originated the idea, to which Charles quickly assented, instructing Sir Christopher Wren to make the designs. Still, the tradition persists in defiance of documentary evidence, and it is not entirely fanciful to suppose that Nell Gwynn contributed in some way, if only by her enthusiasm. It is what we would expect of her, since she never forgot her origins. Besides, if history consisted only in those events and transactions which were recorded on paper, it would thereby be the more impoverished.

There is, anyway, no example of Nell's handwriting, for like most people of her background in the seventeenth century, she was illiterate. The letters that bear her name were written by others, and 'signed' by her with a very hesitant E.G. which looks as if the letters were formed after painstaking care. The loss to posterity is sad, for any written expression of Nell's lively conversation would have given us more insight to her character. That Nell was herself aware of this is hinted by her in a letter where she deplores the inability of her scribe to convey her meaning. 'I have a thousand merry conseets, but I cant make her write um', she said, 'and therefore you must take the will for the deed.' This is a letter to her friend Laurence Hyde, second son of the Earl of Clarendon. In another letter addressed to Madame Jennings 'over the Tub Tavern in Jermin Street', (possibly the mother of Sarah Jennings, who became the great Duchess of Marlborough), she indicates that she has ordered a ring for the Duke of Grafton, Barbara Castlemaine's son by the King, which alone implies an unexpected *bonhomie* existing between mistresses and their various offspring, and she further makes a reference to money that she owes Lady Williams. 'Pray tell my Ladie Williams that the King's mistresses are accounted ill paymasters, but shee shall have her Money the next Day after I have the stuffe.' The fact that Lady Williams was herself a mistress of the Duke of York makes this allusion doubly funny.

Nell probably attempted to write, but gave up as soon as she saw the awful result. At least this can be inferred from a message which she gave to Sir Robert Howard and which he included in a letter to the Duke of Ormonde. 'Mrs Nelly presents you with her real acknowledgements for all your favours', wrote Howard, 'and protests she would write in her own hand but her wild characters she says would distract you [*i.e.* confuse you or drive you mad].'

Even after she had abandoned the profession of acting, Nell Gwynn continued to support and encourage her colleagues in the theatre. There is every reason to suppose that she enjoyed being a member of the audience. In the last four months of 1674, for example, she saw *The Tempest* four times, *Macbeth* once, and *Hamlet* once, always taking a party of guests with her (and incidentally, billing the Exchequer for the tickets). It is recorded that she was present at a performance of *King Lear* in 1675.

Nell may have taken advantage of her position to get a few seats at the theatre free of charge, but her financial requirements were as nothing compared with the enormous fortunes filched by Barbara and Louise. Occasional extravagances were conspicuous by their rarity. She bought a magnificent bed, which cost £1135, and which was elaborately decorated with all manner of ornamental figures, including one of the rope-dancer Jacob Hall, Barbara Castlemaine's sometime lover. She wore dainty petticoats of white satin, which were much admired, and exquisite shoes. But jewellery did not attract her much, unless it was feminine and fairly modest. Being unaffected by nature, she did not like affectation in dress but preferred comfortable clothes.

Evidence shows that Nell regularly received payments of £500 or £1000, which sums were to be regarded as her allowance. Extra was sometimes forthcoming to meet special needs, such as £4000 in 1674 and £2500 in the first four months of 1675, listed charmingly in the Treasury books as 'bounty'. But these sums were derisory when compared to the tidal waves of cash which flowed into the purse of Louise de Kéroualle. Burnet says that the King gave Nell Gwynn a total of £60,000; this may well be, and spread over seventeen years, it is modest enough.

Nell did not entirely escape the vice of the age – gambling. We have seen that she enjoyed giving parties of basset at her house in Pall Mall, often losing sums of money which she could ill afford. £5000 was lost on one evening, a sum which seems monstrously irresponsible, and somewhat colours Nell's character to her disfavour; it is not so easy to applaud her generosity to the poor when it is matched by self-indulgence. Still, Nell's gaming losses were insignificant in Restoration society; she was certainly not avaricious, and her cost to the nation was tiny against the other 'chargeable ladies about the Court'. It is ironic that she, who cost the least, should have given the King the most affection.

It was an affection which survived some tests. More than once the King had occasion to warn Nelly not to confide her trust in all and sundry, as she was liable to do, being friendly towards some whose loyalty to the Monarch was at times questionable. She was not so naive as to be unaware that flatterers would pursue her in the hope that she might use her influence with the King, but she stuck to her opinion of people whether or not they were regarded as unsuitable by the rest of the world. Hence her touching acknowledgement that she relied upon Charles to tell her who her friends really were. She was a staunch defender of the Duke of Buckingham, allowing him to lodge at her house when he was out of favour, and was on especially good terms with the errant Duke of Monmouth. Monmouth, charming and delightful but thoroughly erratic, was banished by the King, who continued to dote upon him in spite of his treachery, during the rumpus over the Popish Plot. Nell interceded on his behalf, pleading with Charles to relent and receive his son, telling him that Monmouth looked ill, pale and haggard, for want of the King's affection. But Charles would not be budged from his resolve.

Nell was as familiarly impertinent with Monmouth as she was with everyone else. His closeness to the throne, even his supposed legitimacy, did not overwhelm her with awe. She called him 'Prince Perkin' to his face, and when once he reproached her with being 'ill-bred', she retorted, 'Was Mrs Barlow better bred than I?'

Throughout Nell's career, we hear very little of her mother, 'old Madam Gwynn', beyond the fact that she was fat and drank an inordinate amount of brandy. We know she lived with her daughter at 79 Pall Mall, for there survives an apothecary's bill delivered to that address for 'plasters, glysters and cordials' prescribed to bolster the old lady's health. Her death in 1679 was inelegant in the extreme. Drunk beyond control, she fell into a ditch in Chelsea, or possibly into the Thames itself, and drowned. With the death of her younger son the following year, this was a time of bereavement and distress for Nell, whose own health was showing signs of weakening.

As her life became more tranquil, Nell may well have spent some period of time out of London, though it is impossible to say for how long in any one place. There are so many houses and places scattered about which claim association with Nell Gwynn, some of them happy to be haunted by her ghost, that she could not in all reason have spread herself abroad so widely. Littleberries at Mill Hill, King's Wick at Sunninghill in Berkshire, Leyton Parsonage in Essex, Philiberts at Bray, Bagnigge Wells, Newmarket, all persist in remembering Nell with affection. Some may have been hunting-lodges where the King and Nelly spent a night or two, as they were known to escape from 'business' in London and pass the time together in jovial companionship. At Sunninghill, there was a double row of lime trees known as 'Nell Gwynn's Avenue', while in Fulham stood a Mulberry tree which was supposed to have been planted by Nell; it was chopped down when Fulham Town Hall was built in 1888, and its branches used as walking-sticks.

Some houses have a more substantial claim to Nell Gwynn. One which was thought to be haunted by her was near Hampton Court, and was later called St Albans (the present Duke of St Albans made an unsuccessful attempt to purchase it a few years ago). Lauderdale House at the top of Highgate Hill, now absorbed into London, was Nell's residence for an unspecified period, and Sandford Manor House in Fulham, now much altered, has always been thought to have sheltered her at regular intervals when she sought to recuperate from the merry life at Pall Mall. It is near the World's End in King's Road, and there is still a pub nearby called the *Nell Gwynn*.

Bestwood Park, in Sherwood Forest, was granted leasehold to Nell in 1681, together with as much acreage of the forest as she could ride round before breakfast. It was the seat of her descendants for many years, though by all accounts it was a monstrosity, and those still alive who remember weekend parties there shudder at the thought. Of all these, the one house in which Nell most certainly lived was in Windsor, assigned to her by the King in 1681, and called Burford House after the title of her son (he was not Duke of St Albans until 1684, this being the last dukedom which Charles created). It was built of red brick, comfortable, and charming, and for the last five years of his life, from 1680 to 1685, the King used frequently to visit Nell there when the court was at Windsor. It was eventually sold to the Royal Family, changed its name for a while, and once more reverted to the name of Burford House, which it retains to this day.

*   *   *

Nell was not present when the King died in 1685. The first she knew of the event was when she heard the sombre tolling of bells all over London. Was she informed that Charles had remembered her with his dying words? Probably yes, for the new King, James II, honoured his brother's request and did not let Nelly starve.

Without the King's support, Nell would have been in dire trouble. Shortly after the death of Charles II, she was outlawed for the non-payment of debts, and would have most likely found herself in prison were it not for James's timely rescue. He arranged for £729 to be paid over to one Richard Graham Esq., in settlement of her debts to tradesmen and creditors, who appeared to have pounced ruthlessly upon her as soon as they thought she might be out in the cold. She also received two gifts of £500 from James II to help restore her financial stability. Stil she found it difficult to survive, so James redeemed the mortgage on Bestwood Park, amounting to over £3000, conveyed the freehold to her and her descendants, and gave her an allowance of £1500 a year. By the autumn of 1687, she was obliged nevertheless to deposit silver at the bank as security for an overdraft, and to sell much of her plate and jewellery, including a pearl necklace with a ruby clasp which she had bought from Peg Hughes, the mistress of Prince Rupert.

Nell Gwynn's descendants have had cause to regret that she was not more acquisitive by nature, for while Barbara's present representative, the Duke of Grafton, lives at Euston Hall, Louise's descendant the Duke of Richmond lives at Goodwood, and Lucy Walter's heirs have, by virtue of a succession of clever marriages, accumulated land approaching a quarter of a million acres in extent with four magnificent houses, the Dukes of St Albans have been forced to sell everything, little by little, until the present Duke had finally to sell the lease on a corner terraced house in Chelsea in 1979. He can perhaps console himself with the certain knowledge that Nell Gwynn was by far the nicest and kindest of King Charles's ladies.

It is not mere hindsight and romance which permits such a rosy view of Charles's most popular mistress, but a justifiable assessment which was held as much by contemporaries as by subsequent idolators. She had the gift of natural ease and genuinely demonstrative affection which normally preclude the kind of selfishness one expects from a royal mistress. Though they were by no means identical in character, they were all three 'normal' in so far as they saw the potential advantage of their position, and pursued it. Lucy did not succeed, Barbara and Louise did. But Nell Gwynn was of different mettle, and she it is who must be thought abnormal, given the opportunities she had to create trouble, and the sorry conditions of life from which she had sprung, never to make a nuisance of herself, never to give Charles a hard time, never to embrace hypocrisy or to feign neglect. She did not seek advancement for herself beyond a gracious acceptance of the favours granted, and though there was a rumour that the King had intended to make her Countess of Greenwich, the fact that she remained Nelly until the

day she died did not, in her sane view of the world, give cause for
complaint. She is more likely to have been amused by the accident
of fate which made an illiterate orange girl the mother of the Duke of
St Albans. She was the only one of Charles's mistresses to be rescued
by a sense of humour, which accounts for her enduring place in the
heart of Londoners.

Colly Cibber accurately summarised the worth of Nell Gwynn in
a few sentences :

> Yet if the common fame of her may be believed, which in my
> memory was not doubted, she had less to be laid to her charge than
> any other of those Ladies, who were in the same state of preferment;
> she never meddled in matters of serious moment, or was the tool
> of working politicians : Never broke into those amorous infidelities
> which others in that grave author [Burnet] are accus'd of; but was as
> visibly distinguish'd by her particular personal inclination to the
> King, as her rivals were by their titles and grandeur.

In other words, she loved Charles, and wanted only that he should
love her, less passionately that he did Lucy, less lasciviously than he did
Barbara, with less infatuation than he showed for Louise, but withal a
more tender attachment than for any of them. He knew she would not
be hysterical, and would not use him. He was indeed as fortunate in
the relationship as was she.

The contemporary playwright Aphra Behn dedicated *The Feigned
Courtezans* to Nell Gwynn, with a fulsome tribute which in the manner
of such eulogies, is perhaps exaggerated, but nonetheless rings true.

> Besides all the charms, and attractions, and powers of your sex [she
> wrote], you have beauties peculiar to yourself – an eternal sweetness,
> youth, and air which never dwelt in any face but yours. You never
> appear but you gladden the hearts of all that have the happy fortune
> to see you, as if you were made on purpose to put the whole world
> into good humour.

*   *   *

Nell Gwynn survived the King by two years, but they were years of
such emptiness and discomfort that she might almost be said to have
died with him. The struggle to pay her way was one problem; the

way in which friends tended to dissolve into the fog was another. Worst of all were the pressures brought upon her to convert from her Protestantism, and her very precarious health.

One of Nell's most rigid characteristics was her firm adherence to the Protestant faith. When she became dependent upon the allowance from James II, the new King tried to wean her away from her chosen creed, pointing out that Charles had finally embraced Catholicism on his death-bed, and that if she expected her son the Duke to be cared for, then she must get rid of the French Protestant tutor she employed, and replace him with a Papist; the French tutor, who had been with Nell's son for some time, was declared a heretic and undesirable. Nell was caused much anguish by this constant advocacy against her wishes; the pressures brought upon her to persuade her son to convert, and the effect of such accumulation of anxiety was to impair her health. Throughout 1687 she was in pain, bedridden and virtually paralysed. 'All agree that it was an inexpressible grief to her that first brought her distemper upon her, and continued upon her heart till her death, that a Papist . . . was made tutor to her son and [the French tutor] displaced.' At any event, the Duke of St Albans remained a Protestant, and was to be one of the first to join William of Orange against the Stuarts.

Another possible explanation for Nell's weakening condition, which has been advanced by other writers without much evidence, is that she had contracted venereal disease transmitted by Charles II. One of the symptoms was severe paralysis down one side. On March 29, Sir Charles Lyttleton wrote, 'Mrs Nelly has been dying of an apoplexy. She is now come to her sense on one side, for the other is dead of a palsey.'

She had to endure eight months of agony before she finally succumbed, in November 1687, at her friend Hannah Grace's house next door to 79 Pall Mall, whither she had moved to receive better care. The previous month she had made a lengthy codicil to her will, obviously with the knowledge that she was about to die. The will itself had not been made until July of that year. In the codicil she requested that her son the Duke of St Albans should see to it that she was buried in the church of St Martin-in-the-Fields, in a plain black coffin, and that the good Dr Tenison, who had visited her frequently in the last months, should preach her funeral sermon. Both wishes were granted, and indeed Nell Gwynn now lies at St Martin's, a stone's throw from the Covent Garden which she had so loved. Tenison, who was later to be the celebrated Archbishop Tenison, did preach her sermon, and suffered some not inconsiderable obliquy for having dignified in such manner the death of a mere whore. But Tenison was a wise man, who appreciated the durability and essential chastity of Nell's qualities. The sermon, alas, has not survived, but we know it was based on the text of St Luke, 'Joy shall be in Heaven over one sinner that repenteth, more than over ninety and nine just persons, which need no repentance', and we are told that Tenison said much to Nelly's praise, and that the church was understandably packed. The date was 17 November.

The costs of the funeral and interment, which amounted to £375, were deducted from the annual allowance of £1500 which James II had settled upon Nell. Her son inherited the bulk of her estate, but since this included some massive bills, he could not entirely be termed a 'beneficiary'. Other small bequests, added in the codicil, tell us more of Nell than could a score of erudite commentators. She wanted a decent pulpit-cloth and cushion to be bought and donated to St Martin-in-the-Fields, out of her money. Her son should provide £100 to rescue the poor from penury, to buy winter clothes for those who had none, and to pay for the release of poor debtors. £400 was left to her sister Rose, who had loyally remained by her side during the last painful months, £10 to her porter, and £10 to her nurses. Most significant of all, in view of her loyalty to the Protestant cause in the face of cruel pressures, she included this bequest :

> That for showing my charity to those who differ from me in religion, I desire that £50 may be put into the hands of Dr Tenison and Mr Warner, who taking to them any two persons of the Roman religion, may dispose of it for the use of the poor of that religion inhabiting the parish of St. James's aforesaid.

Total absence of bigotry should cause no surprise to anyone who can feel, understand, and receive the personality of Nell Gwynn transmitted across the centuries. It was not in her to bear grudges, to harbour resentments, or to sulk. If people did not agree with her, she would not push her point of view. If they spoke against her, she would not curse them, but turn her wit upon them and enjoy the game. She was one of those sunny creatures who see good in everything and give their backs to the bad. She thoroughly enjoyed riding around in her own carriage, with her own coachman and servants, but never would she flaunt these advantages or attach more importance to them than they deserved.

Writers who have suggested that the Cockney folk from whose side she sprung despised her for abandoning her class neither understand that fundamental character of the Londoner, nor the sweet mind of Nell Gwynn, uncluttered as it was by any prejudice. On the contrary, Londoners applauded her, wanted her to enjoy herself, and enjoyed seeing her enjoyment. They relished the extraordinary position attained by one of their number, and they loved King Charles all the more when he demonstrated that he valued Nell as much as they did with his dying words, 'Let not poor Nelly starve.'

*　　　　*　　　　*

SOURCES FOR CHAPTER THREE

Donald ADAMSON and Peter Beauclerk DEWAR, *The House of Nell Gwynn* (1903)
Augustan Satirical Verse 1660–1714 (Yale University Press)
Clifford BAX, *Pretty Witty Nell*
Bryan BEVAN, *Nell Gwynn* (1969)
Gilbert BURNET, *A History of My Own Time* (1724–34)
Colley CIBBER, *Apology for the Life of Colley Cibber* (1774)
Peter CUNNINGHAM, *The Story of Nell Gwynn* (1903)
A. I. DASENT, *Nell Gwynne 1650–1687* (1924)
A. I. DASENT, *The Private Life of Charles II* (1937)
John EVELYN, *Diary*
H. FORNERON, *Louise de Kéroualle, Duchess of Portsmouth* (1887)
Jane HOARE, 'The Death of Nell Gwynn', in *History Today*, June 1977
Samuel PEPYS, *Diary*
Earl of ROCHESTER, *Collected Works*, ed. Hayward
Madame de SEVIGNE, *Letters*
H. Noel WILLIAMS, *Rival Sultanas* (1915)
State Trials, Vol. XIV

CHAPTER FOUR

Louise de Kéroualle

As Nell Gwynn was recovering from the birth of her first son, Charles II was making his way to Dover. He was to negotiate a secret treaty French side was his beloved sister Henrietta, Duchesse d'Orléans, and though he suspected nothing, he was also to make one of the most significant amorous encounters of his life. The chief negotiator on the French side was his beloved sister Henrietta, Duchesse d'Orléans, and one of her newly favoured Maids of Honour was a dark-eyed, baby-faced aristocratic beauty of twenty-one years, Louise de Kéroualle.

It may at first seem strange that the famous Treaty of Dover was fashioned not through normal diplomatic channels but in a personal tête-à-tête between brother and sister, but it was an astute move on the part of Louis XIV to use his sister in-law as intermediary and, as it turned out, even more astute to allow Louise de Kéroualle to accompany her. Since the sojourn in Dover was to have profound consequences on Charles's personal life, and since the love-match which was a side-effect of the negotiations was to carry serious political overtones, it is fitting that we should examine briefly the policies and intentions which locked France and England in a most delicate alliance.

The dazzling Louis XIV, an absolute monarch who presided over a nation which already led the world in fashion and culture, needed to expand territorially in order to consolidate his power. Part of his plan would necessitate a war with the Dutch, a maritime nation sympathetic to England for religious as well as commercial reasons, being overwhelmingly Protestant and having a geographical proximity to England which involved the two countries in cooperative trade. It was essential, therefore, that England's complicity in France's designs be won, a task which would not be easy as far as the English people were concerned, hating and distrusting the French as they did, and detesting the whole notion of absolute monarchy supported by the power of the Roman Catholic church. The English were passionately Protestant, and would look askance at any alliance with Popery.

The King of England, however, was much more malleable and could be persuaded, so Louise thought, to follow a pragmatic foreign policy. Charles was secretly inclined towards Roman Catholicism, and was already tied to France by strong family connections and a personal preference for things French; much of his exile had been spent in France and he had returned to England with an enhanced appreciation of French culture. For his part, Charles needed money, as Parliament was constantly reluctant to provide sufficient funds and the King was permanently hard up. With Louis XIV able to offer attractive financial inducements almost without limit, it was easy to perceive the advantages of an alliance in which Charles would sell his friendship for gold. But it would have to be secret. The people, emotionally prejudiced, would never understand, and Parliament contained few people clever enough to see that Charles's apparently despicable cynicism concealed a political sophistication which gave him a far more subtle intelligence of foreign policy than any of his ministers.

Charles had to proceed in a surreptitious manner because nobody would appreciate his reasons were he to declare them. Besides, he knew better than anyone that diplomacy could not be a shared art and that he must keep his own counsel. In spite of appearances, Charles gained as much as he gave by the Treaty of Dover.

It was a masterful idea of the French king to entrust these confidential negotiations to Henrietta, for she brought not only skill to the undertaking, but a deeply committed desire to see the two countries united in their aims, to see her dear brother embrace the true faith (she was a devout Catholic herself), and to make herself useful. Trapped in a disastrous marriage with Louis XIV's brother, Henrietta was a bright intelligent woman whose gifts were wasted and whose pride suffered daily humiliation at the hands of her disgusting husband. The Duc d'Orléans, more usually known simply as 'Monsieur', was homosexual, bisexual, transvestite, effeminate, spiteful, everything in turns and sometimes all at once. He fathered several children, but fawned upon the foppish Chevalier de Lorraine, whom the King had eventually to have arrested despite the tearful entreaties of his brother, clawing at the King's legs and begging him not to be unkind. He smothered himself in perfumes, wore such high heels that he appeared to be on stilts, dressed like a buffoon, but did not have the saving compensation of being harmless; he was treacherous and nasty. Poor Henrietta suffered agonies from which her main release (though not her only, for she too had affectionate female friends) took the form of letters to her brother Charles in England. Now she was to be given the chance of seeing him, after so many years, and she was beside herself with excitement.

Charles's relationship with his younger sister, whom he called 'Minette', was extraordinarily close, in spite of distance and years of separation. They exchanged tender letters, in which Charles almost invariably declared his fondness. 'You show me so much affection that the only quarrel we are ever likely to have will be as to which of us two loves the other best', he wrote, adding 'In that respect I will never yield to you.' Here is another typical sentence from their correspondence, 'I am sure I would venture all I have in the world to serve you, for I have nothing so near my heart . . . as that tender passion I have for my dearest Minette.' Such outpourings of obviously genuine emotion are almost unique in the correspondence of King Charles; his other affections were becoming soured by cynicism and disillusionment, while his feelings for Minette remained as real and warm as ever. There is a sense in which no woman, not Queen Catherine, nor Lucy Walter, nor the angry Barbara or the funny Nell, was able to touch the springs of Charles's love as did his own sister. To such an extent was this clear that rumours hinted at an incestuous relationship. Nevertheless, the French diplomats were aware of the depth of this attachment, and saw how usefully it could be exploited for political ends. The French ambassador, Colbert de Croissy, reported as much in a letter to Louis. 'The King often says that the only woman who has really a hold on him is his sister', he wrote, trying to discourage Louis from lavishing too generous gifts upon the various mistresses through whom he sought to influence the King of England. And when Charles told Colbert that he passionately longed to see his sister again, the ambassador immediately wrote to counsel quick action. 'I was greatly surprised at the intimation', he said, 'and I lose no time in sending you to say that this is a case, if ever there was one, in which the iron should be hammered while it is hot.'

So it was decided to send Henrietta to Dover, though not as far as London, in the hope that affectionate persuasion would have more chance of success than any amount of diplomatic fencing, and that her wish to see her own country revert to the true faith would so move Charles that his wily political sense might be smothered.

Minette set out with a huge cavalcade. The entourage consisted of 237 persons in a long chain of coaches. To obey the demands of etiquette, Monsieur accompanied his wife as far as Calais, teasing and taunting her all the way, and telling her that he had consulted a fortune-teller who had predicted his imminent bereavement. To look at his wife, he said, he could well believe the prediction might be realised. Minette was in a very poor state of health, coughing and spluttering all the while, and lay on the floor of her coach for hours every day as it bumped and lurched over the primitive roads. Every town brought out flags and arranged entertainment in honour of the travellers, but Minette was more concerned to avoid her husband's appalling company and to get some sleep. In this she was encouraged and supported by the favourite of her four Maids of Honour, Louise de Kéroualle. Louise felt admiration and affection for Henrietta, who had given her this official position at Court and rescued her from a dreary life in the country, and who also, she could plainly see, was a woman whose spirit was breaking under the strain of her artificial life. Henrietta clearly longed for some respite, and Louise, at her side, was hoping that the trip to England would help repair the Duchess's health.

The first signs that she was right were not long in coming. Word arrived that King Charles would be there to greet them in Dover (having bid a fond *adieu* to Nelly and her two-week-old babe), and Minette's vitality blossomed in anticipation. On 24 May, the whole collection embarked at Dunkirk and set sail the following morning. Henrietta and Louise were so excited they barely slept. It was a rough journey, but they were on deck despite wind and water to wait for a sighting of the King. And they were rewarded. Charles came out in a small craft to meet them, Henrietta recognised him, let out a shriek of joy, and pointed him out to Louise. Charles boarded the ship and rushed to clasp his dear sister in a close embrace. Then he saw Louise de Kéroualle.

The Maid of Honour was present at all the private negotiations between Charles and Henrietta which lasted the whole of the first week at Dover Castle, giving the King ample opportunity to observe her and to get to know her. He liked her *soigné* manner, her aristocratic reticence and refinement. Louise was refreshingly proper after the vulgar rantings of Barbara Castlemaine and the lewd banter of Nell Gwynn. Having alarmed his ministers by his taste for the low life, Charles was now aroused by a lady of some decided quality.

We do not know what conversation passed between them, but we may be sure that Charles saw as much of Louise in moments of relaxation as he did during the periods of work. There were such celebrations, frivolous distractions, amusements and fun at Dover, that the Dutch ambassador, who was naturally keeping a wary eye on developments, felt able to reassure his Government that no one could think of raising serious problems in such a flighty, flippant atmosphere. Louis XIV wrote to say that his brother had given permission for Henrietta and her retinue to stay in Dover another ten days. Everyone was overjoyed. Louis XIV told his ambassador, 'You can exaggerate to King Charles the efforts we make and points we stretch to be agreeable to him. Let him feel how much obliged he should be to us, so that when we make demands, he shall be in a humour to yield.'

The Dutch ambassador was wrong. The Treaty of Dover, signed on 1 June 1670, was a document which was to have severe consequences for the Dutch. There were in fact two treaties, one a sham affair for the consumption of Parliament and containing little more that the provision to fight another war with the Dutch in support of the French, the other a secret and dangerous agreement between the two kings, who thereby established their 'perpetual' alliance. In this undeclared treaty, Charles proclaimed his conviction of the truth of the Roman Catholic faith, and promised that he would announce his conversion when the affairs of his kingdom permitted. In other words, Charles left himself completely free to judge when the moment would be right to make this explosive declaration, without committing himself to any time limit. The rest of his reign was to pass by with no such declaration being made, indeed with all the outward display of support for the Anglican church. In return for this 'promise', Louis was to give Charles £166,000 and lend 6000 French troops if and when they were needed. (In the years to follow, Charles was to receive far more than this initial payment; something approching a further £800,000 was to come from the French coffers.) It is important to remember that Louise de Kéroualle, the demure Maid of Honour, was a party to all the stages of this confidential negotiation and knew the provisions of the Treaty rather better than did most of King Charles's ministers.

The formalities over, Henrietta and her suite were free to enjoy themselves for the remainder of their stay in England. Charles took his sister to Canterbury to see a performance specially mounted by the Duke of York's company, and Louise naturally accompanied them and joined in the festivities afterwards. It was noticed that Charles's attentions grew more and more ardent every day.

On the eve of departure for France, Minette sent Louise to fetch her jewel-casket, and opening it in front of Charles, she asked him to choose whatever he wanted as a gift from her. With the art of a practised seducer, the King took Louise's hand in his and said, 'This is the only jewel I want to keep beside me.'

But it was not to be. Charles did everything he could to persuade his sister to leave Louise behind, to no avail; Henrietta had promised the girl's parents that she would bring her safely home, and if she were to abandon her now, it would be quite clear that her fate was being cynically managed for the King's delectation. There is no evidence to suggest that Louis XIV had yet thought of presenting the Maid of Honour to Charles as a camouflaged prostitute; he may not even have noticed her.

So Louise left with Minette. Charles and his sister embraced three times on the ship which was to take her home. The Maid of Honour kept her place in the background.

The event which did finally send Louise de Kéroualle into the Court of Charles II was tragic. Minette returned to France in glory; not only was she popular at Versailles, cherished and admired (and pitied) by all, but now also was she an unofficial stateswoman with a great diplomatic achievement to her credit. Two weeks later she drank a glass of chicory water and collapsed in a state of appalling agony. Her suffering was acute but brief. On the night of 30 June 1670, she died, in the presence of Louis XIV and assembled courtiers. Her last words, addressed to the English ambassador, Ralph Montagu, were intended for her brother Charles. 'I have always loved him better than life itself', she whispered, 'and now my only regret in dying is to be leaving him.'

Versailles was thrown into turmoil by the news. To die at twenty-six was pathetic enough, but to die at that moment, and with such abruptness, was not only a grievous personal loss but potentially a political embarrassment. The suddenness of the event gave rise to evil rumours of poison, as they often did in the seventeenth century, and the finger was pointed at the vengeful Chevalier de Lorraine, her husband's companion. Since other people had drunk the same chicory water, the suspicions were hysterical rather than rational, and the probable cause of death was peritonitis. Still, enough of a fuss was created to alarm King Charles, who was pitifully heart-broken, and to make the French worried lest the Treaty of Dover might be jeopardised. Colbert de Croissy wrote, 'It is to be feared that the grief of the King of England, which is deeper than can be imagined, and the malevolent talk and rumours of our enemies, will spoil everything.'

Bossuet, who had known and liked Henrietta, was moved to deliver one of the greatest of all funeral orations, a piece of living prose which captured the grief and shock of the occasion and is justly celebrated in the annals of French literature. Bossuet was present at the death-bed, and his personal emotion breaks into the formal Ciceronian statement :

O nuit désastreuse ! O nuit effroyable où retentit tout à coup comme un éclat de tonnerre cette étonnante nouvelle : Madame se meurt ! Madame est morte ! Qui de nous ne se sentit frappé à ce coup, comme si quelque tragique accident avait désolé sa famille ? . . . partout on entend des cris; partout on voit la douleur et le désespoir, et l'image de la mort. Le roi, la reine, Monsieur, toute la cour, tout le peuple, tout est abattu, tout est désésperé . . . le roi même tenait Madame serrée par de si étroits embrassements. . . .*

According to Voltaire, at the words, 'Madame se meurt, Madame est morte' Bossuet's voice trembled and the entire congregation burst into sobs. By contrast, the lamentable bereaved husband made all his children wear long black petticoats, converting the sadness into a pantomime. Charles II ever after nursed a steadfast loathing for the man.

To save the situation, the French were anxious to find ways of consoling King Charles. They could not have expected that it would be so easy, or that the solution would eventually turn to their advantage. The French ambassador had noticed the interest Charles had shown in his sister's Maid of Honour, and when the King arranged for her to be offered a place as Maid of Honour to the patient Queen Catherine, intimating his strong desire that she be sent back to England to assume her place at once, the Frenchman was quick to urge compliance. As for Louise, she had nothing much to do with herself now that Madame was dead, and had even thought of entering a convent, so that she would doubtless have been more than happy to oblige whether or not she was ordered to. From the French point of view it was the neatest possible situation, for had not Louise been privy to the recent negotiations, and could she not be relied upon to keep a closer watch over Charles's intentions than any number of ambassadors?

The Duke of Buckingham was sent to France to attend the funeral of Henrietta, and at the same time formally to offer Louise a place at

---

* A disastrous night! A terrifying night in which, like a clap of thunder, reverberated the astonishing news: Madame is dying! Madame is dead! Which of us did not feel stricken by the blow, as if some tragic accident had annihilated his family? . . . everywhere were cries of anguish, everywhere one saw grief, despair, the face of death. The king, the queen, Monsieur, the entire Court, the entire people, all are desolate and laid low . . . the king himself clasped Madame tightly to his bosom . . .

E

Court. He, too, was anxious to find a new mistress for the King, in order to supplant the tedious supremacy of his cousin Barbara Castle-maine, with whom he had quarrelled. (As for Nell Gwynn, she would not take anything seriously.) The Kéroualle girl would be much more suitable in every way. (Buckingham did not know the terms of the secret treaty.) When he saw Louise, Buckingham was reckless enough to strengthen his advocacy with some ill-advised remarks about Queen Catherine which Charles had certainly not authorised him to make. The Queen's marriage was doomed, he said, and Charles would soon have to think of taking a new wife. Thus was the idea of being Queen of England first gently planted in the mind of modest Louise. Thence-forth, ambition turned her nature.

Alas, Buckingham made an enemy of Louise even as he was making her his friend. He arranged that she should travel with part of his retinue to Dieppe, and that she should wait for him there. Then he promptly forgot her, and left her idling away for ten days while the ship he was to send failed to appear. She never forgave the insult. Montagu sent her some money and an escort, while Charles despatched a ship to meet her. On board she made the acquaintance of the Comte de Grammont, who was better placed than almost anyone to tell her what she might expect at the Court of Charles II, as his delightful memoirs testify. On arrival in London, Louise went to stay with Lord Arlington, the very same Henry Bennet who had been Barbara Castle-maine's intimate and whose daughter was to marry her son by the King, the Duke of Grafton. In such a way do the threads of Charles's amorous life cross, connect, and knot.

*　　　　　*　　　　　*

For the first few weeks after the arrival of Louise in London, the King was overcome with tears each time he saw her. Her presence reminded him of his beloved Minette, in whose company he constantly imagined her, so that his intended seduction of the French girl was forever being deflected by sentiment and weeping. This suited Louise perfectly, for she was in no hurry to be bedded, and she soon learnt that a show of tears cooled Charles's libido more quickly than anything. It would serve her frequently in the future.

If one characteristic could be said to dominate Louise, it was pride. She was from an extremely ancient and venerable Breton family, which even as long ago as the fourteenth century had been considered one of the oldest in the land. The original family name was Penhoët, but in 1330 François de Penhoët had married Jeanne de Penancoët, dame de Kéroualle, and the children of this union had assumed their mother's name and arms. Hence Louise's father was Comte Guillame Penancoët de Kéroualle, a stiff, formal and unimaginative nobleman, living quietly in his château near Brest with wife and three children – Louise, Henriette and Sebastien. The Count was a soldier by profession, but had not made any impact on national affairs. It was true to say that the pious Kéroualles had little more than their splendid lineage to be proud of. They were virtually unknown. Family pride was their protection from neglect, and Louise inherited the propensity to boast to a degree which, though understandable, was to bring her many enemies. In England she would always be regarded as a snob.

Louise was educated in a strict convent, where discipline and piety were all, amusement and extravagance nothing. Her mother, *née* Marie-Anne de Ploëuc, was the severest religious influence; she made sure that Louise was brought up a devout Catholic, by conviction rather than mere habit. (She, by the way, was distantly related to the French royal family.) Many English noblemen came to Brest during the years of Charles II's exile, and were entertained by the Count.

A particular English influence occurred when Sir Richard Browne, a distinguished royalist statesman who was the King's resident at the Court of France for nineteen years, was called upon to spend much time in Brest, in 1652–54, and became very friendly with the Kéroualle family. Both then and in later years, as Louise was growing up, Browne would have had the opportunity to tell the little girl about the fate of Charles I, and the character of his son Charles II. In 1670 he lived in retirement at Charlton in Kent, and Louise remembered him with affection. He was, incidentally, John Evelyn's father-in-law.

Piety, isolation and dullness were the essential ingredients of Louise's early life. There was another which was to mark her forever, and have a profound influence on the development of her adult character – poverty; a poverty which, according to the paradoxes of human nature, did not temper her pride but rather reinforced it. The Comte de Kéroualle might have been a nobleman second to none, but he was barely able to provide his daughter with the clothes she needed to hold her own at the Court of Henrietta d'Orléans when she took up her position there in 1668. The four main mistresses of Charles II were all of impoverished origins; Lucy Walter did not live to enjoy the bounty of the Restoration years; Nell Gwynn had a hearty disregard for wealth, and if she had some pretty things, she did not care to pile up riches; Barbara Palmer was simply greedy. Louise was to accumulate more even than Barbara, but whereas the latter's motive force was avidity, Louise was acquisitive not merely because she desired riches, but because she considered them her right; it is a subtle distinction which is essential to an understanding of her personality.

When Louise left with Minette for Dover in 1670, she had no suitable clothes to wear, and was obliged to accept Minette's offer to pay for new garments. Another young lady might have accepted the situation in a carefree manner, thinking it not untoward that she should be provided with things necessary to her position by her employer. Not so Louise. She smarted with undisclosed indignation and determined that, if she could, she would one day live in the style to which her name entitled her.

Louise came to England equipped with not only pride in family, but pride in her virtue as well, which again distinguished her from her three main predecessors in Charles's bed. The Duke of Buckingham may have intended that she should be snatched from France to be the King's mistress, but she had a different view of herself, and was not ready to be so easily seduced. She already had a reputation to live down, gossips having suggested that she was pitchforked into Versailles in order to be Louis XIV's mistress, like her contemporary Louise de la Vallière, and that she had consorted with the debauched young Comte de Sault. Both accusations lacked foundation. Louise was like a daisy among weeds at the French Court, clinging to her innocence while all around her were hurling themselves at each other. Though it is impossible to know, it is more than likely Louise was a virgin when she came to London. If so, that too made her quite unlike Lucy, Barbara and Nell.

In 1669, Louise's brother Sebastien de Kéroualle died from wounds received in battle. At almost the same time, she lost her powerful protector, the Duc de Beaufort, who had secured for her the position as Maid of Honour to Henrietta. Now Henrietta herself had died. From every point of view Louise came to London a vulnerable, lonely young woman, besieged by misfortune on all sides, but with a resilience of character which was beginning to help her cope with the difficulties which beset her. She was calm and sensible, strong-willed, shrewd, calculating, exquisitely feminine, well-mannered, quiet. She did not confide or declare herself, but kept her intentions closely guarded.

She was, in other words, supremely fitted to be a spy as well as a mistress. It is a pity that those who engineered her introduction to the Court of Charles II did not foresee this potential.

Louise's one overwhelming advantage was her beauty. It is becoming repetitive to record *sans cesse* the attractiveness of the women in King Charles's life (and the most beautiful of all is yet to appear), but his good taste must answer for that, and our responsibility must be to reflect the opinion of contemporaries. In the case of Louise de Kéroualle, she had dark melancholy eyes, with the slight caste which prompted Nell Gwynn to call her 'Squintabella', exquisitely fair skin, and dark hair hanging in ringlets to her shoulders. Her demeanour was that of a pubescent girl, a quality which she soon realised gave her beauty a special flavour, and which she cultivated with pouts and a propensity to tears. John Evelyn did not much like her 'childish simple baby face', but his view was not widely shared. Another contemporary called her, with undisguised enthusiasm, 'wondrous handsome'. To accentuate her child-like appeal, she spoke with a soft, tender voice and evolved a manner which was languid and suggestive of frailty. These were tricks she had learnt in Paris, for there was about her whole bearing an affectation and artificiality which had been much in vogue in certain circles in France during the 1660s. The essence of femininity was studied by this côterie, and their behaviour was manufactured to conform with the idea. Sighs, reticence, a languishing look, a delicate response, a fastidious avoidance of rude words, these were all part of the contrived woman whose most exaggerated silly representatives Molière had mocked in *Les Précieuses Ridicules* only a few years before. Indeed, now in the twentieth century 'precious' has come to be a fairly adequate translation of the seventeenth-century *précieuse*, and 'precious' certainly describes Louise de Kéroualle.

Like the *précieuses* she was also romantic and idealistic, not in reflection of deeply held values or of a basic natural predilection, but in conformity with the studied and wholly artificial view of how a woman should think and behave, and how she should be treated by a gallant, honey-voiced man. Flattery was essential to this ideal, and earthy honest lust forbidden. No wonder the English found that Louise and her pretensions grated on their nerves, and no wonder that Nell Gwynn teased her mercilessly. Her chastity, her finely distinguished and much rehearsed manners were a bore.

Also like the *précieuses*, Louise appreciated beautiful objects, gorgeous furnishings, exquisite dresses, painting and poetry, but without any depth of understanding. She was superficially attracted by the obvious, lacking the imagination to see the value of a more discreet appeal, or to enjoy the interchange of ideas. When, years later, some-body wrote that she was 'extremely polite and interesting in her conver-sation', that was because what she had to say was predictably innocuous, not because it really created any 'interest'.

Still, she was protected by naivety and was quite unaware that she could be a figure of fun. French manners were correct, and the English were barbarians; if they chose not to appreciate her *finesse*, then it was their loss. At least she was discreet and circumspect, knew how to protect her own interests and conceal the worst of her opportunism. If this portrait seems unkind, it must be remembered that she was still provincial and naturally succumbed to the tastes and fashions prevalent in the capital. Moreover, she was now virtually alone and would need to construct her own future. The English could laugh at her pretensions, but she would demonstrate that her methods yielded results and their smiles would finally freeze on their faces. She would be patient.

The question was, how patient would King Charles be? Louise arrived in London in August 1670, and took up her unexacting duties as Maid of Honour to the Queen. Before long, Charles had provided her with a suite of rooms in the Palace of Whitehall. Throughout the autumn, he showed her great attention and the eyes of the Court ob-served the growing ardour with which the King pursued his fresh prey and the persistent refusal of that prey to submit; they laid bets on how long the young Frenchwoman could hold out. The closest watch was naturally kept by the French ambassador, Colbert de Croissy. 'The King of England also takes great care to entertain this beauty in the Queen's room rather than any other woman,' he reported back to Paris, 'but he has not been to see her in her own room, as rumour keeps saying that he has.'

By the following year the King's visits were an established regular feature of his day, and he now did see her in her own apartments, at nine o'clock every morning, staying for up to two hours, and again in the evening after dinner, joining her at her gaming tables and seeing that she wanted for nothing. To be sure, they did not reminisce about Minette all the time, yet still Louise resisted the advances of her would-be lover. She flirted, teased, was agreeable but untouchable according to the precepts which she had learnt, and no doubt enjoyed the game she was playing, thinking to do it well. The danger was that Charles, who wanted nothing more than to get down to business, might be exasperated by all this coy prudishness and be tempted to abandon the pursuit.

Louise's motives for keeping herself just beyond reach were mixed. True, she was inexperienced and perhaps cherished her virtue from fear of offending the Almighty. But there was an element of shrewdness in her tactics. If she was going to be pushed into the King's bed, it would be on her terms. She was not going to settle for a lowly position as just another of the bodies used to satisfy the King's desires; he could look to his actress friends for that. Louise was determined to be no ordinary mistress : she would be the senior lady, the surrogate wife, or she would be nothing. Her aims were wilfully of the highest.

She began to accumulate interested acquaintances (they could hardly be called friends), who courted her favour in anticipation of her influence with the King. They in turn exerted pressure on her, openly advising her to give in to the King's desires. Coquetry, they all insisted, could not last forever. Colbert de Croissy reproached her on more than one occasion, and reminded her of her duty to France.

A year passed, and then in September 1671 it looked as if Louise might be pregnant. Colbert was shamefully jubilant. Louise was overcome with an attack of nausea when dining at the French Embassy one evening, and Colbert immediately wrote gleefully to Paris with the news. The Foreign Minister Louvois, wrote back :

> The King was greatly pleased to hear in what manner Mademoiselle Kéroualle suffered when dining the other day at the French Embassy. There was nothing in her conduct since she left France, to lead us to expect that such a piece of good fortune was going so soon to befall her. His Majesty is anxious to be informed of what may grow out of this situation, and of the terms on which she and the King have come to stand mutually.

In less diplomatic language, Louis XIV and his ministers were telling Louise to get on with it. In all this cynical correspondence, there is not a trace of concern for her well-being.

Alas, it was a false alarm; the swooning must have been occasioned by Embassy food, as Louise was not pregnant, nor could she have been. Consternation now erupted among her 'friends' and supporters, who turned on her in a united attempt to bully her into submission. Colbert remonstrated with her for her failure to heed his counsel. Lord Arlington, her closest acquaintance in London, told her to handle the

King carefully and to be sure that she so conducted herself as to make him want to banish all other ladies from his company and seek only to be with her. Arlington's wife, an unprincipled, unscrupulous Dutch-woman, went straight to the point. Either Louise went to bed with the King, she said, or she would have to look forward to spending the rest of her life in a convent; there was no other choice. Even Saint-Evre-mond, who since his exile from France had lived in England as a res-pected man of letters, and had been given by King Charles the unlikely sinecure of Governor to the Isle of Ducks in St James's Park, besought Louise to yield. He addressed her a letter full of circumspect language which purported to be philosophical while advising her to be a whore. Of course you must not be promiscuous, he said, but, dear me, how awful it would be to go through life without having known love :

> Do not repulse temptations too severely – perhaps you are vain enough to be pleased only with yourself, but you will soon get tired of pleasing and loving yourself; and whatever satisfaction you get from vanity, you will need another's love if your love is to be truly enjoyable. And so let yourself go into the delights of temptation instead of listening to your pride.

Saint-Evremond certainly understood the *précieuse* mentality. Maybe Lady Arlington had commissioned this letter, for Saint-Evremond also resorted to threats and painted for the recipient a very glum picture of life in a French convent.

Even after all this time, Charles was so taken by Louise that he once walked all the way from Whitehall to Hampton Court, in very cold weather, to accompany her coach. It was imperative that something should be done, and that a plot should be laid to trap the reluctant girl in a compromising situation. Lord and Lady Arlington and Colbert de Croissy put their heads together and evolved the following plan. In October the King would be at Newmarket for the races. The Arlingtons lived not far away at Euston, the magnificent mansion where there were more coaches in the stables than at any other nobleman's house in England. Colbert would be invited to spend a few weeks there, and would be asked to bring Louise with him as a fellow guest. The King would, in the most innocent fashion, come over from Newmarket and Louise would be enticed to spend intimate moments with him in romantic surroundings. Plenty of wine and a comfortable bed should do the trick.

Colbert, who was supposed to be chaperon, wrote telling Louis XIV of the plan and expressing confidence in the outcome. 'As the King's inclination for Mademoiselle Kéroualle, who is to go there with me, is rising, I foresee that he will often run across from Newmarket to see her.' The French King was greatly amused and sent a reply which suggested Charles was a fool to entrust his intended mistress to the care of someone like Colbert.

Colbert and Louise were not of course the only guests at Euston. There were 200 people, many of them party to the scheme. One who did not approve was, naturally, John Evelyn.

The King was two weeks at Newmarket, finding excuse to come to Euston with the Duke of York every other day, dine, and stay the night. Colbert eagerly observed the growing signs of passion :

The King comes here for his repasts; and after eating he passes several hours with Mlle Kéroualle. He has already paid her three visits, and he invited us yesterday to Newmarket to see the races. We went, and were charmingly entertained, and he seemed more than ever solicitous to please Mlle Kéroualle. Those small attentions which denote a great passion were lavished on her; and as she showed by her expressions of gratitude that she was not insensible to the kindness of a great king, we hope she will so behave that the attachment will be durable and exclude every other.

In a letter to France on 8 October, Colbert gave some inkling of the wise words he used in conference with Louise. 'The advice that should be strongly urged on the young lady', he wrote, 'should be that she should skilfully handle the regard the King has for her, not discuss business with him, not ridicule or show dislike for those who are near him, but to let him find his pleasure exclusively in her company.'

The final scene for the seduction was beautifully arranged. What fun it would be, thought Lady Arlington, to play at weddings! They would enact a country marriage ceremony, with all the traditional games, and Louise could be the bride. The bridegroom? Why not King Charles? So Louise, who was happy to be thought a consort instead of a prostitute, relaxed and relented at last, abandoning herself to the frolic of the evening. She was laid out in bed with all the pomp that attends the real thing, her garters loosened, her friends assembled around the bed laughing and joking, while Charles slipped in beside her. Then mysteriously, they all disappeared, and Louise found herself the object of irresistible embraces.

Exactly nine months later, the future Duke of Richmond was born, which gives Euston Hall a double significance in the amorous history of Charles II : one of his natural sons lived there (the Duke of Grafton), while another was conceived there.

John Evelyn was outraged by the 'fondness and toying with that young wanton' who, he said, was without clothes almost all day. Colbert, on the other hand, was triumphant, and told Louise that King Louis would be very pleased with her, and even more pleased if she kept up the good work. 'Many details lead me to believe that she will do so for a long time to the exclusion of everyone else', he wrote.

As for Louise herself, she is supposed to have defended her honour in broken English (she never learnt the language properly, implying with typical French arrogance that she did not need to); 'Me no bad woman' are the words assigned to her by this story, 'if me taut me was one bad woman, me would cut my own trote'; it is unkind to think that Louise, even in broken English, would sound quite so ridiculous.

Louis XIV was so delighted that he sent Lady Arlington a valuable diamond necklace as a reward for her efforts. King Charles, one may presume, was satisfied.

The rest of the world found the whole affair intensely amusing, taking immediate opportunity to begin the assault upon Louise's reputation. Bussy-Rabutin remarked spitefully that she had benefited from the death of Henrietta Duchess of Orléans, because she would never have been able to secure such an exalted lover in France. Madame de Sévigné said that poor Castlemaine had been cast aside – 'such is the fate of mistresses in that Kingdom'. No one thought to show concern for Louise. While everyone else regarded her as an object of pleasure, it was left to her alone to rescue her reputation and establish respect for her position. To this end Louise now directed all her energies.

It was, however, an almighty struggle. Society ladies openly made fun of her, giggled behind their hands, pointed and mocked her pretensions. None of this, naturally, within a hundred yards of the King, in whose presence everyone treated Louise with reverence. Perhaps the one exception was naughty Nell Gwynn, who teased with impunity and joined the populace in calling Louise 'Mrs Carwell' or, worse, 'Madame Carwell' because the Cockney accent could not cope happily with 'Kéroualle'. Louise almost wrecked her prospects with some very tactless remarks about the Queen's health, which was never very strong, but which Louise evidently hoped would collapse completely. The trouble was, Louise still nursed the silly notion that she might be Queen of England; anyone who knew Charles well, and recognised his sense of honour and decency, would have known it was absurd to suppose that he might discard Catherine, even when all possibility of an heir from her body had evaporated. Those around Louise were slow to disabuse her, rather enjoying the vision of arrogance deflated, and when Dr Frazier erroneously predicted that the Queen had only months, nay weeks to live, poor Louise was bumptious. Colbert de Croissy reported that she was in danger of being mocked out of sight 'because she does not keep her head sober, since she has got the notion into it that it is possible she may yet be Queen of England. She talks from morning to night of the Queen's ailments as if they were mortal.'

In spite of this inauspicious beginning, Louise gradually established her right to be considered not an ordinary mistress, but *maîtresse en titre*, with special privileges and rank. Of all Charles's ladies, she was the only one with the breeding necessary to lend any distinction to such a title (Barbara degraded it, and Nell derided it). Lord Halifax recognised her distinction early on, and spoke of 'some extraordinary solemnities that might dignify, though not sanctify her function'. It was terribly important to Louise to be regarded as a lady of quality.

Imagine her disappointment, then, when the King did not immediately recognise her son as his own, though there could be no doubt of paternity in view of all the witnesses to conception. The boy, named Charles Lennox, was born on 29 July 1672. Charles confessed that he was reluctant to admit paternity because even he, for once, was embarrassed by an excess of progeny, there being no less than four natural children ascribed to him that year, while the world was reminded of a fifth at the betrothal, two days later, of Arlington's daughter Isabella to the infant Duke of Grafton.

If she really were in love with Charles, then Louise's hurt must have been deplorable. There she was, a young woman who had given herself to an insistent seducer, borne him a child in dishonour, only to discover that his insatiable appetites rendered him incapable of fidelity. The termagant Barbara was still in tow and Nell much in evidence. Louise found it difficult to understand how an excess of sensuality should need to be satisfied by variety instead of faithfulness. There were different aspects of the King's personality that responded in turn to the lewd excitement of Barbara, the iconoclastic unconventionality of Nell, and the refinement of Louise. The Queen had by now become used to this complex personality, but Louise had still to learn that she must be content to share Charles with others. No confidences have come down to us which would indicate whether or not she did love him, so we can only risk conjecture based upon what we know of her character. It is more likely that position was more important to her than love, and that she used the latter as a means to obtain the former.

And what of Charles? Was he capable, since the adolescent involvement with Lucy Walter and the frustration imposed by Frances Stuart, of a profound love? Or did his cosy fondness for Nell represent the limit of his errant capacities? Fortunately, there is some evidence much later in Charles's reign which helps to determine the matter, evidence which resides at the County Record Office in Chichester. A letter from the King addresses her in the most affectionate terms. 'I shall not be out of pain till I know how my dearest got to London', he says. 'I should do myself wrong if I told you that I love you better than all the world besides, for that were making a comparison where 'tis impossible to express the true passion and kindness I have for my dearest dearest Fubs.'

This is a patently sincere avowal, which leaves no room for doubt of the King's deep affection for Louise. The nickname 'Fubs' is especially endearing. At other times he called her 'my dear Life', and on his death-bed, where his request to his brother not to let Nelly starve is well-known, it is generally forgotten that he also said of Louise, 'I have always loved her, and I die loving her.'

*   *   *

It was indeed fortunate that Louise had the King's love to support her, for without it she might not have had the resilience to withstand the calumnies which rained upon her. She was deeply unpopular in England almost from the moment she set foot in the country, and not for a week throughout the following years did the antipathy relent. From the highest to the lowest she was reviled, constantly brought down from her high horse and reminded that she owed her position to nothing more than her performance in bed. We have already seen that Nell Gwynn poked fun in asking why, if she really was so high-born, she allowed herself to be a whore. Powerful country families like the Russells and the Cavendishes, who were to found the Whig party, would not countenance receiving her in their houses. Lady Sunderland, who had been present at the Euston 'wedding' and had helped to undress Louise, turned against her, calling her an 'abominable harlot' and putting it about that 'so damned a jade as this would sell us without hesitation for 500 guineas'. The King's own brother, the Duke of York, wisely made a show of getting on well with her, but secretly he could not abide her and did not scruple to indicate as much in private. Even her brother-in-law, the Earl of Pembroke (he married her younger sister Henriette), threatened to drag her to the street-corner and have her hung upside down with her skirts tied up so that everyone could see where her power lay. Lord Shaftesbury belittled her origins and talents, calling her 'a creature of France . . . by birth the lowest of the gentry there, of no fortune, of worse fame . . . a very indifferent beauty, and of wit hardly enough for a woman (her cunning and French mode supplying that defect)'.

At Court, where one might expect Louise to be safe from spiteful treatment, she was frequently harassed and affronted. Two courtiers once waylaid her favourite negro page (we see him standing by Louise in Mignard's famous portrait), gave him money and tried to get him drunk, in the hope that he would reveal some delicious scandal to his lady's detriment. They succeeded only in having themselves banished from Court by the King. And Phyllis Temple, who was in attendance upon the Queen, complained to Her Majesty about something to do with Louise, whereupon Louise burst into tears yet again imploring Charles to seek redress, and he obliged by instructing his wife never to heed derogatory gossip concerning his mistress. Obediently, the Queen deprived Mrs Temple of a quarter's salary forthwith.

The effrontery of Louise's enemies was sometimes amazing. Somebody was once bold enough to pin to her bedroom door a paper bearing the verse:

> Within this place a bed's appointed
> For a French bitch and God's annointed.

Outside, in the carefree atmosphere of the coffee-houses where reputations sank beneath a quagmire of good-humoured satire, Louise was pilloried without mercy. One of Rochester's clever but confused compositions went the rounds and caused, one may presume, much unkind laughter:

Restless he rolls about from whore to whore
A merry monarch, scandalous and poor;
To Carwell, the most dear of all his dears,
The best relief of his declining years,
Oft he bewails his fortune, and her fate :
To love so well, and he beloved so late.
For though in her he settles well his tarse,
Yet his dull, graceless ballocks hang an arse.

Most of the hostility directed at Louise was quite undeserved, deriving as it did from prejudice and hearsay. Though her airs and graces might make her look ridiculous, they could not reasonably be thought justification for vile abuse. She was certainly not the whore that she was painted. But the English detested France, and Louise was, like it or not, the representative of that country at the King's right hand. She had to absorb the hatred intended for an entire nation. She aroused fears which no amount of rational debate could dispel, Protestant fears that the King's infatuation with a Papist was dangerous enough to cause another religious upheaval, and national fears that the French had implanted Louise in Charles's bed as a covert spy, whose purpose was nothing less than the subjugation of England's interests to those of France. Both aspects of this suspicion were to have catastrophic consequences in the future. Meanwhile, it did not help to hear that Louise regularly celebrated Catholic Mass in her private chapel, or to observe that the King declared war on the Dutch in accordance with his secret promises at Dover. It all appeared deeply sinister.

French influence at the Court seemed to become more and more pronounced, even at a surface level. Furniture, fashions, architecture, everything was pervaded by the current French taste. Le Nôtre redesigned St James's Park, the Queen employed a French milliner, Desborde, as her dressmaker, the King's wine-cellar was in the control of another Frenchman, and his tailor, Claude Sourceau, was a Parisian whom Charles persuaded to settle in London. In the popular mind, all this was ascribed, quite wrongly, to the pernicious agency of 'Madame Carwell'.

Louise thought there was one way in which she could force people to give her the respect that was her due. If Charles could be persuaded to bestow upon her the highest titles in the English peerage, surely she would no longer suffer contempt. Besides, it irked her to have to give precedence all the time to such as the Duchess of Cleveland. Louise might profitably have paused to reflect that *la Cleveland's* titles did not earn her automatic respect either: Londoners were not easily hood-winked. Anyway, in order to receive English titles, Louise would need to be an Englishwoman, so the first step was to petition Louis XIV for permission to become an English subject, 'and so benefit by the gifts and honours which King Charles wanted to lavish on her'. This was readily granted.

The King first arranged for her to receive a pension of £10,000 from revenue levied on Irish lands. Then, with the active help of Lord Arlington, Louise was raised to the highest rank as Duchess of Ports-mouth, *suo jure*, with the additional titles Countess of Fareham and Baroness Petersfield. The warrant was made in favour of herself and heirs male of her body, which meant that the honours could not descend to her eighteen-month-old illegitimate son Charles Lennox. Further-more, the new Duchess was appointed a Lady of the Bedchamber, thus attaining the highest position to which she could reasonably aspire.

Still the people sneered, still the smart of disdain made her tense, still the ultimate pleasure of respect for rank eluded her. She had in addition to bear the curse of her upright father, who was not at all impressed that his unmarried daughter should bear a child to the King of England. Louise responded to these disappointments with an increase of ambition. As she saw matters, the English simply did not know how to behave, and rank in that country was not honoured as it should be because manners at Court were too loose, licence too widespread. In France, on the other hand, the vast pyramidal structure of Court etiquette really counted for something, and everyone knew his place in the hierarchy. Now, if Louise could get herself made a French *duchesse*, a rank which conferred the unique and coveted right to sit on an uncomfortable stool called a *tabouret* when in the presence of the Queen, then she could demonstrate to the world (and to her difficult father) that she had arrived, that she was no longer the lowly Maid of Honour in service to a foreign-born princess, nor a mere royal mistress, but a person of significance.

It was Charles again who was called upon to placate his lover by rais-ing the delicate question with Louis XIV. (Lord Arlington, who had pressed for the Portsmouth title, was now forgotten, and complained of Louise's ingratitude.) The estate of Aubigny had been raised to a duchy by Charles VII in 1422, in favour of John Stuart and his descendants. The line had recently come to an end with the death

of La Belle Stuart's husband, the Duke of Richmond, and had therefore reverted to the French crown. (Some authorities aver that it should
not have done, and that the rightful heir to the estate and title was
Charles II himself, but that is another matter.) It was now proposed that
Aubigny should be assigned to the Duchess of Portsmouth. It was a bold
move indeed for a King's mistress to ask for the grant of Crown lands,
especially since Louis XIV was extremely touchy about interference in
his royal prerogatives. Nevertheless, it was becoming plain to Louis that
the French girl was a valuable asset in acting as intermediary between
his English cousin and himself, and might still be used to greater advantage; therefore it would be politic to please her.

The request was transmitted by Colbert de Croissy, acutely embarrassed by his mission and resentful of Louise's effrontery. King Charles
asked him to convey his wishes to France, and he could hardly refuse.
He wrote :

> I own I find her on all occasions so ill-disposed for the service of
> the king, and showing such ill-humour against France (whether
> because she feels herself despised there, or whether she is just
> capricious), that I really think she deserves no favour of His Majesty.
> But as the King of England shows her much love, and so visibly likes
> to please her, His Majesty can judge whether it is best not to treat
> her according to her merits. An attention paid to her will be taken
> by the King of England as one paid to himself.

Louise's son was still not recognised by Charles, and it was altogether
too much to expect that a French ducal estate should pass to an un-
acknowledged bastard. Colbert therefore hit upon a compromise.
Aubigny could be given to the Duchess of Portsmouth, with reversion
to any natural child of the king whom he might appoint to succeed
her. In this way, Louise would have the benefit of a ducal estate, but
would not yet be a French duchess, and the estate could not pass to her
son until such time as Charles recognised him as his natural child.
This is in fact what happened, at the end of 1673, a solution which still
denied Louise her cherished *tabouret*.

Not long afterwards, Louise suffered another, more terrible setback
to her pride – King Charles gave her venereal disease. Far from com-
miserating with her, the new French ambassador, Ruvigny, who had
just succeeded Colbert de Croissy in the post, thought the situation
highly amusing, while her enemies of course welcomed the opportunity

to snigger. Ruvigny wrote in jocular fashion to the Foreign Minister, Pomponne :

> While the King [*i.e.* Louis XIV] wins new provinces, the King of England has won the pox, which he has conscientiously passed on to the Duchess of Portsmouth . . . she has been consoled for such a vexatious gift by another which she finds more satisfactory. She has received a necklace of pearls worth four thousand jacobuses, and a diamond worth six thousand, and she is so delighted that I do doubt she would pay the same price again for such a consolation.

This jibe was, to say the least, unjust; Louise was mortified with indignation, not only because her condition reduced her in the eyes of the world to a creature of human proportions, when she had been trying so hard to assert her superiority, but also because the doctors naturally advised that she should desist from intimacy with the King for some time to come, which would leave the way open for her rivals. The King was quickly cured by the estimable and useful Dr Frazier, but Louise was ill rather longer. The doctors then counselled that she should take the waters at fashionable Tunbridge Wells, where another humiliation awaited her.

Louise rented a house in Tunbridge Wells only to find on arrival that the Marchioness of Worcester had moved into it. Louise pointed out that a Duchess must take precedence over a Marchioness and asked Lady Worcester therefore to make way. Lady Worcester replied with the utmost malice that since titles conferred as a reward for prostitution were never taken seriously by persons of quality, she would refuse to budge. So poor Louise was obliged to turn to the King for help, and leave Tunbridge for Windsor, escorted by a detachment of the Household Guards.

As we already know, Nell Gwynn was delighted to have Louise as bait for her wicked wit. She took all opportunities to ridicule her and aped her mannerisms, her languid walk, her affectations, and pretended in extravagant fashion to be desperately worried whenever Louise was in town because, she said, she feared her rivalry; would she match up to the matchless Duchess?

There is one amusing account of a meeting between the two women, when Nell appeared at Whitehall very sumptuously dressed. Louise unwisely took the chance to make a sarcastic remark, thinking for once to get the better of the impudent actress. 'Nelly, you are grown rich, I believe, by your dress', she said. 'Why, woman, you are fine enough to be a queen.' To which Nell, without pause for breath, replied, 'You are entirely right, Madam, and I am whore enough to be a duchess.'

Louise did manage to score one notable victory over the Duchess of Cleveland, a victory which gave her the deepest satisfaction. She eventually prevailed upon the King to recognise her son Charles Lennox, and to raise him at the age of three to the highest rank in the peerage. The dukedom of Richmond was vacant since the death of la Belle Stuart's husband, and Louise already possessed the duchy of Aubigny which had been associated with the Richmond name. So it was agreed (after what methods of persuasion one can only surmise) that the infant should be created Duke of Richmond, Earl of March, Baron Settrington, Baron Methuen, Earl Darnley and Earl Lennox, should receive a castle and an income of his own, and should benefit from the reversion of the Aubigny estates. But Barbara, Duchess of Cleveland, would not stand aside and see the bastard of a French upstart be honoured above her own offspring. She in turn wanted her second son, Henry Fitzroy, to be created Duke of Grafton, and was determined that he should take precedence over Portsmouth's child. The question of precedence depended entirely upon which patent of creation was the first to be signed. Barbara thought she had won, doubtless because the King, tired of listening to ladies' squabbles, told her so. He secretly hoped to settle the matter in a quiet way by having both patents signed simultaneously. Louise was however more cunning than both of them. She was on terms of affectionate trust with the Lord Treasurer, Danby, and could count on his connivance. She persuaded Danby to receive her attorney at midnight, just as he was setting off in his coach to Bath, and sign the papers there and then. The following day, when Barbara sought to have her papers signed, she found to her fury that Danby had left, and that Portsmouth had outwitted her. To this day, the present Duke of Richmond takes precedence over the present Duke of Grafton as a consequence of Louise's action.

In May of the previous year, 1674, Louise's younger sister Henriette de Kéroualle had arrived in London, ostensibly to seek fortune and a husband. She found both, though it is odd that her father should have allowed her to go in view of his fierce disapproval of Louise. Perhaps he despaired of her finding anyone to marry her in France, for she was not by any means a beauty. King Charles sent a yacht to fetch her, with one gentleman as escort, and assigned to her a pension of £600 a year. Before very long, she was married off to the dissolute and savage

Earl of Pembroke who was suffering from the pox (venereal disease) at the time of the betrothal. (This was the man who threatened to expose Louise by hanging her upside down in public.) Henriette was destined not to have a happy marriage.

When the parents visited London in 1675, they pointedly neglected to stay with either daughter, choosing rather to be guests of their old friend Sir Richard Browne at his quiet home in Kent. There Evelyn met them and recorded his impressions; the Count was military and decent, the Countess beautiful and shrewd. They did not appear at Court, and most wounding of all to Louise, they did not ask to see her son.

They cannot fail to have heard of the overwhelming luxury in which Louise lived. Her apartments at Whitehall, which occupied no less than forty rooms, far exceeded in splendour those of the Queen, who from about this time lived mostly at Somerset House. It began to look as if Louise were Queen in all but name, since Charles preferred to receive the French ambassador and his own ministers in her room, when, that is, they were not crowded with visitors who had come to stare and marvel at the riches they contained. The rooms were hung with Gobelin tapestries and priceless paintings brought from Versailles, their windows were of the finest crystal, their furnishings included Japanese cabinets, rare Chinese *objets d'art*, exquisite clocks, resplendent silver, the whole amounting to a display of refined taste such as London had not seen for years. It was both ostentatious and extravagant, but it nonetheless commanded admiration in its fastidious regard for quality. Those who resented the cost naturally did not share in the general excitement. John Evelyn, who tells us that by 1683 the apartments had been pulled down and rebuilt three times 'to satisfy her prodigal and expensive pleasures', deplored both the self-indulgence and its beneficiary. 'What contentment can there be in riches and splendour of this world', he mused, 'purchas'd with vice and dishonour!'

Expensive furbishments were not, for Louise, mere superficial decoration; they answered a profound need, or rather several needs. She still remembered bitterly the years of poverty. and the humiliation of having nothing suitable to wear at Minette's Court. Again, she felt she had to uphold the prestige of France, and show the vulgar English the fruits of the best taste in the world. Most important of all, she needed solid visible evidence of her pre-eminence to protect her against the poor opinion of her enemies. She was naive enough to believe in the power of material things to impress.

Jewellery, too, had its attraction for the Duchess of Portsmouth. In

March 1674 she coveted a pearl necklace worth £8000, and a pair of ear-rings which Lady Northumberland was trying to dispose of for a sum over £3000. She appealed to the King, who told her his resources were strained and sent her to the Treasurer, Lord Danby. Danby was in favour with the Duchess and was happy to find ways of pleasing her, so she received the cash to buy her trinkets. Presumably Danby thought it politic to oblige, but malicious gossips suggested that she had another hold on him, and that they were secret lovers. There is no evidence beyond tattle, and that, knowing Louise's careful behaviour, it is unlikely.

The amount of money Louise received from the Exchequer varies according to which papers one cares to consult, and what interpretation one wishes to put upon them, but there is no doubt that it was enormous, more even than the fortune accumulated by the Duchess of Cleveland. Apart from the revenue of £10,000 which came from licences given to wine-merchants, Louise frequently received generous lump sums. On 27 October 1676 Charles granted an annuity of £8600 payable out of excise duties to 'our Right entirely beloved Cousin Louise Duchess of Portsmouth'. On 21 July 1677 another £11,000 came as an outright gift. Bryan Bevan has estimated that in the three years between 1676 and 1679 Louise received over £55,000, while at the same time she was gladly accepting gifts from the French King, including a pair of ear-rings worth £18,000. In one year alone, 1681, the enormous sum of £22,952 was assigned to the fortunate Duchess.* These figures, taken with the monies already filched for the benefit of Barbara, add up to a grand fortune, which Parliament viewed with deep disfavour, and led Shaftesbury to make his famous reference to 'chargeable ladies about the Court'.

Yet it is all too easy to exaggerate. King Charles's mistresses and bastards cost the country no more cash than a brood of legitimate children would have rightly absorbed, and the critics, who claimed they did not mind who the King went to bed with as long as he did not pay so dearly for the privilege, would have done well to reflect that the Court of Charles II was really one of the least expensive in Europe. The King's expenditure on women was tame compared to that of some of his cousins abroad.

And what did Louise do with her bounty? Sadly, not as much as she should have done. She had a steward, Dr Taylor, whose job it was to bank the sums received and invest them wisely. A great deal was

* Not £136,000, the figure usually given. See *Complete Peerage*.

stacked away in France, where it could not be touched, in case popular resentment against Louise were suddenly to erupt into dangerous anger. She managed to supplement her income by selling royal pardons to criminals, for which purpose she employed Timothy Hall, whose business was to ferret out those law-breakers who could afford to pay. Nevertheless, with all this, Louise managed to squander a massive proportion in what was the real vice of the age – gambling. In this she was no better than Barbara, whom she tried to treat with disdain. On one occasion she lost 5000 guineas at a throw. She could not prevent herself from getting into debt, even owing her servants money at times. Still, when she left England after the death of the King, Louise had harvested enough to make her more than solvent.

Her sister, Lady Pembroke, appears to have done rather better. Quite as delicately attached to fine things as Louise, the Countess had to charter several ships to convey the colossal booty she eventually took back to France. The list included seventeen dozen pairs of gloves, twenty rare and precious tapestries, lots of tea-pots, and a hundred pounds in weight of pins and needles.

*   *   *

If Louise appeared to be Queen of England in all but name, it was not only because she had taken over most of the official entertaining from Catherine, who was increasingly unwell, retiring and disconsolate, but because it was thought she had undue political influence over the King, as Barbara had had a few years earlier. However much it is pointed out that Charles II did not consult his mistresses in 'business' (Colbert de Croissy had himself reported to France that 'His Majesty is not disposed to communicate his affairs to women'), nevertheless the French always deemed it prudent to seek favour with mistresses in case they could be used as a source of information or as levers for gentle influence. Even after Louise had assumed her role as *maîtresse en titre*, the ambassador was still unwilling totally to discard Barbara. 'I think it safe', he told Louis XIV, 'while undermining that lady, to keep her on our side by appearing to be with her.'

Louise was potentially quite the most dangerous of the mistresses in this respect, being naturally secretive and discreet, and occupying a place midway between the two kings. She received the French ambassador almost daily, which looked innocent enough as she had originally been a French subject herself, but which inevitably aroused suspicions of collusion we now know to be not entirely unfounded.

It was in the matter of Charles's conversion to Catholicism that Louise was most obviously useful. The King had promised in the Treaty of Dover to declare his faith, and thenceforward proved an expert in procrastination. He said that the English Catholics were too weak in numbers, too poor in instruction, that the Pope's health was too precarious (though he would presumably have been succeeded by a more healthy Pontiff), that there was no one in England sufficiently well versed in the rites to give him adequate guidance. At first Louise was disappointed by the King's continual evasions and begged him to follow the right path, but when she changed her tune to inform the French that a declaration at that moment would not carry the English with it, she can only have been echoing Charles own opinion. Of course, the King never intended to risk such public folly, which might have caused another Civil War; it served his purpose to use Louise to temper French entreaties.

By way of appeasement, Charles did publish a Declaration of Indulgence by which he abolished laws discriminating against nonconformists. This was intended to promote tolerance in religious matters and remove some of the harshness with which Catholics were treated. They were to be allowed to exercise their worship in the privacy of their homes. But Parliament, already suspecting the terms of the secret Treaty, would have none of it. A year later, they demanded revocation of the Declaration or they would not vote the subsidies which Charles urgently needed to continue the war against Holland. For the French, the war was the more important consideration, so they used Louise to urge Charles not to be rash. Tearfully (as usual), she implored the King to stay his hand until he was in a stronger position, and the Declaration of Indulgence was duly revoked.

Louise could not of course be seen to have any direct influence with Parliament. When it became essential to French policy to buy the anti-French members with financial bribes, the respectable and honourable Ruvigny was charged with the task of finding complacent victims and paying them off. A man to whom integrity mattered, Ruvigny confessed to Louis XIV that he found it a 'filthy business'. Yet it was hardly worse, from one point of view, than the King receiving huge sums from the French Embassy in return for compliance with French designs. The whole of English power seemed to be sitting in French pockets, and Louise was the *dea ex machina* who had engineered our humiliation. Such as least was the popular version of events.

The duties of the French ambassador demanded someone less squeamish than Ruvigny, and so a new appointment brought Honoré de Courtin to London. He took to the job with relish, enjoying political intrigue, surreptitious manoeuvres, and the company of pretty women; the Court of Charles II was perfect for him. He consulted regularly with Louise, for mixed motives, admitting guilelessly to France that 'I do not believe anyone can be so often in her company without desiring her'.

With the English still at war with Holland, yet yearning to turn their hostility against France, Courtin had a difficult mission. Charles was sensitive to the mood of his people and reasoned with the French not to make his position untenable. He admitted to Courtin that he was compromising himself with his subjects. 'I am resolved to keep my pledged word', he said, 'but I urge him [Louis XIV] to help me a little and to make peace before the winter.' Louise, who thought a monarch should be absolute and had no truck with any system which diluted regal power, urged Charles to put his foot down and keep Parliament in its place. Charles was too subtle to be swayed by such talk, but nevertheless he found himself yet again in an awkward position and was obliged to negotiate another loan with the French in exchange for his neutrality.

Louise was on the periphery of these affairs of state, but her attention was diverted by an event which threatened to overturn her carefully-won position in Court life – the arrival in London of Hortense Mancini, Duchesse Mazarin, whom de Grammont described with impressive simplicity as 'the most beautiful woman I have ever seen'. Louise was thrown into a state of nervous tension, for not only was Hortense amazingly beautiful, but she had a wild, irresponsible and thoroughly captivating personality which made her without doubt the most fascinating woman of her time. As no one could resist her, it was only to be expected that King Charles would not even try. The life of Hortense Mancini is so bizarre, so beyond the bounds of probability, that it compels a disgression to introduce her.

*　　　　*　　　　*

Hortense was Italian by birth, but came to France at an early age under the protection of her uncle Cardinal Mazarin, who had ambitions for her to marry royalty. Her beauty and uncontrolled high spirits soon made her the centre of attention. In his exile, the young Charles II had supposedly fallen in love with her and proposed marriage, but was refused because his prospects were still uncertain. As for Hortense, she did not particularly care whom she married, as long as she could have a good time.

As a child, the 'good time' was divided between flirting and playing pranks upon those who were appointed to control her. She presented her governess, Madame de Venel, with a box of sweetmeats in which she had hidden an army of live mice. When the grateful governess opened her gift, the mice ran all over her, whereupon she screamed like a demon and passed out. As for the flirting, it was directed at men and women alike, causing havoc in the hearts of all around her. This was another jolly game, the self-indulgence of a reckless girl who stubbornly refused to take life seriously. The possession of a fortune which made her one of the richest ladies in Europe made it imperative that maturity should somehow be thrust upon her.

Since she was ten years old, there had been one persistent suitor who had pined for her – Charles de la Porte de la Meilleraye. Now that she was fifteen, she was told that she was to marry him and live in the sumptuous Palais Mazarin, which suited her although she had no strong feelings for her fiancé in one way or the other. He was promptly given the title Duc Mazarin (the 'de' was omitted because his family was not sufficiently noble), and in February 1661 the gay impish beauty was solemnly wed and became Duchesse Mazarin. She could look forward to a life of ease and pleasure.

Or so she thought. What she did not know was that her husband was schizophrenic, psychotic, and getting madder every day. In public he behaved with courtesy and correctness, changing abruptly into a monster of jealousy as soon as he was alone with Hortense. At night, he would wait until she was asleep, then suddenly jump out of bed, light all the candles, and have his servants search the room for evil spirits. If they were not found, it confirmed his view that his wife and servants conspired to hide them from him. He forbade her to stay up late, demanded that she spend most of her waking hours at prayer, and declared that the most sinful crime was to be seated at the dining table with a man. To avoid any such stain on his home, the Duc instructed his servants to turn all visitors away from the door, especially English noblemen.

Unfortunately, this exaggerated protection of the loved one did not flatter Hortense, who submitted bravely for a while before reaching the logical conclusion that if her husband would not like her to enjoy herself, then she would have to do so without his knowledge. She would order her coach; he would send it away; when he went out, she would order it again. Hortense was very adaptable. Her husband, meanwhile, descended further into lunacy when he decided that the angels had told him he must save not only his wife's soul but the morals of the entire world. It would be a Herculean task, but the Duc Mazarin was equal to it. He must grasp the nettle fearlessly. He went to Louis XIV in private audience and said, 'The angel Gabriel has desired me to tell Your Majesty that you must immediately break off your relations with Mademoiselle de la Vallière.' Louis did not ponder his reply. 'The angel Gabriel has told me you are mad', he said, and the audience was swiftly terminated.

There was something almost inspired about Mazarin's imaginings. When a fire broke out in one of his properties, and the servants fought to extinguish it, Mazarin bade them stop, because it was wrong to interfere with God's will; the house burnt down. It was also wrong to have the servants perform tasks arbitrarily dictated by the will of man; let God decide what they should do. The Duc wrote down the various jobs on pieces of paper, and shuffled them before handing them out to the bewildered staff. The valets then found themselves managing the stables, the gardeners had to employ their knowledge in the wine-cellars, and the Head Man was demoted to a washer-up. God's will be done.

God also did not care for nudity. The Duc was horrified to realise one day that most of his collection of statues and pictures revealed private parts which were capable of suggesting licentiousness. Without more ado, he took hammer and chisel and began energetically to deprive the statues of their obscene protrusions, until his curator, Monsieur Turolles, realising what was going on, fell to his knees in tears and pleaded with his master to stop. As there is no reasoning with a lunatic, Mazarin went on with his vandalism until midnight, and continued the next day with the help of half a dozen valets, who were instructed to destroy the statues, while he applied himself with scissors and paint to the offending pictures. By the time he had completed his divinely ordained mission, Mazarin had destroyed or defaced some of the greatest masterpieces in Europe.

The milk-maids, who had for years been handling cows' udders, and had thus been exposed to quite appalling temptations of the mind, were given less dangerous jobs, and the men were assigned to milk the cows whose udders would henceforth be veiled. Perhaps it was too late to save the milk-maids. However, they must be rescued, thought Mazarin, from the dangers inherent in their own prettiness. They were lined up and their front teeth all pulled out.

While the Duc tormented himself with worry, the Duchesse contrived to amuse herself. He took her for six months to Britanny, where she would be so isolated that no man would gaze upon her. That did not prevent the resourceful Hortense from having an affair with a neighbouring woman. She also embarked on a delightful relationship with a sixteen-year-old girl, Sidonie de Courcelles, who had been married a few weeks and decided that she did not care to prolong the experience. Hortense and Sidonie were both placed in a convent to keep them out of trouble, but alas they took trouble with them. The two girls put ink into the holy water, which made the harmless nuns look as if they had the plague. At night, they organised rat hunts through the dormitories, shrieking at the top of their voices. The nuns were told they should not let Hortense and Sidonie out of their sight which, considering the girls' high spirits and the nun's sluggishness in heavy habits, made for wonderful chases through the cloisters.

Eventually, the friends grew tired of their prison, and determined to escape. They climbed up the chimney, Sidonie first and Hortense following. But Hortense was pregnant with her fourth child (not the least astonishing part of this story is that the Duc apparently returned from chopping off penises to work his own into an erection for the glory of God), so she got stuck, and had to be yanked out of the chimney by Sidonie from above, after a twenty-minute struggle. They were both, of course, covered in soot.

Back at home, Hortense secured a ruling by the Court of Requests that her husband should not live with her in the Palais Mazarin. This would certainly make life more equable, but her fortune was fast being frittered away by her husband, one of whose pastimes was foolish litigation. He brought 300 cases to law, and lost all of them. Hortense herself had damaged her reputation by her undignified behaviour in the convent, though no one seems to have objected to her homosexual relationship with Sidonie de Courcelles, except perhaps Sidonie's husband. Hortense, finding herself *persona non grata*, elected to escape again.

Disguised in men's clothes, the Duchesse Mazarin fled to Italy, pausing long enough to have an affair with a young man called Couberville, page to the Chevalier de Rohan. Hortense caused quite a sensation when she bore the page's child nine months later. Back in France, her

husband was now preoccupied by other matters; he had decided that
he was a tulip, and had given instructions to his servants to make sure
he was placed in the sun, and water poured over his head.

Then, quite suddenly, Hortense developed an intelligence which no
one could have predicted. She moved to Chambéry, where she became
interested in philosophical and literary questions, holding her own with
eminent men of learning, and thus she gained an entirely new collection
of admirers. Her teacher was an obscure fellow known as the Abbé
Saint-Réal, a licentious creature, whose real name was César Vicard.
Hortense deserted the books briefly to become his mistress, then on
his advice she wrote and published her memoirs, which were of course
highly successful. It is at this point that Hortense enters our story.
Ralph Montagu and the Duke of Buckingham, anxious to rid Whitehall
of what they thought was Louise's dangerous influence, and to lessen
the King's reliance upon her, were on the *qui-vive* for a woman of
beauty and character who could supplant her. They suggested that
Hortense might like to come to London. Montagu took a house for
her in Covent Garden Piazza, and there she arrived, in characteristically
unconventional fashion, bedraggled and covered in mud, in 1675. She
was accompanied by Saint-Réal, her maid Nanon, and other servants.

Though Hortense had asked to be *incognita*, it was quite impossible
to keep the presence of such a famous woman a secret. She was now
thirty years old, still amazingly beautiful, and adorned with a past
which made her far more interesting than anyone else around. The
details of her life were public property by reason of her memoirs, and
were polished by a reputation which had transformed her over the
years into a creature of fantasy. It was inevitable that everyone should
want to meet her.

Her personality had by this time mellowed, yet retained enough of
the outlandish to fascinate all who came near her. She had the gift of
casualness, was openly friendly and unpretentious, and delightfully
unmindful of problems. Life was still a rich treasure of amusement
to her, which made her naturally optimistic and gave her a sunny
temperament. She was obedient to whim, deploring discipline and self-
control, preferring to place faith in her erratic intuitive powers, which
had always led her to break the rules which others so laboriously honoured, while being childishly unaware that she was doing anything
remarkable. She was indifferent to fashion, in behaviour or in dress,
which gave her a freedom women envied and men admired. Quick-
witted, warm, restless and vital, Hortense was just the kind of woman

whose company King Charles was bound to enjoy; he would especially appreciate the fact that she had not the slightest interest in politics. On top of all, she was quite without vanity, quite unconscious of the qualities she possessed. Her faults? Frivolity, carelessness with both money and the emotions of other people (though not wilfully), a lack of depth. But these were swamped by her sheer loveableness. It was only to be expected that Louise, whose contrived conduct stood in stark contrast to this marvel, should view her arrival with fearful consternation.

De Grammont, whose admiration for the beauty of Hortense we have already recorded, told the French ambassador that all the other mistresses were eclipsed by her, while Ruvigny himself wrote, 'I never saw anyone who so well defies the power of time and vice to disfigure. At the age of fifty she will have the satisfaction of thinking, when she looks at her mirror, that she is as lovely as she ever was in her life.' Moreover, her ease of manner, her knack of knowing what to say and do at every turn, were signs of a great lady, next to which Louise's persistent attempts at the grand manner appeared gauche. Nell Gwynn mischievously went into mourning, because she said the prospects of the Duchess of Portsmouth were now quite dead. The poet Waller made his own contribution to the fun with a piece called *The Triple Combat*, in which Louise, Hortense and Nell were depicted in an almighty struggle for supremacy.

Duchesse Mazarin was actually far less concerned to compete for romantic attention than to replenish her purse. She was near destitution as her husband refused to make her any allowance out of what was, in reality, her own inheritance. Louis XIV being unwilling to intercede, Charles gave her £4000 a year and made sure she was handsomely entertained at Whitehall. Before long, Hortense was presiding over the most brilliant salon in London, far exceeding anything which Louise, with her limited horizons, could produce at Whitehall. All the best intellects and wits flocked to Hortense's salon, where philosophical discussions and readings from Racine would alternate with wild games and dancing. The chief jewel of her set was Saint-Evremond, who now devoted all his time to the fascinating Duchess, providing her with both intellectual stimulation and paternal affection, a state of affairs which put Saint-Réal's nose considerably out of joint. He was now eased into the background. De Grammont was another member of the côterie, with Buckingham and Montagu, and a fine array of ladies, including Montagu's sister, Lady Harvey, and Barbara's first-born, the young Countess of Sussex. The group was completed by King Charles, attracted by Hortense's clever conversation and uncomplicated ease. She was perfectly happy to be his mistress – it was yet another of life's pleasantries.

One of Hortense's most devoted admirers was little Lady Sussex, whose passionate friendship went so deep that tongues began to wag. The two women were virtually inseparable; they provided some rare amusement for Londoners by venturing to St James's Park in their dressing-gowns for a sprightly open-air fencing match. On another occasion they were joined by Lady Harvey and all three pretended to be horses, mounting each other in turn while the men placed bets on them. The new ambassador Honoré de Courtin, a witness to these frolics, commented acidly on the *goûts spéciaux* of Hortense and her friends. Hortense could not have cared less what people said about her; she had always been gloriously indifferent to public opinion, and her continued flouting of the conventions was merely the expression of her impetuous nature. Consequently she caused havoc with men and women, husbands and wives, and sailed on, an improvident, glittering star in society.

All this was torment for Louise, whom fate had so cruelly treated as to give her an eye infection which made her look very unappetising, in addition to an inconvenient pregnancy. People said she was trying to make her eyes as dark as those of la Mazarin. She loathed Lady Sussex, in whose rooms at Whitehall the King secretly met Hortense; Louise suspected her of encouraging the intrigue. The rooms were those formerly assigned to Lady Sussex's mother Barbara, with access by private staircase used only by the King and his faithful procurer Chiffinch, so Louise's fears were probably justified. Courtin went to visit her one day, and found her in despair, shaking with sobs and pouring out her unhappiness in the presence of her maids. Courtin took pity on her, staying with her until midnight in an attempt to soothe and console her. 'I have never beheld a sadder or more touching sight', he wrote to Louis XIV, who was not at all sympathetic, calling Louise *la signora adolorata*. Louise was beginning to realise just how cynical and callous were her so-called protectors.

The strain of coping with day-to-day life when she felt unwanted inevitably had a severe effect on her health. After six years, 'Fubs' had settled into a very real fondness for Charles, and she felt all the pain of a neglected wife. She grew thin and pale and her pregnancy ended in a miscarriage. To make matters worse, public humiliations were carelessly heaped upon her. When the Court made its annual visit to Newmarket, no one bothered to reserve lodgings for her, and she was obliged to find uncomfortable quarters alone in a nearby village. She decided to take the waters at Bath to renew her strength, calling in at Windsor on the way home. She dined with the King, but was not invited to stay, and had to continue disconsolate to London. Further, Louise discovered that her steward had been cheating her, had stolen £12,000 and pawned some of her jewels. She was frequently in tears.

The French ambassador noted that King Charles went through the elaborate ceremony which attended his officially going to bed, waited for the servants to disappear, then got up, dressed, and spent the night with Duchesse Mazarin. He would see Louise during the day, in company with others. 'He gives every appearance of being devoted to her during the day', he wrote, 'but reserves the right to spend the night with anyone he pleases.' Courtin advised Louise to keep control of herself, weep less, and behave with coolness, but he told his masters that her relationship with Charles had subsided into a virtuous friendship.

When Hortense was raised to a position above all other ladies behind the throne, Louise realised that tears were fruitless, and she determined to change her tactics. With that emotional pragmatism which makes women in love such unpredictable creatures, she stopped avoiding Hortense and sticking figurative needles in her imagined effigy, and made instead a great display of seeking reconciliation. The two duchesses could be seen sharing a coach, and even dining together. Hortense, whom nothing troubled, was as content with this arrangement as she was with everything else. They were once left alone together after dinner, and observed tripping and skipping down the stairs hand in hand. Truly an amazing *volte-face*.

When Ruvigny's recall to France was announced, Louise gave an impressive party for him, making sure that the King was present. Mastering her feelings, she instructed the musicians to play a Spanish song, *Mate me con non mirar, mas no me mate con zelos* (Kill me by avoiding your glance, but do not kill me with jealousy). She had made considerable progress if she was now able to point light-heartedly at her own distress. She was given further encouragement by the next ambassador, Courtin, who told her that Louis XIV attached great importance to her retaining the position of official mistress. With the knowledge that she still counted for something, Louise found fresh vigour with which to continue the struggle. It worked. By September 1677, Courtin was able to report that her good health was restored, that she had a beautiful skin, and to give an optimistic opinion of the future. Not only was her health better, but her influence with the King gradually resumed its former level. Courtin advised his successor Barillon (the fourth ambassador to the Court of St James in Louise's time, after Colbert, Ruvigny and Courtin), that it was essential he should be free to call at any hour of the day on Madame de Portsmouth. Barillon confirmed this impression shortly after taking office, sending a report to Paris which included the remark, 'I have no doubt that the King talks everything over with her and that she is able to draw him to her way of thinking.' As we know, Charles hoodwinked all four ambassadors in this regard, but at least their view points to Louise's restoration of favour.

The next time Louise fell ill, she was confined to bed for six weeks and actually thought she was going to die. Clutching her crucifix, she repented all her sins and did everything she could to persuade the King to renounce women and lead a virtuous life. We do not know his response to these pious exhortations, but he visited her frequently, and was accustomed to receive Ambassador Barillon in her room. When she recovered, Henry Savile wickedly said that her confessor had ascribed her miraculous cure to the Virgin Mary, whom he had promised in her name that 'in case of recovery she should have no more commerce with that known enemy to virginity and chastity the monarch of Great Britain, but that she should return to a cloister in little Britanny and there end her days'. Far from retiring into the shadows, Louise dragged herself out of bed to be present at a play where she knew the King would be with Hortense, and placed herself firmly by his side. Thus asserting her authority, she would see to it that never again would impertinent courtiers speculate as to her future.

Hortense, meanwhile, continued to worry about money. She resented the parsimony of Louis XIV, who would not bestir himself to help her, and loudly proclaimed that the English King was much more understanding of the needs of a lady in distress. (Indeed he was.) There was a danger that she would entrench herself in enmity against France and cause embarrassment to the French ambassador, who advised handling her with some caution. Louise's fortunes were further assisted by a typically reckless love affair into which Hortense threw herself like a woman accustomed to following her instincts. The Prince of Monaco came to London for a short stay. Louise entertained him lavishly, and introduced him to Hortense, who immediately pursued him. Charles was offended, Louise jubilant, Hortense temporarily deprived of her income. The affair ended long before the Prince returned to Europe,

having pined and moaned for months with Hortense cheerfully indifferent to his fate. It was a trivial interlude, after which amity was
resumed, but with a shift in emphasis. Henceforward, the loyalty of
Louise, who never shared in the common promiscuous habits around
her, assured her a lasting place in the King's affections.

*   *   *

A national catastrophe which erupted at the end of 1678 took Louise's
mind off her personal troubles and had such serious implications for
her that it almost drove her out of the country. This was the period of
collective madness which has become known to history as the Popish
Terror, a bland expression which does little to convey the horrifying
irrational hysteria which gripped England for weeks and reduced the
capital to a barbaric city where life was at the mercy of witch-hunters.
As so often, religion was the root of the trouble.

The Protestant English had been whipped up over the years into a
state of fearful tension by recurrent rumours of a Catholic take-over.
These had by now so instilled themselves into the unconscious that the
slightest spark could ignite a dread that was only just below the surface
and was shared even by normally rational folk. It was said that an
invasion by His Most Christian Majesty Louis XIV was imminent, or
that a *coup d'état* would rob the people of their liberties overnight.
The French Embassy was profoundly distrusted, and any cardinal an
automatic object of suspicion. The very seat of royal power (they said)
was poisoned by Catholic influence : Queen Catherine was Popish, so
was the heir to the throne, so too the most enduring mistress, the
Duchess of Portsmouth. The Whig landed aristocrats feared that their
vast properties, acquired in many cases from monastic lands, would be
surrendered back to Rome. In such an atmosphere, any suggestion of a
Catholic plot, however far-fetched, was bound to carry conviction.

Such a suggestion came in August 1678. Taking a walk in St James's
Park, King Charles was stopped and warned that a dastardly attempt
on his life was being planned by the Jesuits. Charles referred the matter
to his Treasurer and gave it no further thought. But by September he
was alarmed to discover that the story had assumed such proportions
as obliged him at least to make a show of taking it seriously.

The plot was revealed by two 'patriots', Titus Oates and Israel
Tonge, who in reality were rogues and criminal liars. Oates in particular had a past of villainy. He had been expelled from school, and from

a Jesuit college, and from a naval chaplaincy. He had been imprisoned for perjury. He now claimed to be a renegade Jesuit, privy to the Jesuits' deepest secrets, and was using a fraudulent degree as Doctor of Divinity to which he had no shadow of a right. Oates had been un-popular all his life, with a fearfully ugly face, the mouth placed dead centre on a full moon, the chin hanging on a neckless torso. For these defects Oates compensated with arrogance and bluster.

Oates and Tonge declared that the Jesuits planned to assassinate Charles II and massacre the Protestants, in order to secure the succes-sion of a Papist, the Duke of York. Pope Innocent XI and King Louis XIV were both party to the conspiracy, which was nothing if not thorough. Two Jesuits had infiltrated the Palace and were placed to shoot the King, four Irishmen had been delegated to stab him to death, and Sir George Wakeman, the Queen's doctor, was going to poison him. Three thousand cut-throats hired by the Jesuits were in waiting to slaughter the citizens of London in their sleep. That one man should have been able to invent such absurd stories and be believed, and by his agency the country plunged into darkness, exposes the raw nerves of the populace.

Titus Oates was deemed serious enough to be examined by the Privy Council, in the presence of the King. Charles himself was not fooled for a minute; he asked pertinent questions, to which Oates, emboldened by his own effrontery, gave such ludicrous replies as betrayed his fun-damental ignorance of affairs. The King was, alas, virtually the only person who kept his head. He knew the man was an impostor, and hoped the truth would dawn on everyone else. But it did not. A farrago grew into the most serious crisis of Charles II's reign and almost de-prived him of the throne. Only his own level good sense saved the day.

Before long, everyone knew about the Popish Plot and informers flocked from all over the country to betray neighbours and seek reward. Anyone who looked like a priest was clapped into prison. It was suffi-cient to say that someone wanted to be a priest, even if it were a cock-and-bull story, for that person to be deprived of his liberty. Everything was possible where the Papists were concerned. A story went about that an army of monks had arrived from Jerusalem to sing a *Te Deum* in support of their friends, and it was believed. More ominously, the Duchess of York's secretary, Coleman, was accused of being a prime conspirator. Letters and papers had been found proving that he was in correspondence with Louis XIV's confessor, an innocent thing enough, but in the present climate a gross act of treason. Then, in October,

F

an event occurred which brought passions to an hysterical pitch.

Sir Edmund Berry Godfrey was a popular Justice of the Peace, a Protestant though a friend of Coleman's; he had recently taken depositions from Titus Oates. He was a wise and sensible man, who may well have seen through the bogus cleric. On the morning of Saturday, 12 October, Sir Edmund left home at nine o'clock, was later seen at Marylebone and St Martin-in-the-Fields, and then disappeared. Five days later his dead body was found in a ditch on the south of Primrose Hill. He lay face downwards, his own sword thrust through his body. At the inquest the next day, two surgeons swore that marks around his neck indicated that Sir Edmund had been strangled, and stabbed after death. The murder of Sir Edmund Berry Godfrey was immediately laid at the door of the Papists, without a jot of evidence, and was seen to confirm all that Titus Oates had said. The man was right. There was a conspiracy. Had not the Papist Duchess of Portsmouth spat upon the dead body of the poor man?*

Oates next testified against a group of terrified Jesuits, and was again tripped up by King Charles in cross-examination. He asked Oates to describe Don Juan, and laughed out loud when he was told that Don Juan was tall and dark, whereas he was really short and red-headed. But it was too late to shake popular conviction; the conflagration had spread too far, and the mood of the nation was eager for blood. Charles knew that if he persisted in treating Oates like a harmless buffoon he would be out of tune with his people and would risk a confrontation with unpredictable results.

The King tried to introduce some calm. He told Parliament that he would not countenance the introduction of Popery by foreigners, but would leave the present matter in the hands of the law. But this was not enough. Parliament insisted that Titus Oates be celebrated as a hero, given a pension of £1200 a year and a personal bodyguard, and worst of all, lodged in his own apartments at the Palace of Whitehall. Though it stuck in his throat, Charles deemed it wise to give his assent. In the overwhelming passion of the moment, other measures were passed to banish all Catholics ten miles from London and keep them under house arrest, and to remove the Duke of York from the Council. A Bill was passed in both Houses to exclude Catholics from sitting in Parliament; though introduced in a moment of panic, it remained law until the nineteenth century. An unscrupulous man like Lord Shaftesbury took advantage of the prevailing fears to lend the weight of his

---

* An unjust accusation; it was not in Louise's nature to behave in this way.

support to Oates's accusation for his own political ends. The King was helpless to hold back the wave of feeling which surged around him. He seemed to be the only sane judge of men, but sanity is quiet and ineffectual against the manic derangement of an entire nation. He could only attempt to mitigate the frenzy by example. He admitted privately that he did not believe one word of the plot.

Danger loomed ever closer for Louise as panic-induced accusations accumulated. The wretched Edward Coleman was found guilty, condemned of nameless crimes without even a hearing, and executed on 1 December in barbarous fashion; he was cut open alive, his bowels torn out and burnt before his eyes. It was a day of shame for England. Then Oates, from the safety of his Whitehall apartments, accused Duchesse Mazarin of complicity in the famous plot, and even went so far as to say he had heard the Queen herself consent to the murder. At this King Charles was furious. He imprisoned Oates until the Commons, still credulous, clamoured for his release. Queen Catherine wept copiously at the idea that anyone could suspect her of plotting her husband's death, for apart from the monstrous treason of which she was simply not capable, she still loved him. Charles sprang to her defence. 'They think I have a mind to a new wife', he said, 'but for all that I will not see an innocent woman abused.' He told Burnet that he knew full well he had treated her abominably, and would not dream of abandoning her now. The King's steadfast adherence to decency saved the day, and for the first time since the crisis began, shifted the mood in favour of reflection. The House of Commons petitioned for the Queen's removal, but the House of Lords refused its support by a narrow margin.

Throughout all this, Louise remained as discreet and hidden as she could, but she was terrified of what might befall her, for she well knew that if the Queen herself could be accused, she was in a very precarious position and could easily fall prey to the howling mob. Barillon told Louis XIV that Louise was seriously thinking of escaping to France. 'There are many persons who are minded to name her in Parliament', he wrote, 'as conspiring against the Protestant religion for the King of France . . . Her presence here, she is afraid, must embarrass King Charles, and she would prefer to get away while he preserves some kind of feeling for her, than, by staying longer, to expose herself to the rage of a whole nation.' Louise and Catherine comforted each other in the midst of turmoil, while the King removed the French musicians he normally kept at Court, and Louise asked Barillon if he would give them lodging at the Embassy. It seemed a prudent thing to do in the circumstances.

As the terror abated, Charles took stock of the damage. He had fought almost alone for the preservation of common sense, against a campaign of crazed vilification which a less popular monarch could not have survived. The high favour he enjoyed with the people was his strongest card, and his sagacity in the face of crisis revealed a statesman-like security which his philandering with countless mistresses had tended to obscure in the public mind. There is no doubt he grieved as he watched the nation revert to the worst excesses of the Middle Ages. Signing the death warrants of indiscreet but innocent folk, he told Thomas Bruce, 'Let the blood lie on those who condemn them, for God knows I sign with tears in my eyes.'

In the months and years to follow, ripples of the Popish Terror continued to be felt, and Louise was not out of danger for a long time. In June 1680 Lord Shaftesbury appeared before the Court of the King's Bench in Westminster and demanded the indictment of the Duke of York. For good measure, he denounced the Papists and asked the tribunal to condemn the Duchess of Portsmouth as a public scandal. Louise was so frightened she fell ill. She had been careful enough to give guarded support for the Exclusion Bill, which sought to deprive the Duke of York his rightful succession to the throne, an act which must have caused her some distress when one remembers the enthusiasm with which she welcomed the provisions of the Treaty of Dover ten years earlier. She had wanted to bring the true faith to England, now she was having to pretend to fight for its prohibition, to save her own skin, and even then was named before a Grand Jury. Lord Chief Justice Scroggs, one of the cruellest judges during the Terror (he alone condemned twenty-one men to death) included the indictments on the list, then dismissed the jury before they had a chance to examine them.

At the same time, the House of Commons was invited to consider *Articles of High Treason and other High Crimes . . . against the Duchess of Portsmouth*, a document which specified Louise's intimate relations with the King and deplored her 'foul, nauseous, and contagious distempers'. Amongst other things, she was accused of employing a French Catholic confectioner in order to tempt the King into eating poisoned sweets. There was only one way in which the King could prevent this slanderous invention from being widely disseminated, as it would have been had the Articles of Treachery been discussed in the Commons: he dissolved Parliament. The finger was again pointed at

Louise, who was supposed to have bullied the King into this intemper-
ate act. Again thoroughly alarmed, Louise prepared to dismiss her
Catholic servants and repeated her desire to return to France.

Perhaps confused by her fears in these trying times, Louise showed
embarrassing signs of political naivety. She tried to emulate Charles's
pragmatism, and succeeded only in making herself look foolish and in
exasperating the French Embassy. She gave vocal support to William of
Orange, who had married Charles's niece Mary, then switched her
loyalty to the Duke of Monmouth when it looked as if he might have
the succession. Secretly she hoped that, if Monmouth's case could receive
serious consideration, why should not her son, the Duke of Richmond,
also be in line for the English throne? There was a moment when
Monmouth seemed perilously close to succeeding. The King fell dangerously ill after playing tennis in the cold at Windsor. The occasion
is worth recording if only to picture the reconciliation of Louise and
Nell Gwynn, who wept in each other's arms. But quinine restored
Charles to vigour, and Louise moved her allegiance to the Duke of
York. Charles showed no sign of being annoyed by this chameleon-like
behaviour, simply because he knew that the 'influence' of his mistress
counted for little, and he grew more and more dependent upon the
solace of her company. For the last five years, 'Fubs' was certainly
the most important woman in his life.

The French, however, under-rating Charles's wisdom, continued to
believe that Louise was an important barometer which should dictate
the direction of their policy. Barillon wrote to Louis XIV :

> I saw Madame de Portsmouth, to whom the King has confided all
> his affairs. She told me that if your Majesty would pay four millions
> a year for three years, the King would agree to carry out Your
> Majesty's wishes; but that without this sum it would be impossible
> for him to refuse to call Parliament. The King said to me last night
> that he was ashamed and that he felt a profound displeasure in
> having to traffic in this way with Your Majesty.

It is evident that Charles was using the French, not the other way
round; if they expressed confidence in the Duchess of Portsmouth, he
was quite happy to transmit his desires through her from time to time.

Louis XIV wrote to Louise to express 'the respect I bear towards you
and the pleasure I know you have in carefully fulfilling all you know of
my intentions and those of the King of Great Britain, my royal brother'.

That Louis should give her the ultimate accolade of addressing her as
'ma cousine' made her beam with pride. In French eyes she was virtually Queen of England and she imagined that henceforward no one
in London would dare to cross her. At the apogée of her power, Louise
now thought it would be safe for her to visit France without losing the
King of England's affection. She had emerged safely from a period of
intense danger, and was still the undisputed reigning *maîtresse en titre*.

*   *   *

At the beginning of 1682, doctors advised the Duchess of Portsmouth
that the general fragility of her health would benefit from taking the
waters at Bourbon, a fashionable spa in France noted for its restorative
powers in calming the nerves. Louise welcomed the opportunity, for
she still nursed one potent and unfulfilled ambition : to shine at the
most brilliant Court in the world, where, when she had quit France
twelve years before, she had been looked upon as a lowly and insignificant Maid of Honour, too humble to compete with the mighty. She
wanted now to have the great rank she had achieved recognised where
it really mattered, to dazzle her countrymen with the wealth she had
amassed and could display with pride. Charles and the Court were
due to go to Newmarket for the annual visit so Louise, who never really
cared much for country life, elected to take advantage of the King's absence in order to make her triumphant progress into France.

Elaborate plans were laid to ensure the Duchess travelled in suitable
style. A yacht was entirely refitted especially for her, and she set sail
from Greenwich in March with her sister the Countess of Pembroke
and her eleven-year-old son the Duke of Richmond, now a pretty lad
bearing a strong resemblance to the young Charles II whom the French
had last seen twenty-two years before. His presence alone would serve
to remind the Court how high in the world Louise de Kéroualle had
risen. Through Barillon, the King asked Louis XIV to receive his
mistress with the utmost favour :

He has charged me to supplicate Your Majesty [wrote Barillon] to
accord to her your protection, for the arrangement of her private
affairs in France. I turned the conversation to another subject, when
he spoke about her wish that your Majesty should withdraw the
domaine of Aubigny from the Crown to give it to her. But I made
him hope that Your Majesty would give her other marks of kindness.

The truth about her is, that she has shown great, constant, and intelligent zeal for Your Majesty's interests, and given me numberless useful hints and pieces of information.

In addition, Charles wrote asking that Louise be given the honour afforded to the Duchess of Cleveland at Versailles, the peerless privilege of sitting on a *tabouret* when she paid her respects to the Queen of France. He need not have worried. Louise was received not merely as a favourite, but with all the ceremony and multiple special attentions normally reserved for a visiting sovereign.

Paris was taken aback by the ostentatious display in which Louise now luxuriated. The English ambassador had leased for her a magnificent establishment to which she invited the cream of French society, making them gasp at the prodigal splendour of her entertainment. Whenever she went out, it was with four coaches and more than sixty horses, the coaches decorated with the royal arms, and the coachmen wearing Charles II's livery. She was overwhelmingly spendthrift, losing vast sums at the gaming tables without a trace of anxiety, dressed with a dazzling quantity of jewels. Nothing could be more calculated to astonish. Was not the Court of Charles II supposed to be beggarly? Had not the King himself been embarrassingly shabby? Surely it was true the English did not appreciate and could not afford style and elegance? Yet here was a calm, beautiful woman, glowing with satisfaction, haughty, regal, and spectacular with riches.

'There has never been a parallel for the treatment she meets with', wrote Saint-Simon. Louise was given every attention and fêted wherever she went. The Capucine nuns in the rue Saint-Honoré formed a procession to greet her, with Cross, holy water and incense, as if she were not only a Queen, but God's representative in England. With commendable reserve in the light of Louise's ecstatic account of her reception, King Charles wrote to King Louis with 'his best thanks for the kindness he had shown to the Duchess of Portsmouth'.

At the end of April, Louise went to her estates at Aubigny, which she had not seen before, then proceeded to take the waters at Bourbon. In June she was back in Paris, busily investing her fortune (she had not come to France simply to enjoy herself), and afterwards went to Brittany to visit her parents and buy back the Kéroualle estates which her hard-pressed father had had to sell. Her final stay in Paris took place in July, when she was smothered with yet more indications of esteem. The King gave her a pair of diamond ear-rings, the Queen took her out in her own carriage, and the former ambassador Colbert de Croissy arranged a sumptuous banquet in her honour, at which she was permitted to make her own seating plan. The homage paid her by Louis XIV was, in Barillon's words, 'like sunshine gilding and glorifying an insignificant object'.

Louise returned to London in glory at the end of July. Henceforth no one would dare treat her as anything less than a person of great consequence, clothed with the dignity of approval from Versailles. Everyone at Whitehall had heard of her success. The Duke of York, mindful of the future, became almost obsequiously friendly with her. Charles had not been able to meet her, but he had sent her the touching letter quoted earlier* which showed how much he had missed her. Burnet says that the King grew more demonstratively affectionate towards her, caressing her in public with a tenderness which courtiers could not remember having witnessed before. Louise could comfortably smile at Lord Sunderland's malicious remark a few months earlier : 'Are you stupid enough to let the King see he can live without you ?' he had asked. The answer was now manifest : he could not.

Charles took Barillon aside one day to confide that Louise and her son were the two people most dear to him in the world. As if to demonstrate that these were no empty words, the King piled unparalleled honours upon his son during the last four years of his reign. The boy had been Duke of Richmond since the age of three; he was made Master of the Horse when he was nine, and shortly afterwards he was invested a Knight of the Garter. Inspired by her respect for French traditions, Louise was responsible for an innovation at the Garter ceremony which continues to be observed to this day. It was customary for the garter ribbon to be hung around the neck, with the St George medallion in front, but Louise made the little boy wear the Garter over his left shoulder, so delighting the King that he directed the new style should be adopted by all Knights of the Garter from that moment. Next, at the invitation of the second city in the kingdom, the young Duke was made High Steward of York, letters patent conferring the honour being delivered to the proud mother in a golden box.

The ambitions of the Duchess of Portsmouth for rank and wealth were insatiable. As soon as one honour had been granted, she busied herself thinking of another. The King had been adroit in providing for his offspring by securing marriages to wealthy heiresses, but Richmond remained unbetrothed. At ten, he risked being left on the shelf.

* See page 140.

Louise, aiming for the highest, wanted her son to be married to the richest heiress in the kingdom, the unfortunate 'Carrots' of Northumberland, Lady Elizabeth Percy, who was pursued by every eligible bachelor as well as every greedy old man, and was destined to be married three times to three virtual strangers before she was sixteen. The Percy family had died out with her father, the last Earl of Northumberland, in 1670, making the girl sole owner of Alnwick Castle, Syon House, and most of the county of Northumberland. The Duchess of Cleveland had more than once sought her hand in favour of her sons, with a conspicuous lack of success. Louise was also to remain unsatisfied, for the surviving Countess of Northumberland, Carrots's mother, detested her and would not countenance such a match.

What would happen to all Louise's property and wealth in France if she were suddenly to die? As foreigners could not inherit French possessions, and the Duke of Richmond was indubitably a foreigner, there was no route by which the son could be heir to the mother. This state of affairs needed to be altered. Louis XIV was approached with the problem which called for an obvious solution; the French King signed letters of naturalisation, permitting 'his dear and beloved cousin, Prince Charles Lennox, Duke of Richmond, to enjoy, in the same manner as his mother, the privileges, franchises and liberties which the nobility of our realm enjoy'.

Only one prize remained to be won. Louise owned the Aubigny property, had been treated like a French duchess on her recent visit home, had sat on the inestimable *tabouret*, but the fact remained that she was not a French duchess at all; she still wanted to sit on the *tabouret* by right, not by permission. King Charles made it known that he would be deeply obliged if Louis XIV would surrender the duchy of Aubigny to his mistress, with reversion to her son and his future issue. Barillon thought this was going too far, but Louis no longer had any hesitation in acceding to the request. When the news arrived in London, Charles ran across the room to tell Louise, who was congratulated by the whole Court on this, the pinnacle of her achievements. What a long way she had travelled, and what a change in the fortunes of her son, whose paternity had not even been acknowledged when he was born. In consequence of this gift, while the title of Portsmouth died with Louise, the title of Aubigny has passed down with her descendants, and the present Duke of Richmond is also Duc d'Aubigny in France.

Having settled into a comfortable *quasi*-domestic life with the ageing King, even so far as to assume the rôle of hostess at grand banquets while Queen Catherine withdrew to the background, Louise threatened in the last few years to upset everything with a surprising, uncharacteristic love affair. She was, as we have said, a faithful woman, not the easygoing whore her enemies attempted to depict; in twelve years she did not stray, gave no cause for King Charles to suspect her of emotional disloyalty. Now thirty-five years old, she was entering a period when most women, unsure of their attractiveness, are especially vulnerable to flattery.

One of the men who had been impressed by the Duchess of Portsmouth's victorious visit to France in 1682 was the Grand Prior of France, Philippe de Vendôme, a great-grandson of Henri IV through a bastard line. His mother was Laura Mancini, sister to Hortense Mancini, Duchesse Mazarin. From an early age, Philippe had been blessed with ravishing good looks, of which he took full advantage. He had been the lover of Madame de Ludres when he was eighteen, and subsequently won over Ninon de Lenclos. At twenty-eight he was an experienced and vicious creature who boasted of the number of women he had bedded (not to mention the men and the boys), an atheist, a rake, an unscrupulous manipulator. He had not been to bed sober in his life, he said, celebrating his depravity like a medal. His brother was the even more horrid Duc de Vendôme, who spattered his clothes with foodstains, and received visitors sitting on the lavatory. Philippe had no need of such an example; from being the handsome spoiled darling of the Court, he had degenerated into an odious and arrogant creature. That he, of all people, should succeed in tempting the fastidious Louise was a terrible misfortune.

Vendôme came to London in the spring of 1683 on the pretext of visiting his aunt Hortense. He lost no time in courting Louise. At first, Charles was tolerant of the flirtation, understanding that for Louise there was comfort in the company of one of her countrymen, with whom she could converse in French and exchange gossip about Versailles. But when it became obvious to all that the pair had exceeded the demands of friendship, Charles's jealousy was aroused as never before. Normally indifferent to the infidelities of a mistress, the King had not been worked into a frenzy by Barbara's gross behaviour except in so far as it embarrassed him. This was different. Not since Lucy Walter had Charles discovered his emotions to be so possessively and deeply attached.

The King sent Lord Sunderland to convey his displeasure, forbidding Vendôme to visit the Duchess of Portsmouth forthwith. A few days elapsed, during which Vendôme arrogantly defied the order and continued to be present at Louise's apartments. The King then commanded the Grand Prior to leave England, sending word through the harassed ambassador Barillon, who had somehow to respect the man's high rank and at the same time intimate that he was unwelcome. Vendôme once more refused obedience, saying that he would not even consider leaving unless he heard the order from the King's own mouth.

Louise was by this time thoroughly alarmed. She realised her mistake in giving herself to such a vulgarian who she feared might disclose the contents of letters which had passed between them. Not only did she risk losing Charles's affection, but she could also arouse the far less tolerant notice of Louis XIV. She implored Barillon to do what he could to get rid of the Grand Prior.

Several times Charles refused an audience, but eventually gave in to Barillon's imprecations. He told Vendôme quite bluntly that he must leave England, and received the astonishing reply that Vendôme did not intend to leave, owing to the uncertainty of his reception in France. The whole Court gasped at the insolence of a man who dared to disobey a reigning monarch at his own Court. In the end, Charles had to resort to unmannerly dismissal, treating Vendôme virtually as a criminal. He sent the Lieutenant of the Guard to give Vendôme two days to get out of the country, or he would be escorted to his ship by force. Obviously, the usually amiable unruffled King had lost his patience in the face of such brazen impertinence.

Vendôme said that he would retire to the country, or perhaps leave on the understanding that he could come back whenever he wished. Louise, frightened of the possible consequences which a fully-fledged row might involve, begged the King to agree to this compromise. Charles would not, however, have his authority challenged. Eventually the creature went, after receiving word from his brother the Duc de Vendôme that he should return to France, and must not say anything against the Duchess of Portsmouth if he did not wish to incur the French King's displeasure. Louise sighed with relief, Charles's irritability subsided. What no one dared to admit was that the Grand Prior had left England not in obedience to the voiced command of King Charles, but as the result of the implied order of King Louis.

Louise was not required to pay for her indiscretion. On the contrary, Charles gave every sign of happiness that his beloved Fubs had been relieved of a burden for which she bore no real responsibility. All the blame attached to the abysmal Vendôme. Charles was not a man to be blinded by his jealousy; his maturity of attitude made him perfectly aware of the frailty to which a flattered woman is subject. One of the reasons why he adored Louise so much as they grew older was her sheer femininity, a distinction which set her apart from all his previous lovers. Lucy, Barbara and Nell had in their different ways been aggressive creatures with minds and wills of their own. They had commanded the King's interest by their ebullient personalities, whereas Louise had earned his love by her absence of any masculine attribute whatever. Quiet and subdued, sweet, deferential and loyal, she was many men's ideal mate, a pretty, alluring, uncomplicated individual who would come when she was called and not interrupt the pleasantness of life with unnecessary opinions or wild tempers. It was part of her weakness to fall an unwitting victim to an adventurer, and Charles was not about to chastise her for it. His openly expressed affection increased rather than diminished after the Vendôme episode.

The qualities which endeared Louise to the King all derive from her fragile femininity. Unlike many of the great Frenchwomen of the seventeenth century, she did not read books, philosophise or indulge in intellectual debate. Her letters are dull, betraying no sense of style or appreciation of phrasing nor, for that matter, any desire to impress. She appears to have had no pretensions to intelligence, being quite happy to make her mark with jewels and rank. Docile, lazy, given to tears as her only articulate expression, Louise de Kéroualle devoted all her energies to one overmastering ambition – to be the best-kept mistress in Christendom. She was, as Miss Delpech has pointed out, 'greater than nature intended'. Her more positive qualities were also feminine – gentle unimaginative kindness and instinctive compassion. She was a dutiful and affectionate mother to her only son.

Charles understood her well. Embarrassed by Lucy, exasperated by Barbara, amused by Nell, he reserved for Louise his most attentive fondness, for she was the wife that Catherine of Braganza might have been had she been able to give him an heir.

*   *   *

On 1 February 1685, there took place at Whitehall the celebrated evening party which John Evelyn so vividly deplored.

I can never forget the inexpressible luxury and profaneness, gaming
and all dissoluteness, as it were total forgetfulness of God, [he wrote]
the King sitting and toying with his concubines, Portsmouth, Cleveland and Mazarin, a French boy singing love-songs in that glorious
gallery, whilst about twenty of the great courtiers and other dissolute persons were at basset round a large table, a bank of at least
two thousand in gold before them.

This scene which so excited Evelyn's *pudeur* involved no more repre-
hensible activity than had been a regular feature of Court life for years,
even if it was the Sabbath; indeed, it was a remarkably innocent affair
compared with the nocturnal corridor-creeping of earlier days. We
now find it rather a touching picture of autumnal amiability in a
middle-aged man still young at heart and still able to surround himself
with former loves on friendly terms. It was to be the last pleasant
evening at Whitehall.

The next morning, the King's good humour had evaporated. He
looked worryingly pale, and paced up and down as if preoccupied. Once
he nearly fell, for no apparent reason. Sitting in the barber's chair
for his daily shave, the King suddenly collapsed in a fit, his mouth
foaming and distorted. Immediately, the physicians lanced a vein, bled
him profusely, poured medicaments down his throat. When he came to
he asked for his wife; Catherine was already there, rubbing his feet.
Everyone pretended nothing drastic was happening, but the King,
ever an enemy of humbug, was the first to acknowledge that he was
dying.

For the rest of the day, a veritable army of doctors applied every
conceivable remedy to the King's weak body. Privacy was denied him.
He managed to survive the night in spite of their attentions, to be
tormented again throughout the following day in front of a muttering
crowd of courtiers. By 4 February he seemed better, but on Thursday
5 February, Charles broke out in a horrible sweat and complained of
intense pain. As the news passed through the palace that the doctors
had given up hope, men of all degrees openly wept.

Protestant bishops gathered round the bed. Louise, whom decency
bade should remain apart in her own rooms, told Barillon that that
King was at heart a Catholic, and that some way must be found to
administer the last rites before it was too late. Barillon then took the
Duke of York aside to urge him into some prompt gesture for the King's
soul. While a crowd pressed at the open bedroom door, York knelt

beside the bed for a quarter of an hour, whispering into his brother's ear. The King's words in reply were heard distinctly only once. 'With all my heart', he said.

Urgently and secretly, a priest had to be found. Fortunately, Father Huddlestone was at hand, was ushered in heavily disguised through a side door and brought to the royal presence to administer the sacrament. The King confessed his sins, and hoped to be forgiven by all those whom he had offended. Then he received Extreme Unction. When the throng was again admitted, his life was ebbing away. The Queen came in at midnight and knelt weeping beside the bed until she could bear the ordeal no longer and was led away in a faint. She sent word to beg his forgiveness. 'Alas, poor woman!' said Charles, 'She asks my pardon? I beg hers with all my heart. Take her back that answer.'

Having given his blessing to all his sons (except Monmouth), the King asked his brother to look after Queen Catherine, his children, and Louise, not forgetting Nelly. Then he apologised for being so long in dying. The Duke of York was beside himself with grief.

The next morning, Charles said, 'Open the curtains that I may once more see day.' As the early hours passed, he sank into the deepest slumber. By noon he was dead.

When Louise was given the news in her apartments, she broke down and wept copiously. We do not know if the new King James II told her then of Charles's moving reference to her on his death-bed. 'I have always loved her', he had said, 'and I die loving her.' As soon as she recovered, aware that the day's event had plunged her at a stroke into insignificance, she gathered her belongings and retired to the French Embassy.

Louise felt sorely treated after the death of Charles II. Her interests were neglected, her debts allowed to soar. She had expected to continue to receive £25,000–£30,000 a year from the Irish taxes, and further to benefit from the confiscated estate of Lord Grey, which Charles had intended to settle on Grey's heirs until Louise prised it into her own hands. To the former, James II turned a deaf ear, and as for the latter, it was her son Richmond who would receive the revenues – when he was older. James allowed her a miserable £2000 a year, with £3000 a year for her son, whom he immediately deprived of the post of Grand Equerry, conferred upon him by his father. Louise was furious. Did the new King not realise who she was? Did he not remember that she had been the means by which the pockets of England had been filled from the coffers of France? Were it not for her, England would have starved. For once in her life, Louise spoke bluntly and with passion.

James II soon changed his tune. He was well aware that he would still need France as a source of finance; it would be folly to upset the Frenchwoman. Louise finally accepted that her son would not make a very good equerry at the age of thirteen, and proclaimed her desire to return to France. There was nothing for her in England any more. The hatred of the English for this foreigner, who was blamed for all the ills which befell the country and roundly chastised for her friendship with rogues like Rochester and Sunderland, grew more bitter now that her one value, that of making King Charles happy, had disappeared.

Louis XIV told her that, in consideration of her zeal in his service over the years, he would offer his protection 'en quelque endroit de mon Royaume où vous choississiez votre retraite'.*

Barillon wrote to Louis XIV to announce her arrival, warning that her requirements included payment of all her debts and the provision of a dwelling-house in Paris. James II promised to keep on her apartments in Whitehall in case she ever desired to come back. Secretly, he hoped never to see her again.

In August 1685, Louise set sail for France with an armada of ships to carry her furniture, jewellery, all her worldly goods, which explains why there is nothing of her at Goodwood, the home of her descendants in England. She also took her son the Duke of Richmond.

In Paris also Louise was made to realise her changed position. No longer was she treated like a Queen, no longer could she run up debts with indifference. Still, she was slow to learn the lesson which circumstances imposed. She continued to gamble recklessly and to play the part of a *grande dame*, until she was rudely reminded to temper her behaviour. She was once rash enough to speak ill of Madame de Maintenon, a folly which Louis XIV could not tolerate. Letters were issued banishing her into exile, to be reprieved only on the intervention of her old friend Honoré de Courtin, who bravely pointed out that her great services to France in the past earned her some leniency. The King threw the *lettre de cachet* on the fire.

In 1686–87 Louise spent almost a year in England, and was there again in 1688 for the marriage of her niece Charlotte, the daughter of Henriette and Lord Pembroke, to the notorious Judge Jeffreys. She

* In whatever corner of my kingdom wherein you should choose to retire.

cut a pathetic figure, vainly clinging to past glory only to find that her jewels did not impress and her opinion was not sought. Back in France, she was forced to recognise that her bleak future was destined to keep her lonely, bored, and for the most part unnoticed. She yet had almost fifty years of life left to her.

With the Revolution of 1688 all her sources of income in England dried up. Louis XIV came to the rescue with generous pensions assigned to both her and the Duke of Richmond, but they were insufficient to meet the huge appetite of her extravagance. In 1691, a disastrous fire at Whitehall destroyed her apartments there and consumed what remained in England of her fabulous furniture. Slowly, Louise descended into poverty.

When her son absconded from the French army to go over to the Prince of Orange, Louise admitted that she was ready to die of despair. Again, Louis XIV sustained her by assigning the miscreant's pension to her favour. Throughout her middle age, Louise's energies were bent upon one object – to escape a horde of creditors who threatened to have bailiffs confiscate her belongings. She appealed successfully to Louis XIV to have the creditors ordered by royal decree to desist from pursuing her for a year. As she was unwilling or unable to make ends meet, the order had to be renewed time and again to keep the enemy at bay. It is not easy to summon sympathy for an unhappy woman who made others suffer for her own selfishness, however unconscious it may have been. As Forneron has written, 'Louis suspended the course of justice, ruined tradesmen who sold in good faith, and shook the security of commercial transactions. She had only to write to him, that the present state of her affairs did not allow her to pay her debts, and the sovereign's hand was stretched out to drive away her creditors.' In the old days, letters had been unnecessary; King Charles would remove her embarrassments with a wave of the hand. Now she, Duchesse d'Aubigny in France, was reduced to the humiliation of writing from her estates in the country in this vein :

I came here in the hope of finding some peace and quiet; but the misery all around is so dreadful that no one can find a single sou, there is nothing with which to buy a single seed for the sowing; and if you don't take pity on me, my fields will not be sown at all.

Thus in a letter to Desmarets, the Controller-General of Finance. Here is another such :

I remain, Monsieur, sufficiently unhappy that you do not seem to have any concern or humanity for my cruel condition and dire need.

In spite of all this, and of being required to live in the country because she could not afford town life any more, we hear that she bought land to augment her status and had the course of a river diverted to avoid the sound of a water-mill which disturbed her sleep.

In 1697 Louise obtained leave to visit England again. William III let it be known that he would prevent her landing. Nevertheless, she was in England in 1698, taking the opportunity to remind King William that she had urged Charles II to allow William's marriage with Mary, and had done everything in her power to support the exclusion of James II and the Duke of Monmouth from the throne of England. Her protestations went unheeded. The fiercely Protestant William was unlikely to think well of an avowed Papist who had regarded England simply as a purse to be looted.

Louise did not move from Aubigny in the last ten years of her life. She abandoned the house in Paris which she had taken, at what is now numbers 3 and 5 Quai Voltaire, and watched Aubigny fall into neglect, unable to meet any bill for repairs. She went so far as to petition the Crown to pay for repairs, claiming that as *Duchesse* she should not be responsible for the upkeep of what had been Crown property. All logic must have deserted her in the face of threatening poverty. In 1714, she was obliged to sell the lands and Seigneury of Kéroualle.

Her heart at least emerges, shadowy but secure, in this painful autumn. She corresponded regularly with her grandson, who was to be the 2nd Duke of Richmond, her letters showing a fondness and loving interest which do her credit. She gave money and time, lavishly as always, to an order of nuns in Brittany. Voltaire saw her in extreme old age and tells us that she retained her beauty. On 14 November 1734, she died at the age of eighty-five and was buried in the Church of the Barefoot Carmelites in Paris. She had survived into an age which already considered her an historical figure.

Apart from portraits, the only trace of Louise de Kéroualle at Goodwood is indirect. In an attempt to exercise some control over the errant conduct of her son, she had sent over to England an old friend and servant called Monsieur Carné, to act as some kind of guiding influence. In 1743 her grandson built a small house on the Goodwood estate and called it Carné's Seat, with a beautiful view of the Sussex countryside.

It is now the modest home of the present Duke and Duchess of Richmond.

*   *   *

SOURCES FOR CHAPTER FOUR

Bryan BEVAN, *Charles the Second's French Mistress* (1972)
BOSSUET, *Oraisons Funèbres*
Arthur BRYANT, *King Charles II* (1931)
Hester CHAPMAN, *Privileged Persons* (1966)
Sir G. CLARK, *The Later Stuarts 1660–1714* (1955)
Jeanine DELPECH, *The Duchess of Portsmouth* (1953)
John EVELYN, *Diary*
H. FORNERON, *Louise de Kéroualle, Duchess of Portsmouth* (1887)
Goodwood Papers, West Sussex County Record Office, Chichester.
C. H. HARTMANN, *Charles II and Madame* (1934)
C. H. HARTMANN, *The Vagabond Duchess* (1926)
Hortense MANCINI, DUCHESSE MAZARIN, *Les Illustres Adventurièrs, où Mémoires d'Hortense et de Marie Mancini* (ed. Carno, 1929).
DUC DE SAINT-SIMON, *Memoirs*
H. Noel WILLIAMS, *Rival Sultanas* (1915)

CHAPTER FIVE
Destinies

THE DUKE OF MONMOUTH After the accession of James II, Lucy Walter's only son led a rebellion against the Crown, claiming that his supposed legitimacy made him the rightful heir to Charles II. In fact, Monmouth was a compliant tool in the hands of unscrupulous politicians, rather than the purposeful instigator of any solid plan. As soon as the Monmouth forces invaded England, and had the feeble Duke proclaimed 'King Monmouth' at Taunton on 20 June 1685, all his English titles and dignities were cancelled by Act of Attainder, and a price placed on his head. The rebellion was over within a matter of days. On 5 July, Monmouth's troops were routed, and he himself fled into the countryside, disguised as a farmer. For three days he wandered, until he was discovered hiding in a ditch by a search party, who conveyed him to the Tower of London.

Whilst imprisoned, Monmouth put his name to a document which was intended to settle once and for all the question of his birth.

I declare yt ye Title of King was forct upon mee [he wrote], & yt it was very much contrary to my opinion when I was proclaimed. For ye Satisfaction of the world, I doe declare that ye late King told me that hee was never married to my Mother.

With rather too keen an eye for the omissions in diplomatic language, some historians have pointed out that this statement merely testifies to what King Charles is reported to have said, not to what the Duke of Monmouth himself believed. How on earth could the King have said anything else? The defenders of Monmouth's legitimacy maintain that the question must remain open.

Hours after signing the document, Monmouth was dead, the sorry victim of his own vanity and irresolution. He was executed for treason in a scene of grisly horror. Pressed by the bishops to repent of his rebellion, he refused to use that word, implying legal justification for the invasion while expressing sorrow to have caused so much bloodshed. In spite of their pestering, he would budge no further, and displayed such strange laudable courage as death approached that one wondered why he could not have discovered such qualities earlier. 'I will make no speeches,' he said, 'I come to die . . . I shall die like a lamb.'

Monmouth declined the customary blindfold and tying of hands. Of his own will, he placed his head on the block. He turned and asked to see the axe, then ran his thumb along the edge. 'It is not sharp enough', he said, but the executioner reassured him, and he turned his head back to face the ground.

The first blow merely wounded the Duke on the neck. He looked at his executioner, and said nothing. Nor did the second stroke sever his head. He crossed his legs. At the third stroke, seeing the wretched man was still alive, the executioner understandably lost his nerve and threw down the axe. Monmouth's head was finally cut off with a knife.

Although Monmouth's progeny could not inherit the English titles, which had been forfeited, his Scottish titles have passed down to the present day. Thus he was succeeded as 2nd Duke of Buccleuch by his grandson, and is currently represented by the 9th Duke of Buccleuch, born in 1923. H.R.H. Princess Alice, Dowager Duchess of Gloucester, is another descendant, being a daughter of the 7th Duke of Buccleuch.

The subsidiary English titles (Earl of Doncaster and Baron Scott of Tindal) were restored to the family by Act of Parliament in 1742, though the dukedom of Monmouth remained under attainder, presumably because there was then living an Earl of Monmouth with whom confusion might have caused embarrassment. It is still within the Queen's power to reverse this attainder and restore the historic dukedom in favour of Lucy's senior male descendant.

CATHERINE PEGGE, who bore two of Charles II's bastards, was married in 1667 to Sir Edward Green, Bart., and died the following year. Her daughter Catherine, by the King, died unmarried. Her daughter by Sir Edward died in 1717.

THE EARL OF PLYMOUTH King Charles's son by Catherine Pegge was known as Charles Fitzcharles, but more generally called 'Don Carlos'. In 1675 he was created Earl of Plymouth. After serving in the Dutch army as a volunteer, Plymouth married in 1678 Lady Bridget

Osborne, daughter of the 1st Duke of Leeds (known to history under his more familiar name of Danby, Charles II's Lord Treasurer). The Earl died at the siege of Tangier in 1680, of a 'bloody flux'. He was only twenty-three years old. The earldom of Plymouth was thereupon extinct, and the first and only bearer of this creation of the title lies buried in Westminster Abbey.

LADY SHANNON Her daughter by King Charles, Charlotte, born in 1650 or 1651 first married James Howard, and second, the Earl of Yarmouth. She died childless in 1684 at her house in Pall Mall, aged thirty-four.

ROGER PALMER (Earl of Castlemaine) As a known Papist, Roger was an early victim of the Popish Terror. On 24 October 1678 he was accused by Titus Oates before the House of Commons of being a Jesuit priest and of having wished success to the Popish Plot within Oates's hearing. Sent to the Tower of London in October, he was released on bail the following January without having been formally charged. Roger used his time in prison profitably to write a book about the Terror and the trials which it spawned. In November 1679 he was again pursued by Oates, and again sent to the Tower on a charge of High Treason. Once more he was released.

With James II, Castlemaine naturally stood in high favour. He was appointed a Privy Councillor and entrusted with an embassy to Rome. On 28 October the House of Commons impeached him for High Treason, charging him with 'endeavouring to reconcile this kingdom to the see of Rome'. Since that was precisely the mission which James II had ordered him to make, one was bound to ask to whom was the act treasonable? Off once more went Roger to the Tower, to be released once more on bail in 1690.

Castlemaine died on 21 July 1705, thus leaving his estranged wife free to tie the knot (or so she thought) with Beau Feilding. He was buried at Welshpool; his will left everything to his presumed daughter, the Countess of Sussex.

ANNE PALMER (Countess of Sussex) Barbara Castlemaine's first child, the daughter of either Roger Palmer (whose name she bore) or Charles II (who claimed her), the friend of Duchesse Mazarin and the victim of Ralph Montagu's seduction, was born in 1661, married Lord

Dacre (Earl of Sussex) in 1675, and died in 1722. Her sons having died young, the earldom of Sussex became extinct, but the Dacre title passed on through her second daughter, whose direct descendants today are Viscount Hampden, and his niece the Baroness Dacre, wife of William Douglas-Home.

THE DUKE OF SOUTHAMPTON Barbara's second child, Charles Fitzroy, born 1662, though his father was Charles II, was passed off as Roger Palmer's son until 1670 and therefore bore the title subsidiary to Earl of Castlemaine, namely Lord Limerick. He was created Duke of Southampton in 1675, and inherited the dukedom of Cleveland from his mother in 1709. He had an uneventful life. He married twice, having three sons and three daughters by his second marriage, but the Cleveland and Southampton titles were extinct with the death of his eldest son in 1774 (the other boys died unmarried). The dukedom of Cleveland was however re-created in the nineteenth century, in favour of a descendant of one of his daughters, to be extinct again in 1891.

THE DUKE OF GRAFTON Henry Fitzroy, Barbara's second son, was created Duke of Grafton in 1675. He was the most accomplished of the family, and his descendants have continued to be prominent. Grafton was made Vice-Admiral of England in 1682, and was Lord High Constable of England at the Coronation of James II. He commanded the King's army against the invasion led by his half-brother the Duke of Monmouth. Deserting the Stuarts to lend support to William of Orange, Grafton was fighting with William's forces when he was mortally wounded at the siege of Cork, and died at the age of twenty-seven.

His son the 2nd Duke was, as we have seen, kindly disposed towards his grandmother Barbara, but otherwise not much admired; he was variously called a 'booby', a 'slobberer' and 'totally illiterate'. He did however build Euston Road in London. His grandson, 3rd Duke of Grafton, was Prime Minister from 1767 to 1770, making time when out of office to beget fourteen legitimate and eighteen illegitimate children. The line continues to the present day, with the 11th Duke of Grafton still living in a somewhat diminished version of Euston Hall in Norfolk. He is one of the most active and responsible peers of the realm.

The title of Southampton was resurrected for a grandson of the 2nd Duke of Grafton, who became Baron Southampton by a creation of

1780. His descendant is the 5th Baron, but he prefers to be known simply as Charles Fitzroy, having disclaimed the use of his title in 1964. He cannot however disclaim his descent from Barbara Palmer and King Charles II.

Yet another offshoot of the same family is Robert Fitzroy, Viscount Daventry.

THE DUKE OF NORTHUMBERLAND George Fitzroy, Barbara's third son, was created Duke of Northumberland in 1683. John Evelyn regarded him as 'the most accomplished and worth owning' of Charles II's children, 'a young gentleman of good capacity, well-bred, civil and modest . . . extraordinarily handsome and well-shaped'. In 1686, he was 'bubbled into marriage' with one Catherine Lucy, the heiress of a poultry merchant, having first kidnapped her with the help of his brother Southampton. King James II was said to be enraged by the marriage. He, too, deserted James II for William of Orange. He married again in 1715, but died without heirs in 1716 and was buried in Westminster Abbey. (The present Duke of Northumberland descends from a creation made in 1766, and has nothing whatever to do with Charles II and Barbara.)

CHARLOTTE FITZROY This was Barbara's second daughter, who in 1674 married Sir Edward Lee, Bart., thereupon ennobled as Earl of Litchfield. Though Charlotte produced thirteen sons before her death in 1718, this was not sufficient to secure the Litchfield line, which was extinct in 1776 with the death of the 4th Earl. But the blood of Charlotte Fitzroy flows through a female line to the present day, in the veins of the 20th Viscount Dillon.

BARBARA FITZROY The Duchess of Cleveland's daughter by John Churchill, 1st Duke of Marlborough, having had a child by the Earl of Arran (later Duke of Hamilton), retired to a nunnery where she was known as Sister Benedicta. She rose to become Prioress of the institution, at Pontoise, and died in 1737. Her son Charles Hamilton, brought up in Chiswick by his grandmother Barbara, eventually settled in Switzerland (as 'Count of Arran') and devoted himself to classical studies. He died in Paris in 1754 and was buried in Montmartre. He had a son, who died in 1800, but it is difficult to trace his descendants further.

THE DUKE OF ST ALBANS Nell's elder and only surviving son prayed with his half-brothers at the death-bed of Charles II in 1685. Only weeks before he had been appointed Hereditary Grand Falconer of England, with reversion to his male heirs. The Duke continued to live at 79 Pall Mall until he was forced to sell the house in 1694. On 17 April of that same year, he married Diana de Vere, daughter of the 20th and last Earl of Oxford, and heiress to one of the greatest families in the land. Unfortunately, the greatness of her name was not reflected in her dowry, most of the family wealth having been squandered by the 17th Earl. (The 20th Earl of Oxford's first wife, incidentally, was Anne Bayning, a sister of Barbara Villiers's mother Mary Bayning.) St Albans's early career was in the army, which he relinquished on his marriage to take up a more lucrative appointment as Lord of the Bedchamber. Like his half-brother, he had deserted the Jacobite cause to support William of Orange against the Stuarts. He died in 1726, aged fifty-six.

The Duke assured the perpetuity of Nell Gwynn's line by having eight sons by his beautiful wife, with the result that there are now hundreds of people who can claim descent from the union of the King and Nelly. In 1901 a list was drawn up showing 311 such persons, a number which by now might well be doubled. They comprise a fittingly motley crowd of Duchesses. Countesses and commoners. Nell's senior descendant is the 13th Duke of St Albans, who came to the title in 1964 after a varied career in the Intelligence Service during the Second World War (for which he was decorated) and in the Central Office of Information. An active City gentleman, he is unusual among dukes in having no landed estate and being dependent upon salary or wise investment of initially small capital. He lived in a leasehold house in Chelsea, overlooking the Albert Bridge, but now spends much of his time abroad.

It is a paradox that neither King Charles's nor Nell Gwynn's ancestry is remembered in the family name – de Vere Beauclerk. Beauclerk is the name which the King gave to his infant son (most of the other bastards were allowed the name of Fitzroy, though not all of them used it), while de Vere recalls the ancestry of the Earls of Oxford, who came to England with the Conquest in 1066. De Vere Gardens in Kensington likewise reminds us of this illustrious heritage, as does the popular area of London known as Earls Court, which occupies the site of the Earl of Oxford's manor house. The Duke's grandson is Lord de Vere.

THE DUKE OF RICHMOND Shortly after he arrived in Paris with his mother in 1685, the young Duke was ceremoniously received by Louis XIV, who was most anxious that he should be formally admitted into the Catholic faith. The Duchess of Portsmouth being more than agreeable to the plan, Richmond was given the necessary instructions and became a Catholic a few weeks after his arrival, on 21 October 1685. The very next day, Louis XIV put his signature to the fiercely anti-Protestant revocation of the Edict of Nantes, so the conversion may be said to have taken place in the nick of time. Richmond was handsomely treated by Louis XIV and acquitted himself well in the French army, first as *aide-de-camp* to the Duc d'Orléans, and then as commander of his own cavalry regiment. But as he grew to adulthood, he determined to manage his own destiny. He left France secretly, turned up in England to give allegiance to William of Orange, and married Anne Bellasis who gave him three children and secured the succession of the Richmond line. It was he who in 1720 bought Goodwood House, which has been the seat of the Dukes of Richmond ever since, and is currently the home of the heir to the title, Lord March.

Richmond lost no time in renouncing his Catholicism, to be reconverted to the Anglican church in a ceremony which took place at Lambeth Palace on 15 May 1692. It is unfair to accuse him of tergiversation, for he had been a mere thirteen years old when he embraced Catholicism, far too young to be held responsible for such a step.

Richmond led a wayward life which caused many to mutter reproaches and to lament the fate which brought him from a handsome young man to the ravages of a dissolute life. But the evidence is scanty, and his wife certainly remained loyal and defensive. He died in 1723 and is buried in the family vault at Goodwood.

Of the various families which descend from Charles II to the present day, Richmond's is the only one which has travelled in a direct line from father to son through nine generations.

MOLL DAVIS It is not known when Moll Davis died. She had the distinction of bearing the last of Charles II's fourteen bastards, born on 16 October 1673, two years after Louise de Kéroualle had established herself as *maîtresse en titre*. This was Lady Mary Tudor, who married three times and died in Paris in 1726. Her first husband was the Earl of Derwentwater, by whom she had three sons, two of whom died tragically on Tower Hill owing to their Jacobite sympathies. The eldest son, 3rd Earl of Derwentwater, was a simple, earnest and admirable young man, much beloved by all who knew him, and a devout Catholic. He held a command in the Jacobite army, was arrested and found guilty of High Treason, and despite entreaties to the King from an impressive number of people, he was beheaded in 1716, aged twenty-six. The *aurora borealis* shone especially bright that night, and is still known in some parts of Cumberland as 'Lord Derwentwater's Lights'. Derwentwater's brother was likewise arrested and sentenced, but managed to escape to join the Stuart family in Europe. When he returned to England in 1746, he was condemned to death under the sentence passed thirty years before, and though technically not a nobleman (the titles having been attained) he was granted a nobleman's death by beheading. Thus two of Moll Davis's grandchildren ended on the scaffold. The male line of her issue came to an end in 1814. However, the hapless third Earl had a daughter, who married the 8th Baron Petre in 1732 and is the ancestress of the 17th and present Baron. So Moll Davis's and Charles II's blood continues in the Petre family.

LA BELLE STUART Frances Stuart, Duchess of Richmond (old creation), Duchess of Lennox, settled down quite sensibly in her maturity after a somewhat vapid youth. She remained for many years at Court, attending both the *accouchement* of Mary of Modena in 1688 and the coronation of Queen Anne. She died in 1702, without issue, and was buried in the Henry VII chapel in Westminster Abbey. Her will contained some curious bequests to ladies who were charged therewith to look after her cats. She left to her nephew, the Earl of Blantyre, the estate of Lethington with the request that it should thenceforth be called 'Lennox love to Blantyre'. It is at Haddington, not far from Edinburgh, and is now the seat of the Duke of Hamilton; it is still called 'Lennoxlove'.

QUEEN CATHERINE OF BRAGANZA Overwhelmed with grief at Charles II's death, Catherine retired to her bed at Whitehall where she remained for two months in a room made gloomy with black drapes and pale, barely flickering candles. She then removed to Somerset House, staying from time to time at her own little retreat in Hammersmith, where she had established a convent of nuns. Never ostentatious, she spent the years of widowhood dressed with a spartan simplicity which made the resplendence of the mistresses in their heyday the more meretricious. Catherine was not treated as a person of great consequence in subsequent reigns. She became difficult in her dealings with William of Orange, and 1692 she left the country for good, to return to Portugal, declining to visit Versailles and Louis XIV *en route*. Back home, she lived as quiet a life as she had done before she ever left Portugal, with a household reduced to the barest minimum and in an atmosphere rendered austere by her unrelenting piety. She acted as regent for her brother King Pedro, and died of colic in 1705. As we have said, she is responsible for making tea-drinking popular in England.

HORTENSE MANCINI (Duchess Mazarin) After Charles II's death, Hortense dried her tears and resumed her life of indomitable frivolity. Still she was unconventional, still she beguiled everyone in sight, trailing lovers of both sexes, giving huge parties, riding at five in the morning, playing with her dog, her cat, her parrot, even once piercing the ears of her father confessor so that he might wear the ear-rings she gave him. Nothing ordinary or prosaic happened to her, every move she made was lit with the *éclat* of a firework display. After an affair with the Swedish Baron Banier, her nephew the Chevalier de Soissons came to England, fell ridiculously in love with her, fought a duel with poor Banier and killed him. Madame de Sévigné said with some justice that the madness of her husband exempted Hortense from the normal rules, but she did compensate in an extravagant fashion.

As she grew old and grey, Hortense retained alike her unparalleled beauty and invincible charm. Gradually, however, her followers thinned out, until she was left with perhaps half a dozen friends, supreme amongst whom was the ever faithful Saint-Evremond. When she fell ill in 1699, her children set sail for England, and arrived in Dover to discover that she was unlikely to survive more than a few hours. They did not bother to continue the journey to London, having ascertained that all she could leave them was an assortment of pets and debts; they turned back and sailed again for France. Hortense died on 2 July of that year.

Even in death, her story breaks through all barriers of reasonable expectations. Her body was conveyed to France and received there by her lunatic husband, who thenceforth carried it on a bizarre progress through his estates, from Brittany to Alsace. As the months passed, the Duchesse Mazarin became a legend. Peasants laid rosaries in her coffin and offered their sick children to it for miraculous cures. Eventually in 1700 Hortense's remains were laid to rest next to those of Cardinal

Mazarin in the vault of the Collège des Quatre Nations. At the Revolution ninety years later, a crazed mob stole the coffins, broke them open, and consigned the skeleton of the beautiful Hortense to a bonfire.

OTHERS By the proliferating mathematics of the generations, there are naturally a few hundred people who can trace their ancestry to Charles II and one or more of his mistresses. They include many of the present Dukes (in addition to the four in direct male line, that is), as it has long been desirable in ducal families that the heir should marry the daughter of another Duke. The Duke of Northumberland, to take just one example, (though as we have said his title is not connected with that created for Barbara Villiers's third son) is nonetheless descended from Charles II and Louise, his mother being a daughter of the 7th Duke of Richmond. His son, Lord Percy, multiplies the connections yet again, for his mother, the present Duchess, is a daughter of the Duke of Buccleuch, and therefore descended from King Charles and Lucy Walter.

To give the whole list would require a small reference book, and is anyway unnecessary for those who have the patience to jostle with the intricacies of Burke's *Peerage*. Just three are perhaps worth a special mention. The Dowager Duchess of Portland, who is now (1979) ninety-two years old, is descended three times from Charles II, through Nell Gwynn, Louise de Kéroualle, and Barbara Villiers. Lord Montagu of Beaulieu, world-famous for his unique collection of antique motor-cars, is a great-grandson of the 5th Duke of Buccleuch, and is therefore of Lucy Walter's stock. Finally, the youngest daughter of the 5th Duke of Richmond, Lady Cecilia, married the 4th Earl of Lucan; her great-grandson, the present Lord Lucan, is by this connection descended from King Charles and Louise de Kéroualle. As he has been missing for some years, he is in no position to share the pride of his multitudinous kinsmen in their colourful descent.

Pride there certainly is, and why not? King Charles was an admirable and amiable man, his four principal mistresses interesting women in their different ways. There is no longer any horror engendered by the thought of bastardy, and there might well on the contrary be very real happiness in the reflection that the various conceptions which resulted from Charles II's amorous nature were not owed to any cold, loveless duty, but to hot-blooded joyous pleasure.

*   *   *

SOURCES FOR CHAPTER FIVE

Donald ADAMSON and Peter Beauclerk DEWAR, *The House of Nell Gwynn* (1974)
Burke's *Peerage*
Hester CHAPMAN, *Privileged Persons* (1966)
Complete Peerage
Jeanine DELPECH, *The Duchess of Portsmouth* (1953)
Dictionary of National Biography
Bernard FALK, *The Royal Fitzroys* (1950)
H. FORNERON, *Louise de Kéroualle, Duchess of Portsmouth* (1887)
Goodwood Papers.
Brian MASTERS, *The Dukes* (1975)
Philip SERGEANT, *My Lady Castlemaine* (1912)
John TIMBS, *Romance of London*, Vol. 1

INDEX

Acton, Lord, 10
Alice, H.R.H. Princess, Duchess of Gloucester, 180
Anne, Queen, 91, 93, 186
Aretino, Pietro, 69 and *n.*
Arlington, Earl of (Sir Henry Bennet), 68, 86, 88, 130, 135, 136, 143
Arlington, Lady, 136, 137, 138
Atholl, Dukes of, 48
Avon, Lord, 48

Barillon, Paul, 159, 163, 165, 166, 168, 169, 171, 173, 175
Barlow, Mrs, *see* Walter, Lucy
Barnwell, Sir Frederick, 27
Bayning, Anne, 184
Bayning, Mary, 49, 184
Beauclerk, Lord James, 111, 116
Beaufort, Duc de, 132
Beaulieu, Lord Montagu of, 188
Bedford, Dukes of, 48
Behn, Aphra, 119
Bellasis, Anne, 185
Bennet, Sir Henry, *see* Arlington, Earl of
Bennet, Isabella (Duchess of Grafton), 86, 139
Berkeley, Sir Charles, 68, 70, 73, 75
Berkshire, Earl of, 82
Bernard, Edward, 88
Bevan, Bryan, 148
Bloxham, Matthew, 28
Bossuet, Bishop of Meaux, 128, 129
Bowman, Harry, 108
Braybrook, Bishop, 83
Brouncker, William, 12
Browne, Sir Richard, 131, 147
Bruce, Thomas, 164
Buccleuch, Duchess of (Lady Anne Scott, Duchess of Monmouth), 42, 70, 75
Buccleuch, 2nd Duke of, 180
Buccleuch, 5th Duke of, 27, 28, 188
Buccleuch, 9th Duke of, 180
Buckhurst, Lord, *see* Sackville, Charles
Buckingham, George Villiers, Duke of, 9, 48, 55, 80, 85, 116, 129, 130, 132, 155, 156

Bussy-Rabutin, Roger de, 138
Byron, Lady, 20

Carbery, Earl of, 11, 13
'Carlos, Don', *see* Plymouth, Earl of
Carné, Monsieur, 177
Carteret, Marguerite de, 10
Castlehaven, Lord, 39
Castlemaine, Countess of, *see* Villiers, Barbara
Castlemaine, Earl of, *see* Palmer, Roger
Castlereagh, Lord, 48
Catherine of Braganza, Queen, 21, 24, 57, 58, 59, 60, 61, 62, 63, 64, 65, 66, 68, 69, 72, 73, 74, 75, 76, 78, 79, 82, 129, 130, 139, 140, 141, 142, 147, 149, 160, 163, 170, 172, 173, 174, 186, 187
Chapman, Hester, 41
Chappell, Nicholas, 12, 13
Charles II, King
  and Lady Byron, 20
  and Moll Davis, 81, 82, 105, 110
  and Marguerite de Carteret, 10
  and Duchesse de Chatillon, 18
  and Louise de Kéroualle, 123–78
  and Nell Gwynn, 95–122
  and Duchesse Mazarin, 151, 157–60
  and Mlle de Montpensier, 17–18
  and Catherine Pegge, 19–20, 38
  and Lady Shannon, 19, 30
  and Electress Sophia, 18–19
  and Frances Stuart, 70–9
  and Barbara Villiers, 45–94
  and Lucy Walter, 7–43
  and Mrs Weaver, 105
Chatillon, Duchesse de, 18
Chatillon, Marquis de, 88
Chester, Lady, 87
Chesterfield, Lord, 49, 50, 51, 52, 55, 60
Chiffinch, William, 107, 157
Churchill, John, Duke of Marlborough, 85, 86, 183
Churchill, Sir Winston, 48, 86
Cibber, Colley, 119

Clarendon, Earl of, 15, 21, 22, 32, 38, 46, 48, 55, 56, 57, 62, 63, 64, 65, 67, 68, 79, 80, 82
Cleveland, Duchess of, *see* Villiers, Barbara
Colbert de Croissy, 125, 128, 134, 135, 136, 137, 138, 139, 144, 149, 168
Coleman, Edward, 161, 162, 163
Coleraine, Lord, 83
Cooper, Samuel, 12, 16, 35
Cosin, Bishop, 26, 29, 42
Courcelles, Sidonie de, 154
Courtin, Honoré de, 151, 157, 158, 159, 175
Creeton, Dr, 81
Crofts, James, *see* Monmouth, Duke of
Crofts, William, 41
Cromwell, Oliver, 33, 36, 38, 41, 45, 49

Dacre, Baroness, 182
Danby, Earl of, *see* Leeds, Duke of
Davenant, Sir William, 97, 98
Davis, Mary ('Moll'), 81, 82, 105, 107, 110, 185
d'Aulnoy, Baronne, 14, 15
de la Cloche, James, 10
de Lenclos, Ninon, 170
d'Orléans, Duc, 124, 125, 129
d'Orléans, Duchesse de *see* Henriette dOrléans
de Vere, Lady Diana, 184
de Vic, Sir Henry, 32
Deleau, Mrs, 92, 93
Derby, Lady, 46
Derwentwater, Earl of, 105, 186
Digby, Sir Kenelm, 12
Dillon, Viscount, 183
Disney, William, 26
Dorset, Earl of, *see* Sackville, Charles
Dryden, John, 85*n*, 102, 105

Edward I, King, 11
Elizabeth I, Queen, 84
Elizabeth II, Queen, 48
Erskine, William, 42
Evelyn, John, 11, 12, 14, 42, 45, 46, 54, 56, 59, 65, 78, 84, 90, 107, 131, 133, 137, 138, 147, 172, 173, 183

Falmouth, Lady, 80
Fanshawe, Mary (d. of Lucy Walter), 25, 30, 31

Feilding, Robert, 91, 92, 93
Ferguson, Robert, 26, 27
Fitzroy, Barbara (d. of
    Barbara Villiers by John
    Churchill), 86, 88, 183
Fitzroy, Charles, Duke of
    Southampton, 57, 59, 66,
    84, 87, 88, 182
Fitzroy, Charles, 5th Baron
    Southampton, 183
Fitzroy, Charlotte (d. of Lady
    Shannon by Charles II),
    19, 181
Fitzroy, Charlotte (d. of
    Barbara Villiers by
    Charles II), 77, 87, 183
Fitzroy, George, Duke of
    Northumberland, 77, 84,
    87n, 88, 90
Fitzroy, Henry, Duke of
    Grafton, 68, 72, 73, 84, 86,
    87n, 88, 90, 91, 114, 118,
    130, 138, 139, 146, 182
Fitzroy, Robert, Viscount
    Daventry, 183
Forder, Richard, 29
Fox, Sir Stephen, 114
Frazier, Dr, 78, 139, 145

Gerard, Sir Filbert, 26
Gerard, Lady, 67
Germaine, Sir John, 110
Gilbert, G. D., 15
Godfrey, Sir Edmund Berry,
    162
Goodman, Cardonell, 90, 91
Gosfright, Mr, 13, 17, 23, 25,
    26
Gosfright, Mrs, 12, 26
Grace, Hannah, 120
Grafton, 1st Duke of, see
    Fitzroy, Henry
Grafton, 2nd Duke of, 93,
    182
Grafton, 3rd Duke of, 182
Grafton, 11th Duke of, 182
Grammont, Comte de, 130,
    151, 156
Grey, Lord, 174
Gwyn, Mrs, 99, 100, 116
Gwyn, Nell, 82, 87, 88,
    95–122, 123, 126, 130,
    132, 133, 138, 139, 140,
    145, 146, 156, 165, 172,
    184, 188
Gwyn, Rose, 99, 121
Gwynne, Thomas, 99

Halifax, Lord, 139
Hall, Jacob, 82, 83, 115
Hall, Timothy, 149
Hamilton, Lady Anne, 50
Hamilton, Charles, 86, 93,
    183
Hamilton, Duke of, 48, 86,
    183, 186
Hamilton, James, 55, 70
Hampden, Viscount, 182
Harriot, Thomas, 11

Hart, Charles, 82, 98, 99,
    101, 102, 104, 111
Harvey, Lady, 156, 157
Henrietta Maria, Queen, 8, 9,
    17, 18, 19, 23, 24, 30, 49
Henriette d'Orléans, 32, 46,
    71, 95, 106, 123, 124,
    125, 126, 127, 128, 129,
    130, 131, 132, 138
Hill, Anne, 33, 36, 37
Holles, Denzil, 12
Howard, Lady Katherine, 11
Howard, Robert, 102, 114
Howard, Tom, 33, 34, 36, 37,
    38
Huddlestone, Father, 174
Hyde, Sir Edward, see
    Clarendon, Lord
Hyde, Laurence, 114

James II, King, see James,
    Duke of York
Jeffreys, Judge, 175
Jennings, Mrs, 114
Jermyn, Henry, 70, 72, 80, 84

Kéroualle, Comte Guillaume
    Penancoët de, 131, 143,
    146, 147, 167
Kéroualle, Henriette de, 131
    141, 146, 147, 149, 166,
    175
Kéroualle, Louise de
    (Duchess of Portsmouth),
    53, 84, 86, 87, 88, 101,
    106, 108, 109, 110, 112,
    115, 118, 119, 123–78,
    185, 188
Kéroualle, Sebastien de, 131,
    132
Killigrew, Elizabeth, see
    Shannon, Lady
Killigrew, Harry, 78, 99
Killigrew, Thomas, 12, 78,
    97, 98, 99

Lacy, John, 99
Lang, Andrew, 10
Leeds, Duke of, 20, 146, 148,
    181
Lely, Sir Peter, 12, 53
Litchfield, Earl of, 87, 183
Lorraine, Chevalier de, 124,
    128
Louis XIV, King, 75, 89,
    123, 124, 125, 127, 128,
    132, 135, 137, 138, 143,
    144, 145, 149, 150, 151,
    153, 156, 157, 158, 159,
    160, 161, 163, 165, 166,
    167, 168, 169, 171, 175,
    176, 185, 187
Lower, Sir William, 11
Lucan, Lord, 188
Ludres, Madame de, 170
Lyttleton, Sir Charles, 120

Maintenon, Mme de, 175

Mancini, Hortense, see
    Mazarin, Duchesse
Mancini, Laura, 170
Marlborough, Duke of, see
    Churchill, John
Marshall, Rebecca, 101, 102,
    104, 111
Mary, Princess, 23, 24, 25,
    33, 46, 49
Mazarin, Cardinal, 151, 188
Mazarin, Duc, 152, 153, 154,
    155, 187
Mazarin, Duchesse (Hortense
    Mancini), 151–60, 163,
    170, 173, 187–8
Meggs, Mary, (Orange Moll),
    98
Melbourne, Lord, 48
Mersey, Lord, 27–8
Middlesex, Earl of, see
    Sackville, Charles
Molière, Jean-Baptiste
    Poquelin de, 133
Monaco, Prince de, 159
Monk, General, 45–6
Monmouth, Duke of, 8, 15,
    16, 17, 21, 26, 28, 29, 35,
    36, 38, 39, 40, 41, 42,
    43, 70, 76, 87, 116, 165,
    174, 177, 179–80
Monmouth, Duchess of, see
    Buccleuch, Duchess of
Montagu, Duke of, see
    Montagu, Ralph
Montagu, Sir Edward, 52,
    70, 77
Montagu, Ralph, 88, 89, 90,
    128, 130, 155, 156
Montpensier, Mlle de, 17,
    18
Mottet, Giles, 39, 40
Motteville, Mme de, 9

Needham, Eleanor, see Byron,
    Lady
Newburgh, Earl of, 23
Nicholas, Sir Edward, 9, 21,
    68
Norfolk, 2nd Duke of, 11
Norfolk, Duchess of, 110
Northumberland, Duke of
    (son of Barbara Villiers
    by Charles II), see
    Fitzroy, George
Northumberland, 10th Duke
    of, 183, 188
Northumberland, Countess
    of, 148, 169
Norwich, Bishop of, 78

Oates, Titus, 160, 161, 162,
    163, 181
O'Neill, Daniel, 25, 31, 33,
    34, 35, 41
'Orange Moll', see Meggs,
    Mary
Orford, Earl of, 12
Ormonde, Duke of, 25, 38,
    39, 40, 84, 114

Osborne, Lady Bridget, 20
  181
Otway, Thomas, 112

Palmer, Alice, 51
Palmer, Anne (Countess of
  Sussex), 55, 87, 88, 89,
  90, 156, 157, 181–2
Palmer, Barbara, see Villiers,
  Barbara
Palmer, Charles, see Fitzroy
  Charles
Palmer, Sir James, 51
Palmer, Roger (Earl of
  Castlemaine), 51, 52, 55,
  56, 57, 58, 62, 66, 77,
  78, 90, 181
Pegge, Catherine, 19, 20, 38,
  112, 180
Pembroke, Countess of, see
  Kéroualle, Henriette
Pembroke, Earl of, 141, 147,
  175
Pepys, Samuel, 15, 20, 21,
  50, 52, 53, 54, 56, 60,
  65–6, 68, 69, 70, 72, 73,
  75, 76, 77, 78, 80, 81,
  90, 100, 101, 102, 103,
  104, 105
Percy, Lady Elizabeth, 87,
  169
Percy, Lord, 188
Petre, Baron, 186
Plymouth, Earl of, 19, 20, 87
  112, 180–1
Pomeroy, Sir Henry, 23
Portland, Dowager Duchess
  of, 188
Portsmouth, Duchess of, see
  Kéroualle, Louise de
Povey, Thomas, 75
Prodgers, Edward, 23, 35, 41
Protheroe, John, 11, 12

Repas, Denis de, 77
Richmond, 3rd Duke of
  (Charles Stuart), 79, 144,
  146
Richmond, Duchess of, see
  Stuart, Frances
Richmond, 1st Duke of
  (Charles Lennox, son of
  Louise de Kéroualle by
  Charles II), 88, 112, 118,
  138, 139, 143, 144, 146,
  165, 166, 168, 169, 174,
  175, 176, 185
Richmond, 2nd Duke of, 177
Richmond, Dowager Duchess
  of, 56
Rochester, Earl of, 69, 96,
  141, 175
Rohan, Chevalier de, 108, 154

Russell, Bertrand (Earl
  Russell), 48
Russell, Lord John, 48
Ruvigny, Marquis de, 144,
  145, 150, 151, 156, 158

Sackville, Charles (Lord
  Buckhurst, Earl of
  Dorset, Earl of
  Middlesex), 103, 104, 111
St Albans, Duke of, (son
  of Nell Gwyn by
  Charles II), 106, 112,
  113, 117, 118, 119, 120,
  121, 123, 184
St Albans, 13th Duke of,
  184
Saint-Evremond, Charles de,
  136, 156, 187
Saint-Réal, Abbé de, 155
Sandwich, Earl of, see
  Montagu, Sir Edward
Sault, Comte de, 132
Savile, Henry, 159
Scott, Lord George, 15, 28, 31
Scroggs, Lord Chief Justice,
  164
Sedley, Sir Charles, 103, 104
Sévigné, Madame de, 106,
  138, 187
Shaftesbury, Lord, 141, 148,
  162, 164
Shannon, Lady, 19, 30, 181
Shrewsbury, Countess of, 110
Sidney, Algernon, 15, 16
Sidney, Robert, 15, 16, 35
Slingsby, Sir Arthur, 38, 39
  40, 41
Soissons, Chevalier de, 187
Sophia, Electress, 18, 19
Southampton, Duke of, see
  Fitzroy, Charles
Strickland, Agnes, 65
Stuart, Frances (Duchess of
  Richmond, la Belle
  Stuart), 70, 71, 72, 73,
  74, 75, 79, 186
Sunderland, Earl of, 90, 168,
  170, 175
Sunderland, Lady, 141
Sussex, Countess of, see
  Palmer, Anne
Sussex, Earl of, 87

Taafe, Lord, 30, 34, 35
Taylor, Dr, 148
Temple, Mrs, 141
Tenison, Archbishop, 120,
  121
Tonge, Israel, 160, 161
Tudor, Lady Mary (d. of
  Moll Davis by Charles
  II), 105, 185

Turolles, Monsieur, 153

Vallière, Louise de la, 132,
  153
Vane, Sir Henry, 12
Vaughan, Elizabeth, 11
Vendôme, Duc de, 170, 171
Vendôme, Philippe de, 170,
  171, 172
Venel, Madame de, 152
Villiers, Barbara (Mrs Palmer,
  Countess of Castlemaine,
  Duches of Cleveland),
  14, 21, 45–94, 95, 101,
  104, 105, 106, 108, 110,
  112, 115, 118, 119, 126,
  130, 132, 138, 139, 142,
  146, 148, 149, 166, 169,
  170, 172, 173, 188
Villiers, Dame Barbara, 86
Villiers, Charles, Earl of
  Anglesey, 49
Villiers, Elizabeth, 48
Villiers, George, Duke of
  Buckingham, see
  Buckingham
Villiers, Sir George, 47, 48
Villiers, Susan, 48
Villiers, William, Viscount
  Grandison, 48, 56, 77, 82

Wadsworth, Mary, 92, 93
Walter, Elizabeth, 11, 12, 13,
  25
Walter, Lucy, 7–43, 45, 47,
  49, 116, 118, 119, 131,
  140, 170, 172, 179, 188
Walter, Justus, 11, 36, 37
Walter, Morris, 11
Walter, Sir Richard, 11
Walter, Richard, 11
Walter, William, 11, 12, 13
Whalley, Sir Edward, 52
William of Orange, 165, 176,
  177, 182, 183, 184, 185,
  187
Williams, Lady, 114
Williamson, Sir Joseph, 107
Winter, Sir John, 12
Wood, Mary, 87
Worcester, Marchioness of,
  145
Wren, Sir Christopher, 114
Wycherley, William, 85

York, James, Duke of
  (James II), 15, 28, 29,
  30, 46, 53, 55, 74, 78,
  89, 97, 99, 104, 108, 111,
  114, 117, 118, 120, 121,
  137, 141, 160, 161, 162,
  164, 165, 168, 173, 174,
  175, 177, 179, 181, 183